Children in Prison

D1603014

Children in Prison

*Six Profiles Before, During
and After Incarceration*

JEROME GOLD

McFarland & Company, Inc., Publishers
Jefferson, North Carolina

ISBN (print) 978-1-4766-7741-5
ISBN (ebook) 978-1-4766-3735-8

LIBRARY OF CONGRESS CATALOGUING DATA ARE AVAILABLE

BRITISH LIBRARY CATALOGUING DATA ARE AVAILABLE

Front cover photograph by Saranya Loisamutr (Shutterstock)

Printed in the United States of America

McFarland & Company, Inc., Publishers
Box 611, Jefferson, North Carolina 28640
www.mcfarlandpub.com

For Jeanne

For those I wrote about in this book

And for the staff of the Saw Mill
where I wrote much of this book,
who allowed me time
and space and unlimited coffee.

Table of Contents

People in This Book

Ash Meadow Staff

Anna—Whale Cottage director
Meg Ballardine—Ash Meadow mental health resource coordinator
Celia Barney—Ash Meadow associate superintendent
Clara Beam—Ash Meadow associate superintendent
Marty Biggs—Ash Meadow associate superintendent; Jan's supervisor
Caroline Bloodworth—Whale Cottage case manager
Herman Boats—Swan Cottage director; Jan's husband
Jan Boats—Wolf Cottage director
Clare—Wolf Cottage case manager
Curly Cook—singer/guitarist; founder of Blues in the Schools
Debra—Crane Cottage case manager
Tony Dell—Peacock Cottage case manager
Kathleen Foreman—Ash Meadow associate superintendent; Anna's and Jan's
   supervisor following Marty Biggs' tenure
Gil—Wolf Cottage case manager
Jake Gorman—Serpent Cottage staff supervisor and case manager
Grant—leader of youth group
James—Wolf Cottage case manager
Jerry—case manager at Swan Cottage, Whale Cottage, and Wolf Cottage; author
   of this book
Ms. Johns—Ash Meadow school administrator
Layton—Wolf Cottage staff supervisor
John Loring—Swan Cottage case manager
Margareta—Wolf Cottage case manager
Marie—school psychologist
Don Martino—Ash Meadow associate superintendent
Michael—Swan Cottage case manager
Dr. Nader—Ash Meadow superintendent
Charlie Patterson—Wolf Cottage case manager
Frank Payne—Wolf Cottage case manager

Dick Peck—Ash Meadow chaplain
Danielle Priest—Peacock Cottage case manager
Rob—Swan Cottage staff supervisor
Sandra—Serpent Cottage case manager
Bernie Sanford—Wolf Cottage case manager
Newt Smith—chief of security at Ash Meadow
Stan—Swan Cottage case manager
Dick Teall—Wolf Cottage case manager
Dr. Williams—chief of psychiatric services; Lyle Munson's psychiatrist

Residents

David Banks—Wolf Cottage resident
Marcus Bellows—Wolf Cottage resident
Casey—Wolf Cottage resident
Jeremiah Court—Dolphin Cottage resident
Durrell—Wolf Cottage resident
Derek Evans—former Ash Meadow resident
Reggie Greene—Swan Cottage resident
Paul Grise—Wolf Cottage resident
Jessica Johnson—former Ash Meadow resident
Norah Joines—Wolf Cottage resident
Johnny Kerwood—Wolf Cottage resident
Laurel—Wolf Cottage resident
Linsey Lopez—Wolf Cottage resident
Cassandra Martin—Wolf Cottage resident
Sonia May—Wolf Cottage resident; inmate at Washington Corrections Center for Women
Michael—Wolf Cottage resident
Lyle Munson—Wolf Cottage resident; inmate at Clallam Bay Corrections Center and Stafford Creek Corrections Center
Oren—Wolf Cottage resident
Caitlin Weber—Wolf Cottage resident; inmate at Washington Corrections Center for Women
Jamal Willson—Wolf Cottage resident

Persons Known to Residents or Ash Meadow Staff from the Outside

Anthony—Helen Martin's boyfriend
Benjamin—Shari's boyfriend
Geraldine—Norah Joines' foster mother

Grandma—Cassandra Martin's grandmother; Helen Martin's mother
Sacha Greene—Reggie Greene's sister
Stecia Greene—Reggie Greene's sister
Guillermo—Norah Joines' boyfriend
Tony Hunter—Reggie Greene's friend
Jane—Rashif's mother
Jeanne—author's wife
June—Reggie Greene's girlfriend
K.—Norah Joines' boyfriend; father of Lily
Kiki—Cassandra Martin's friend
Cami Lessing—parole officer; former Wolf Cottage case manager
Lily—daughter of Norah Joines and K.
Cherice Martin—Cassandra Martin's daughter
Helen Martin—Cassandra Martin's mother
Keisha Martin—Cassandra Martin's sister
Louis Martin—Cassandra Martin's father; Helen's husband
Yvette Martin—Cassandra Martin's sister
Meika—Reggie Greene's friend
Nancy—social services agency representative
Patrick—Norah Joines' uncle
Rashif—Cassandra Martin's boyfriend; father of Cherice, Cassandra's daughter
Ruth—Cassandra Martin's housemate
Shari—Cassandra Martin's friend
Richard Stern—attorney representing juvenile residents of state prisons
Eugene Weaver—Norah Joines' husband; father of Eugene Weaver, Junior, Norah's son
Eugene Weaver, Junior—son of Norah Joines and Eugene Weaver

Introduction:
Throwaway Kids

Wolf Cottage

Nestled in the western foothills of the Cascade Range in Washington State, Ash Meadow is only a few hundred yards off the interstate. Yet, screened by forest, it is invisible to drivers. Not long ago, an upscale housing development was built about two miles away, but buyers, at least at first, were unaware that a prison was so near. Later, some of the children of the new householders would occasionally go through the woods to the edge of Ash Meadow's campus and throw rocks at the residents through the fence surrounding the recreation yard of the maximum-security unit.

Ash Meadow is one of two juvenile prisons in the state. It takes the youngest boys of all the institutions and, for most of the time I worked there, it took all of the girls. During the years I was there, there were five prisons for juveniles in Washington, but owing to the state's adoption of ways other than prison to manage juvenile offenders, and because of a decrease in the overall number of offenders, three were later closed.

Ash Meadow was built in the mid–1960s to house youth at risk, kids who were considered by social workers and the courts to be doing things worrisome enough to attract the attention of law enforcement agencies. A sentence served in Ash Meadow was considered a kind of intervention. It was assumed by the courts, if not always the social workers, that it was flawed thinking, poor choices on the part of the kids, that brought them to prison. But by the Eighties, owing to the drug economy and the rise of youth gangs, Ash Meadow was getting kids who had committed serious offenses and it had become a true prison, even if it did not look like one.

When I think about it, I think about the kids I knew there, and then I think about some of the staff I knew, and then I think about Ash Meadow itself. In its pastoral setting, surrounded by forest made up mostly of ever-

1

greens but with some madrona and ash and other deciduous trees and a small
pond on one side, Ash Meadow's grounds were home to a gaggle of non-
migratory Canada geese, crows and other birds, raccoons, blacktail deer, does
and fawns for the most part, although occasionally I saw a mature stag, and
other, less often seen wildlife—minks and bobcats and, once, a lynx—though
"wildlife" might be a mischaracterization of most of these animals. On my
walk from the parking lot to Wolf Cottage at the far end of the campus, I
often had to maneuver between the geese, reluctant to move aside for a
human, and walk beneath the crows perched in the branches of the poplars
and ponderosa pines on either side of the asphalt path, calling out with the
raspy, grating sound they make to warn one another that someone is
approaching, and then, sometimes, a group of five to eight deer would move
to let me pass and then gather behind me as I neared the cottage door. They
wanted apples.

One night in late winter, as I was leaving work, a gale was blowing and
the geese, facing into the wind in flying formation, were hunkered down on
the earth, their legs crooked back, their bodies so low you could hardly see
their feet, the small feathers on their heads swept into tiny coifs. I felt as if I
were flying with them, or sitting alongside them in a painting, so still and
silent were they, the storm like an oiled brush slicking their feathers tight
against their bodies. When I think of Ash Meadow, that is one of the things
I think of, the geese in V-formation, illuminated by the lamps along the walking paths, facing into the wind, flying nowhere.

I worked at Ash Meadow as a rehabilitation counselor for fifteen years,
the last seven in Wolf Cottage, maximum security. In Wolf, I usually managed
a caseload of three kids, and monitored and interacted with all of the kids in
the cottage. There were sixteen bedrooms in the cottage and sixteen residents;
in Wolf, as opposed to other cottages, we never doubled kids up in a room.
I conducted treatment groups, acted as a surrogate parent, broke up fights
and did whatever else I was called on to do that was necessary for the func-
tioning of the cottage. I worked with two other staff. As we did not usually
have the same days off, the staff I worked with were not always the same. My
favorites were Bernie Sanford and Dick Teale. I felt certain that, together, we
could handle whatever might arise.

During my time at Ash Meadow—almost all of the Nineties and the first
several years of this century—every resident but two, as far as I know, had
been convicted of a felony. One of the exceptions was a boy serving four consecutive sixteen-week sentences, each for a count of fourth-degree assault—
i.e., fighting, a misdemeanor. Ordinarily this would have earned him time in
county detention or on probation, but, the boy said, his family and the judge's

family were at odds over another matter and the judge saw this unusual punishment as a way of striking at the boy's family. In any event, it was the judge's decision to make the sentences consecutive rather than concurrent, thereby lengthening the boy's incarceration time enough to justify sending him to prison instead of detention. He did well at Ash Meadow, earning average or better grades in school and staying out of fights. He was released early owing to good behavior and I didn't hear anything more about him.

The other exception was a homeless girl who had asked her probation officer to incarcerate her so she could kick her heroin habit. She knew she would die, she told me, unless she got off the streets, and she didn't have a safe place to go to withdraw. Her probation officer persuaded a judge to send her to Ash Meadow. The girl came first to maximum security because we had more staff than the girls' cottages and could attend to her more assiduously as she went through withdrawal, and then she went through the Phoenix Program, Ash Meadow's drug-and-alcohol rehab, and then she was released. She became an advocate for homeless kids. I saw her in this role on the local news a couple of times and then I didn't see her anymore.

I knew other kids who came to Ash Meadow to stay alive, but they had finagled their sentences by committing crimes where they knew they would be caught.

There are thirteen living units at Ash Meadow, called "cottages," as though people who could afford it would send their children to us for a couple of weeks in the summer so they could learn woodcraft and leather craft and how to use the stars to navigate at night and how to cook over a campfire and some of the other things kids with advantages might learn at camp. As if we taught those things, although a volunteer did come in occasionally to teach beadwork.

Several cottages have specialized programs. Andromeda is a mental health unit, Fox and Crane take male sex offenders—there is no cottage that exclusively houses female sex offenders, although there are girls who are sex offenders—Eagle runs the twelve-week rehab program, Goldfish houses the youngest boys, down to age nine. Other cottages house older boys.

When I was at Ash Meadow, one cottage in particular, Swan, and sometimes a second unit, dealt primarily with boys having gang affiliations. Two cottages housed only girls. For several years, Andromeda, Eagle and Wolf were coed, but then Andromeda became a girls' mental health unit and Dolphin, which had been a unit for older boys, became a mental health unit for boys and occasionally girls for whom there was not enough room in Andromeda. I worked in Swan for five years, then a girls' cottage, then another boys' cottage before going to Wolf.

Compared to the way kids lived in other cottages, the living conditions of the residents in Wolf were austere. Most kids in Ash Meadow attended the school on upper campus, near the health center, the security office, the gym, the cafeteria and the administration building. Kids in Wolf went to school in a small, two-room structure behind the cottage, enclosed by a metal fence that also spun around the recreation yard next to the classroom. Kids in other cottages had access to the gym and the swimming pool, attended campus-wide "socials," or parties, in the gym, or smaller ones hosted by one or another cottage. Kids in Wolf did not attend socials and did not get to play basketball or volleyball on wooden floors or work out in the weight room or swim. Kids in Wolf played ball games on asphalt out of doors. On days when it rained or snowed, they stayed in the cottage except to go to class.

Residents in other cottages wore their own clothes, clothes they had bought themselves, or that their parents or other relatives had sent them, or that they got gratis from the prison commissary if they were wards of the state. Residents in Wolf wore orange jumpsuits supplied by the institution.

Residents in other cottages were permitted to have personal items in their rooms—clothing, books, toiletries, CD players, posters on the walls— and had shelves built into the walls to hold their belongings, and a desk and a chair to do their homework or write letters or write in their journals or draw. Residents in Wolf had none of these: no clothing except a spare jump-suit, extra socks and underwear, all of which they stacked neatly on the floor at the foot of their bed; no desk or chair; no shelving; no posters; no CD players. Residents in Wolf were permitted to have one book in their room, unless their case manager allowed them more. Toiletries were kept in the staff office and given to kids in the morning before breakfast and collected after breakfast and showers, and again in the evening just before bedtime so kids could wash and brush their teeth, and were returned before the kids went to their rooms.

In other cottages, residents could earn bedtimes as late as ten or eleven o'clock. In Wolf, all residents had an eight o'clock bedtime.

Kids came to Wolf directly from county detention if they had not done well there while awaiting sentencing—they had been aggressive, had gotten in a fight, had stolen from other kids—or if they had committed unusually severe crimes, those in which the victim or victims had been killed or badly injured or could have been. Some of the kids we got had committed murder or tried to, one had committed residential arson, and another had fired a handgun into the ceiling of his school cafeteria, although he had not shot anybody or tried to.

Kids would be sent to us from other cottages if they became overly aggressive or too disruptive for the staff in those cottages to manage. Of course, cottages' ability to dump a resident into maximum security was abused, so that often enough a cottage sent us a kid who complained too much or was slow to comply with staff's directives, but was not a threat to anyone and eventually did what he was told. Many, many of the kids we got were mentally unbalanced, a few psychotic. Wolf, in fact, was also an undesignated overflow cottage for kids who belonged in mental health units but who were too difficult, physically, for the mental health staff to manage, or for whom there were simply no beds available.

Wolf could be violent. Kids rarely assaulted staff, but some of them went after one another, and staff had to be alert. We were trained in "Dealing with Resistive Youth," techniques by which to manage kids who didn't want to be managed. In less euphemistic terms: we were trained to try to talk a kid into doing what we wanted him to do—go to his room, put his meal tray down—and if that didn't work, if he was so hot that he couldn't hear you, or so enraged that he couldn't comprehend anything but his desire to hurt someone, almost always someone in particular, to take him to the floor where he could be handcuffed and, if necessary, shackled before being moved to an isolation cell.

Some staff were more willing than others to get physical with a kid. In Swan I worked with a woman who liked to wrestle boys to the ground. In Wolf I worked with a woman who told her colleagues that she would not participate in restraining kids—we preferred a staff-to-kid ratio of two to one in this kind of situation; it made for efficiency and kids often did not feel obligated to resist when staff outnumbered them—but then broke up a fight by taking a kid down without assistance. I worked with a man who ran away, leaving me to handle a boy by myself.

Although staff were occasionally injured during restraints, back injuries being the most common type, I can recall only two incidents in which a kid was hurt. The first occurred when one of the staff slipped on a wet floor and fell on the kid, breaking the boy's clavicle. The second was when a staff member fought with his fists a resident who had taken another staff hostage and was threatening to stab her.[1] But most days in Wolf were without incident. We could go for weeks, even months, without a fight in the cottage.

Cottage staff were hired as rehabilitation counselors, and most of the people I worked with took their job title to heart. In the United States there is always a tension between the desire to punish and the desire to rehabilitate prisoners. When I came to Ash Meadow, the balance between them was tilted in favor of those who would rehabilitate. Over the years, with a change of superintendents and other administrators, the balance shifted so that those who saw prison as a place for punishment rather than a place to rehabilitate children—or "habilitate" them, some staff said, as many of the kids sent to us had never known a life without deprivation and fear and violence—became more influential.

The Residents

When *Paranoia and Heartbreak*, one of my earlier books on life in a children's prison, was published I gave readings from it in bookstores and libraries. I used to say, to emphasize the relevance of the book to the lives of those in the audience, that everybody in the United States knows someone who is in prison or who has been in prison, or knows someone who knows someone in prison or who has been. I could see the audience thinking—no one ever contradicted me. I had not gotten my information by searching out Census Bureau or Department of Justice statistics, but had inferred it by the fact that at any given moment in the United States between two and three million people, adults and children, are in prison. And when you consider that the level of imprisonment began its meteoric rise more than a generation ago, and take into account inmate turnover—people are released and other people come in—you realize that tens of millions of people have served time.[2] Even presidents of the United States have known, or do know, people who are in prison, or who have been.

Aside from the kids I knew at Ash Meadow, I've known other people who had been or would be locked up. I went to high school with two boys who had been in prison. (One became a high school principal; I don't know what became of the other.) When my parents owned a restaurant, they hired a former inmate as a cook. One of my closest childhood friends spent a year locked up when we were in our early twenties. Eighteen years later, I worked beside a man who had served five years, and another man, in the cubicle on the other side of mine, would be found to be a serial killer—he got life without parole. When I was in the army, a friend went to the stockade at Fort Leavenworth for several months for having gone AWOL. I ran across him ten years later; he was driving a cross-country bus.

There have been others. A mechanic who worked on my car had, as a juvenile, served time in Elk Grove, one of Ash Meadow's sister institutions. His boss, hearing him tell me this, asked me if he could donate clothes or anything else to Ash Meadow, and what the procedure was. I met a woman, a state employee, who had been locked up at Ash Meadow when she was a teenager, and another woman who had served time in a federal prison for selling drugs. And, oh yes, I had a cousin who spent five years in San Quentin, got out and died a few months later from a heroin overdose; I had forgotten about him until I remembered the woman who had been in federal prison.

As I write this, I think of others I have known who had been locked away, though I would not have known this had they not told me. I don't ordinarily think of their having been imprisoned, but see them in my mind as I knew them: as someone I worked beside, telling jokes between phone calls; as a political activist, speaking with irony and rage about an injustice; as a friend describing the sculpture she was working on; as a collector of antiquarian books talking about a series, published during the Great Depression, on American rivers. I find it hard to believe that the course of my life has been unusual in placing me in the proximity of people who had been prisoners. I grew up in the middle class. My father was a manager in one of the large aerospace companies. My mother was a housewife who occasionally worked part-time as a salesperson for Sears.

The purpose of this book is to acquaint the reader with six young people, four male, two female, all of whom I knew when they were children in prison, all of whose lives I have been able to follow, to some extent, after their release. Their lives have been difficult, both before and after they were locked up, but some, with help, have been able to improve on what they were born into.

The people I have written about in this book were not selected at random. I was the counselor, or case manager, for four of the six young people I describe here during part of the time they spent in Ash Meadow. I knew all but one, Reggie Greene, when I worked in maximum security. Reggie was on my caseload when I was in Swan Cottage. I wrote about him before, in *Paranoia and Heartbreak*, and I wrote about Cassie Martin and Norah Joines and Kyle Payment also in that book. I have written about them again because the structure of my earlier book did not permit inclusion of some information, and also because, in some cases, I learned more about them—what their lives were like before they came to Ash Meadow, what became of them after they left—since completing *Paranoia and Heartbreak*.

Readers of both that book and this one will find that I have summarized aspects of the lives of these kids as they were depicted in the former book, and presented these summaries in *Children in Prison* as a kind of introduction to what follows, or, in Reggie Greene's and Cassie Martin's cases, integrated the synthesis into the main narrative. In these instances, I have presented information on the earlier parts of their lives that I did not present in *Paranoia & Heartbreak* but which helps to clarify why these kids came to Ash Meadow.

I have not written about Marcus Bellows or Jamal Willson before. I chose not to include Marcus in *Paranoia and Heartbreak* because I thought I had already talked enough about gang kids. What I did not appreciate until later was Marcus' use of violence and intimidation, his gang involvement aside, as a way to avoid being demeaned, or to retaliate against others for having abased him, or to keep them at bay because he was afraid of them. Although the evidence existed in my journal, I did not understand it until I wrote Marcus' story.

Jamal Willson was not on my caseload. He is hardly mentioned in my journal, and other than a newspaper article and discussions about him with former colleagues at Ash Meadow, what I've written about him is drawn entirely from memory.

Except for the chapter on my concluding thoughts and observations, the chapter on Kyle Payment was the last one I wrote. I had not thought of writing about him again. Readers of *Paranoia & Heartbreak* may recall that Kyle was the only resident in my time at Ash Meadow that I took to the floor when I didn't have to, but was angry enough to want to. I had not been his case manager. I had no information about him other than what I had already written. But then, after I had written about the other five people in *Children in Prison* and had put the manuscript in a drawer to allow it time to mature away from my eyes and pen, I received a letter from Kyle. He had read *Paranoia & Heartbreak* and, despite my efforts to disguise his identity, had recognized himself in it. A correspondence of several years ensued during which I learned a great deal more about him, including the answers to questions that had troubled me for more than a dozen years. My portrait of him in this book is drawn largely from our exchange of letters.

Though none of the major "characters" I write about in this book had known any of the others before coming to Ash Meadow, several had certain things in common. All had attached themselves to older people, either adults or older kids, who later, directly or indirectly, led them toward trouble. All, except for Jamal and Cassie, had a history of chronic or resurgent anger. None, for various reasons, had a father at home, or anyone who routinely took the place of a father, although all, except perhaps for Jamal, had fathers who had lived with them earlier in their lives. All had known poverty, but not all had been poor their entire lives.

All but Cassie had used drugs. Both Cassie and Reggie sold drugs. Norah's mother was an alcoholic and Reggie's mother smoked marijuana regularly. Many in Kyle's family were addicted to methamphetamine. I became acquainted with Marcus' and Cassie's mothers and believed, and continue to believe, that both women were doing the best they could under very difficult circumstances. Perhaps Norah's and Reggie's mothers were also doing the best they were capable of, given their infirmities, but I find that I cannot sympathize with Norah's mother, even though I never met her. Health problems overwhelmed Norah's and Reggie's families in concert with other problems, including substance abuse.

Both Norah and Cassie were the victims of sexual abuse, one directly, one collaterally, before coming to Ash Meadow. In Cassie's case, her sister was the primary victim, but the entire family suffered from the consequences of the abuse. Also, three of the boys had been sexually violated, one collaterally.

In the work I used to do as a rehabilitation counselor, I learned to expect that part of the story of a girl's being sexually assaulted by an older relative or by her mother's boyfriend was her mother's refusal to believe her when she told, even accusing her of lying. One explanation for this denial is the mother's economic dependence on her husband or boyfriend, but another explanation is that the mother suspects her daughter of trying to destroy her relationship out of rivalry or jealousy. Of course, these two explanations are not mutually exclusive. Whatever the cause of the mother's denial of her daughter's abuse, the girl would invariably tell me that this was the worst part of the experience, her mother's refusal to believe her.

Boys who were abused by their uncle or grandfather or stepfather or mother's boyfriend—I did not hear of a boy being sexually abused by his father, although physical abuse by parents, both fathers and mothers, was common—depicted their mothers as tending to dismiss their abuse as insignificant. One boy's mother told him not to worry about it; her brother had done the same thing to her when she was his age. Or they were told by their mothers or grandmothers not to tell anyone about it because it would bring shame to the family if anybody outside it found out.

All the boys had started getting into trouble around the onset of puberty and the time they entered middle school, although the conditions for behavioral discord—at home or in the neighborhood—had been present since they were small, or even before they were born. For Marcus and Reggie, the pattern was this: domestic disruption followed by behavioral problems at school culminating in suspension, expulsion, or the boy's refusal to return, concomitant with or followed by drug use, theft, and gang involvement.

Jamal remained in school until his arrest and had no record of theft or gang involvement. I know little about Kyle's problems at school, if any. I do know that he was not involved with a gang. Certainly he experienced domestic disruption—for a time, according to his case manager, Kyle, his mother, and his siblings lived in a tent.

The pattern of domestic instability and leaving school also fits Cassie, even though she was not associated with a gang and was not involved with criminal activity other than selling drugs. Domestic violence was a part of Norah's life too, but she didn't leave school and she didn't steal or sell drugs, though the gang she was involved with probably did.

Often kids at Ash Meadow were not aware of life's possibilities, of possibilities for their own lives, or they had lost confidence in themselves to achieve what, earlier, they thought they could. Although Norah had been a child fashion model, modeling as an adult became an impossible fantasy for her in late adolescence and she decided not to try to re-establish the relationships she had had with people in the modeling agencies.

Another kid, a boy not mentioned in this book, was unaware that there were other colleges in Seattle than the University of Washington, which had the reputation among African Americans of being racist. The boy was highly intelligent—his I.Q. was in the genius range—but he didn't have the information he needed to seek a future for himself outside of crime and prison, and he didn't trust people who weren't black to provide valid information.

All of the young people I have written about share a general distrust of the larger world and its institutions. Only particular people may be trusted, and they must be watched and must prove themselves before trust may be invested in them. Help may be found only with these people. Usually they are family members, or are close enough to one's family to be regarded as a part of it. In lieu of a family that functions effectively, on which one can rely for shelter, food, money, and a sense of security, a child often turns to other, older kids. That may mean a gang, though not necessarily. Sometimes a child is simply left to his own devices, or abandoned.

*   *   *

These are not stories in the sense of having a beginning, middle, and end, and somewhere near the end is a climax that has been foreshadowed by elements of the beginning and middle. Rather, these are small histories, biographies or profiles of persons whose lives are not yet finished, and about whom we have incomplete information. Because I wanted to get as close as I could to what was true about each person and the context of his or her life, I have not manufactured a climax, and the ending, except in one case, arises out of my loss of contact with the person rather than from a desire to tie things up in a neat package.

Hemingway said somewhere that a story may be a comedy or a tragedy, depending on where you end it. These unfinished stories are neither entirely comedic nor tragic (with possibly one or two exceptions), though you may want to weep at various parts in all of them. But the lives these stories represent are hard lives. They have to do with the effects of prison on children, and the events and environment that brought them to prison, and the lives they found themselves living after they were released from Ash Meadow. All of these stories, too, deal with human connection. Each of them, whatever else it may be, is a love story and deals with love lost and, in some cases, love found or regained.

As I did in *Paranoia and Heartbreak* and *In the Spider's Web*, I have used a variety of techniques in this book to avoid revealing personal identities. Everyone's name except Kyle Payment's, Curly Cook's—Curly, since deceased, was a professional musician who taught intermittently at Ash Meadow and its sister institutions—my wife Jeanne's, and my own has been changed, as well as many place names. When I told Kyle Payment that I wanted to include him in this book, he made it a proviso that I use his real name.[3] The reader should be aware that most of the information about them prior to coming to Ash Meadow or, in some cases, after leaving Ash Meadow, comes from these young people themselves.

Paranoia & Heartbreak was taken from the journal I kept during my years at Ash Meadow. In *Children in Prison* I have again used my journal, but also I have relied on my memory, although I recognize some, at least, of the problems of memory. I know, for example, that on at least one occasion I integrated another person's memory of an event at which I was not present into my own store of memories.[4] But knowing this, I believe I have been able, through a kind of self-interrogation, to separate my own memories from others.'

My memories of conversations are, I think, accurate. A conversation has its own logic, though it may jump from one subject to another, seemingly without transition. With each I tried to discern its underlying logic and to follow it out through the dialogue of the speakers, capturing its tone as I was able. In this, as do more formal interviews, a recalled conversation may have as much in common with the art of translation as of reportage.

The six stories in this book, then, are informed by my journal and by memory, but also by emails to and from Norah Joines, essays I had assigned Reggie Greene to write, an unfinished memoir written by Cassie Martin, and the letters Kyle Payment and I wrote each other.

About Cassie Martin: when she was in Ash Meadow, she began to write about herself. I believe she wanted to understand herself better than she did and saw writing as a vehicle to accomplish this. But also she thought that if other, younger girls knew her story they might spare themselves the pain and dislocation she had experienced, or at least they would know that someone else had endured, and this might give them the courage to persevere. As she completed a portion of her autobiography, she gave it to me to comment on.

I had agreed to assist her in her writing, but I soon realized that I could not read it in the small bits she gave me, and I decided not to read any more until I had the entire book. But she didn't complete it and never mentioned it to me again. I forgot about it until, having left Ash Meadow, I was going through my papers and came across it, as much as she had given me. Her unfinished memoir has informed my thinking about her, and helped me to understand how she regarded her own history.

I

Cassie Martin
The Accommodation of Loss

Earliest Years

She was born in the same small town in Texas that her mother and her father and her mother's mother had been born and had grown up in. She was the third and last child that her parents would have together. All three were daughters. Her mother, Helen, was close to her own mother, talking to her daily and walking to her house to visit several times a week. When she visited her mother, Helen would leave the older girls with a neighbor but take Cassie with her. Cassie went wherever Helen went. If Helen closed the door behind her when she went into the bathroom, Cassie cried.

Sometimes when Cassie and her mother visited Grandma, she would hear her mother talking about her longing to return to school and her grandma telling her that she would watch her daughters for her if she did go back to school. Helen would say that she'd never had a job and that she knew she needed more education before she could support her family. Grandma would say she wanted Helen to go to school so that she didn't have to depend on Louis, her husband, whom both considered unreliable.

At home again after a visit to Grandma, Helen would prepare dinner. When Cassie's father came home, Helen would pretend nothing was amiss. She would pretend that she was happy to see him and would ask him how work went. Cassie had never seen her parents argue or fight, so she did not know what to think about what she heard at her grandmother's house.

* * *

Helen began to take night classes with the goal of becoming a secretary. Cassie and her sisters stayed with their grandmother or their father when Helen was at school.

Louis did not want Helen to go to school, and told her that her high school diploma was enough. After a while he began to come home late from work. Some nights he did not come home at all. There were nights when Cassie pretended to be asleep but lay awake listening to her parents argue. One night she heard her mother say, "You do what you think you have to do. Just pay the bills around here. I don't care if you never come home."

Sometimes, when Helen thought she was alone, Cassie would see her on her knees, praying to God to help her leave her husband. She knew his children needed him, she told God, but she needed to leave. As the weeks passed, her prayers grew longer, thanking God for giving her and her children life and for bringing her this far in her secretarial training, and imploring Him each time she prayed to help her leave Louis.

Louis was gone sometimes for days at a time now. When he returned he always brought gifts for the children—dolls, stuffed animals, candy. Once, after talking quietly with Helen in the bedroom, they came out and announced that they were all going out for ice cream. In the car, Cassie sat between them. She felt good because she hadn't been with her parents together in a long time. She enjoyed seeing them sit together in the ice cream shop, even sharing their ice cream with each other.

Afterward, they rented some videos and went home and Helen popped popcorn and made Kool-Aid. Watching the videos, Louis and Helen cuddled on the couch. Cassie was confused. She had seen her mom beg God to help her leave Louis, but now it looked like she didn't want to leave him. But later, when they thought the children were asleep, they began to fight again, Helen demanding to know where Louis had been, and Louis responding by saying she had told him she didn't care what he did as long as he paid the bills, and that he made sure his kids had everything they needed. They were still fighting when Cassie fell asleep.

*   *   *

Helen had been working at the phone company for over a year, her mother caring for the girls while she was at work, when she learned for certain that Louis had another woman. She told her mother that it was too much, that she had to leave him now. Her mother agreed, saying Helen didn't deserve what Louis was doing to her. Her mother said she and the children could come back home—Helen could have her bedroom back and they would make room for the kids.

One evening after Louis had been gone for a week, he came home as though he had been there only yesterday and Helen treated him as though he still lived in their house. He asked her how her day had gone and she called him "Honey." When she was cooking he came up behind her and kissed her on the back of her neck. He told her that he loved her cooking and kissed her again.

Supper wasn't ready yet and the other girls went outdoors to play with the gifts their father had brought. Cassie stayed inside, ostensibly to color in her new coloring book, but really to listen to what her parents were saying. Soon they were arguing again. Helen told Louis that if he continued to do what he was doing, she was going to take the children and leave him. Louis told her not to threaten him with his kids. Then Helen burst out: "You fucking that little ho and you think I don't know? But I know!"

Louis said Helen was crazy, he wasn't messing with anybody.

"Okay, if you say I'm crazy, then I'm crazy," Helen said. "The kids need shoes for school."

"All you had to do was tell me," Louis said, and he handed her some money. "There's enough for shoes and something for you. Buy yourself something nice."

"I don't need your money," Helen said. She called the kids in for dinner. It was strange having their father eat with them, but they enjoyed it. Louis made everyone laugh.

He spent the night. He went to work the next morning, then returned in the afternoon. He did the same thing the next day. It was as if he regarded the house with his wife and children in it as his home again. Every day he left for work at six in the morning and was back by four in the afternoon. He played games with the girls and helped the older ones with their schoolwork. Cassie felt like she had a family again. Her mom called her dad "Honey" and he called her "Darlin'" or "Baby." Cassie did not hear them fighting any more and she did not hear her mother praying. It was like that for weeks.

One day at her grandmother's house Cassie overheard her mother telling Grandma that she was going to leave Louis. She said she was taking the children and going away with Anthony. Cassie did not know who Anthony was. Grandma said it was good that Helen was leaving and offered to give her some money. But Helen said she didn't need it. She had saved some from what she had earned from her job.

That night everything was the same. Helen cooked dinner, did some ironing and acted as she usually did. But later, when she thought everyone was asleep, she prayed. She informed God that Louis' drinking had gotten worse and that she was leaving him. And she thanked Him for sending her Anthony, who was a good man. Cassie had not known that her father had a drinking problem.

A few days later, Helen woke the girls up early and took them to her mother's house. Everybody was there, Helen's brother and his family and her aunt and her family. There were cousins everywhere. They had gathered to say goodbye to Helen. Her brother told her he would miss her, that things would not be the same with her gone, and thanked her for keeping him straight when he was growing up. Helen's aunt told her that if she ever needed to come home, just call and she would send for Helen and the kids. Grandma told Helen that she wanted her to stay, but knew it was better that she leave. She said she had confidence in Helen, but that her room was right down the hall and she could come home anytime. Helen cried. Cassie had never seen her mother cry before. Helen assured everyone that she was going to be all right.

She took the kids home and waited for Louis to come back from work. He came through the door a little after eight and kissed the children and hugged them. Helen did not even say hello to him. When Louis asked what was wrong, she said, "I'm tired of your shit."

"Don't do this in front of my children," Louis said.

"Your children? You ain't gonna have no children after tonight. I'm leaving your ass!"

"Y'all go to y'all's room," Louis told the girls.

"For what? Louis, they know what's going on. It's too late to hide it from them. I'm done with you, Louis. I can't make up no more lies for why you don't come home at night."

"Helen, quit talking crazy. Y'all go to y'all's room. Me and your mama need to talk."

The girls went to their room, but even so, Cassie could hear every word her parents said. She had never heard her mother talk to her dad like that before.

"I know what you been doin'! I'm not takin' this shit! I watched my mother go through this shit and I'm not going to go through it myself! Not any more! You ain't worth it. Go be with your bitch!"

"Helen, I don't know what you're talking about. You're crazy."

"I'm crazy? Okay, here are your papers. I want a divorce."

*   *   *

They drove for three days and then they were in a city called Seattle. The houses were big, and there were trees and grass and small lakes, and there were streetlights on all the streets.

They lived in a two-story, three-bedroom house. Cassie shared a bedroom with Yvette, her next older sister. Keisha, the oldest, had her own bedroom. There were blinds on the windows instead of sheets, and, for the first time, they had a washer and a dryer. The kids liked this big house. Helen was optimistic about her and her children's future. She began to take classes at a community college.

Anthony was working. He was a construction worker and had arranged for a job before they left Texas. He loved Helen and was glad to provide for her and her children. On Sundays, the family went to a movie, a museum, the zoo—there were a lot of things to do and see in Seattle that the kids hadn't had in Texas. They always did something, even if the weather was bad, and then they would go out to eat. There was a restaurant that Cassie particularly liked because you could eat as much as you wanted, even desserts. Helen began to take the kids to church a couple of times a month before their family outing. Cassie always looked forward to both, to going to church where she could listen to the choir, and then to going out with her mom and Anthony and her sisters.

After two years of taking classes at the community college, Helen graduated. She found a job immediately, working with handicapped people, even though Anthony wanted her to be an at-home mom. She had Sundays and Mondays off, so she could still take the children to church and then out for Family Day. And she got off work in time to get home before the children came back from school. Cassie looked forward to coming home and helping her mom prepare dinner.

They began to have what Helen called "mother-daughter talks" when she gave Cassie her bath at night. Sometimes Cassie would have to take her bath with Yvette, but other times Helen would bathe her alone, washing her hair and her back where she couldn't reach. Their talks consisted of Helen talking about and advising on certain topics: independence, perseverance, trying your best, love, forgiveness, success, and life's struggles. Cassie came to feel that she knew her mother's life as if she had lived it herself.

Helen said, "Cassie, I want you to be strong, to never give up. Even when things are hard for you, never quit."

She said, "In life, you may have to fight to get where you want to be, and you may have to fight for what you want. But if you keep at it, in time you will get what you want."

She taught Cassie how to cook, clean house, wash clothes, and how to present herself to other people.

Cassie believed her mom got as much from talking to her as she got from listening to her mom. Sometimes Helen would cry, but she would say, "Baby, these are tears of joy." Other times she would cry and Cassie would hug her and Helen would say over and over, "Cassie, I love you so much, Baby." Cassie hated to see her mother cry, whether it was from joy or sadness.

The more they talked, the more Cassie wanted to know.

"Mom, how did you meet my father?" "What did you like about him most?" "Were you close to your mother when you were my age?"

And Helen answered. "I fell in love with your father the day I met him. He was tall and handsome. He was a gentleman. He opened doors for me and picked me up from school. Later I learned never to go out with a man who's prettier than you."

"I was really close to my mother," she continued. "There were times when it seemed like my mother was all I had. That's why I named you after her, Baby. I could talk to her about anything. My mother went through a lot with my father when I was young, and me and my brother saw it all. I didn't want y'all to see any of that. That's why we left Texas, before things got to that point."

"Mom, what happened?"

"It's a long story. Someday I'll tell it to you, but not now."

* * *

One night during their mother-daughter talk, Helen asked, "Do you like Anthony?"

"He's nice. And he makes you happy."

"Yeah, he's a good man. And I love him."

"You loved my father too, didn't you?"

"Cassie, I loved your father for too many years."

"Mom, when are you going to tell me what happened with Grandma?"

"Oh, Baby... Well, I'll tell you now."

When she was young, Helen said, her father became involved with another woman, got her pregnant, left Helen's mother and moved in with her. Helen's mother would not let Helen or her brother see their father. Her brother grew up angry with his mother for not allowing him to have a relationship with his dad. Eventually their mother told them about their father and his other family. Their father died in a car accident only a few years after he moved out of their house.

"Did you love him?" Cassie asked.

"I loved him, but I hated him for what he put my mother through and for what my brother went through. It took years for my brother to understand that what happened was not his fault or my mother's fault."

Helen began to cry and Cassie, still sitting in her bath water, hugged her. Helen said, "Cassie, I don't want you to ever have to go through the pain that I've gone through."

Cassie couldn't sleep that night. She lay awake thinking about her mother and what she had suffered when she was with Cassie's father. Cassie knew her parents had loved each other, but now her mom was with Anthony. Cassie thought he was all right. Yvette thought he was all right, too. Cassie began to pray silently some nights when she lay in bed. She asked God to help everyone in her family, even those she didn't know.

* * *

Helen asked Cassie what was going on with Keisha. She was keeping to herself even more than she usually did.

Cassie didn't know, but she had also noticed that Keisha was withdrawn, although she still helped Cassie with her schoolwork.

Helen was working a graveyard shift now. It was okay because the kids were older and pretty much looked after themselves. Also, Anthony was home at night. Helen was home by the time the kids left for school and was home when they returned, so they felt all right about her schedule.

* * *

Yvette told Cassie that something was wrong with Keisha. She didn't know what it was, she said, but it had to do with Anthony. Cassie thought Yvette did know what it was and insisted she tell her.

Yvette began to cry. Anthony had touched Keisha "down there," she said. He had done it not only once, but a lot. And he forced Keisha to kiss him and he kissed her. Mama didn't know and Keisha was afraid to tell her because Anthony had said that Mama wouldn't believe her because Mama hates her because she's just like Dad.

Cassie said she was going to talk to Keisha, but Yvette said no, Keisha had told her not to tell anyone.

I have to, Cassie said.

It was a little before midnight. Helen had already left for work. Cassie knocked on the door to Keisha's room. She asked Keisha to come into the bathroom with her because she had gum stuck in her hair and she needed Keisha's help in getting it out. Yvette had already tried, but she couldn't do it.

In the bathroom, Cassie locked the door and turned on the tap to get the sound of the running water. She asked Keisha if it was true that Anthony had touched her. Keisha was angry that Yvette had told, but admitted it was true.

Cassie said Keisha had to tell Mom.

Mom wouldn't believe her because she loved Anthony and hated her, Keisha said. Anthony had told her that Mom was always talking about how much she hated her because she acted like Dad.

Anthony was lying, Cassie said. Mom was always saying how smart and pretty you were. Cassie asked what Anthony did to her.

Keisha turned the handle of the tap so that the water ran louder.

He made her touch his thing, Keisha said, and he touched her and kissed her chest. He made her take a bath while he watched after Helen had gone to her job. Keisha begged Cassie not to tell their mother. Helen wouldn't believe her anyway. And besides, what could their mother do? Anthony said she wouldn't leave because they had nowhere to go.

Back in their room, Cassie told Yvette that Keisha had told her everything but didn't want her to tell their mom.

Cassie didn't know what to do. She wanted to cuss Anthony out. He had messed with Keisha and had turned her against their mother. Cassie had never hidden anything from her mother. Her mother had always told her that she wanted her children to be able to talk to her about anything. Cassie asked God to tell her what she should do. The clock on the dresser read 12:40. She decided to wait until one o'clock to call her mother. Anthony would be asleep by then.

* * *

"Mom? This is Cassie."

"Cassie, why are you whispering? Why are you up so late?"

"Mom, you have to come home."

"What's wrong? Where's Anthony?"

"It's Anthony."

"What happened? Is he okay?"

"Mom, he's been doing bad stuff to Keisha. He's been touching her and kissing her and making her touch him down there."

"What! Where's Keisha?"

"She's in her room. She told me not to tell you. Anthony told her you wouldn't believe her. He said you hate her because she's like dad."

"Does Keisha believe him?"

"Yes, Mom. She's really scared. She begged me not to tell you."

"Cassie, don't say anything to anybody. I want you to sleep in Keisha's room until I get home. I'm going to try to get off early, but I'm the only one here and I can't leave until my relief comes in. I'm going to call her now. I'll be there as soon as I can. Don't let Keisha out of your sight. If anything happens, you call me back, do you hear?"

"Yes, Mom. Mom, Anthony told Keisha not to tell you because we have no place to go."

"He did, huh? Okay, you do what I told you. I'll be there as soon as I can. I love you."

"I love you too, Mom."

Cassie went to Keisha's room. She was afraid that Anthony might do something to Yvette, but she did what her mother told her to do. She lay down beside Keisha. She wanted to stay awake, but dropped off.

When the bedroom door opened, she woke up. Anthony was in the doorway. He looked at her but didn't say anything. He backed out into the hall and closed the door. Cassie listened hard: he didn't go into her and Yvette's room. Keisha's clock read 5:31. Anthony left for work at six. Helen got home between 6:35 and 6:45.

At 5:40 Cassie heard her mother's car pull into the driveway. She looked through the window to be sure it was her mom, then she lay down again. She heard the door open and her mom say, "Hi, Honey."

"Baby, why you home so early?" Anthony asked.

"Oh, my relief came early and she said I could leave. The girls ain't up yet?"

"They don't get up till after I leave. For some reason, when I went to check on Keisha, Cassie was in the bed with her."

Cassie couldn't hear what her mom said. She heard Anthony leave—first the sound of the front door, then those of the car door closing and the engine starting.

Helen got the kids up and brought them into the living room. She asked Keisha if what Cassie told her was true. Keisha began to cry and said it was.

"Don't cry, Keisha. I believe you. I believe you. I would never pick a man over my children. I believe you." Helen was crying too.

"I'm sorry, Mom," Keisha said.

"Baby, it ain't your fault. We are leaving. You'll never have to see Anthony again. I promise you that. Now y'all get y'all's clothes on and bring all the things you'll need. We are leaving. I want y'all to know that I would never ever pick a man over my children. I love you all. Y'all are the reason I live and work so hard. I love all of you. Keisha, do you hear me? I love you. That punk is going to jail for what he did."

Post-Trauma and Dislocation

They lived in a one-bedroom flat above a church. The girls slept in the single bed. Helen slept in an armchair. Most of what they owned had been left behind. They had their clothes and Helen had her car. Helen tried to reassure her children that their situation was only temporary.

Keisha blamed herself for what had happened to her family. Sometimes

Cassie would wake up at night and find Keisha sitting on the edge of the bed, unable to sleep. She was doing badly in school.

Helen found a counselor who would see them. In counseling, Helen would sometimes get upset, but nowhere near the extent to which Keisha did. Listening to Keisha, Cassie could not imagine herself suffering as her sister was suffering. You always want to know why, Cassie thought years later, but even the best answer in the world wouldn't have lessened Keisha's pain. "It was in her voice, her eyes, the way she sat, the way she felt around men now, and in the way she blamed herself," Cassie said. Helen began having mother-daughter talks with all of her daughters instead of just Cassie alone.

After two months in the shelter, they were able to move to a house. Later, Cassie would feel that their time in the shelter was their lowest as a family. It was a time when the family almost disintegrated. But it was also a time when Helen and her girls learned to depend on each other. They decided on a code to let one another know that something was wrong, that one of them was hurt: "Your love is my love." Helen warned the girls never to play with those words, that they meant only what they said, what they were intended to mean. "Your love is my love."

Once they moved into the new house, Keisha did better. She began to enjoy school again and she began to laugh again. Helen found a new job, one that allowed her to be home most evenings. She felt guilty about what had happened to Keisha, especially because it had happened with the man with whom she had chosen to live.

*   *   *

Louis had learned what happened, whether from Helen or Keisha or Yvette, Cassie didn't know, and he came to Seattle where he and Helen tried to repair the damage between them.

He stayed for a month, then returned to Texas. Helen had discovered that she didn't need him anymore. She had made a home for herself and her children, and a man, even if he was her children's father, had no place in her house. The girls were sad to see Louis leave, because they knew their parents would not try to reconcile again.

Helen continued her mother-daughter talks. "Never give up," she said.

"Say no and mean no."

"Don't come in second best."

The dictum that Helen most impressed on Cassie was "A person should only have to deny you once. Never give him the chance to do it twice."

A Mother's Love, a New Life

Cassie was twelve. She and her best friend, Kiki, and some other girls skipped sixth period to hang out at the corner store near the school. Neither Cassie nor Kiki had any money and neither knew how to take the Metro bus home anyway, so they didn't want to be far from where the school buses collected to pick up the kids at the end of the day. Although their friends were skipping school regularly, and some even stole from the store, the two girls had not stolen anything and this was the only time they had ever cut class.

On the bus ride home, Cassie and Kiki were frightened of being found out. They knew the school would call their parents about 6:00. They made a plan: Cassie would call Kiki at 5:45 and they would talk for half an hour so that they would be on the phone when the school called. Cassie felt guilty and she was afraid her mother would learn what she had done. Still, she behaved as she normally did around the house after school and nobody acted as though anything was out of the ordinary.

At 5:45 she called Kiki and they talked for a few minutes just to take up time. But then Cassie heard the beep from another call coming in. Instead of the school, it was one of Helen's friends from church. Cassie told Kiki she had to go. Kiki begged her not to, telling her she was going to mess everything up, but Cassie felt she had to give the phone to her mom.

While conversing with her church friend, Helen got the cue from another call. Cassie had been eavesdropping. Now she looked at her mother; Helen was glaring at her. Thank you, Helen said into the phone. Then she told her friend she would call her back: something had just come up.

"Cassie, where were you during sixth period today? Don't lie to me."

"I was at school."

"Cassie, don't lie to me. Where were you? You weren't at no damn school. The school just called here. Now where were you?"

Before Cassie could say anything more, Helen slapped her. She was yelling, "Where the hell were you? Do you know what could have happened to you? What were you doing? Who were you with? How long have you been doing this?" She kept yelling, not giving Cassie an opportunity to answer. When Cassie tried to respond, Helen screamed, "Shut the hell up! I don't want to hear any bullshit! Shut up! Just shut up!" Helen was yelling at her just like she had yelled at Cassie's father that time before she and the girls left Texas. Cassie was crying. She tried again to speak but her mother only got more upset.

"You think you're grown up? You think you don't have to go to school? Well, you can get the fuck out of my house! You get out now!"

* * *

Kiki's father said Cassie could not stay with them.

Cassie was sitting on a bench at a bus stop when a young woman came up to her and told her not to cry and asked her what was wrong. Cassie told her. Shari said Cassie could come with her. Shari was nineteen.

* * *

They lived in a motel room whose smallness reminded Cassie of the shelter she and her family had lived in. Everything Shari owned was in this room. For the first couple of days Cassie continued to go to school, but she couldn't concentrate. Her mind was on other things. She wondered what would happen if her mother came to the school or if Shari did not pick her up when school was out. Sometimes she fell asleep in class. She saw Kiki. Kiki felt bad for her, but there was nothing she could do—her father didn't want Cassie to stay with them because he didn't want to be responsible if anything happened to her. After two days, Cassie didn't return to school.

Shari showed her how to sell crack cocaine. "Remember to get your money first. Give them as much as they want to pay for, but don't go anywhere with them. Are you scared?"

"Yeah."

"Don't be scared. It's easy. Girl, this is the only way to make some fast money." Shari warned her not to tell anybody how old she was. "Say you're seventeen and that you're my little sister. Okay?"

"Okay."

The only clothes Cassie had were on her body. Shari bought her some sweat suits, socks, underwear, shampoo and deodorant, and told Cassie to give her twenty dollars when she started earning money. Cassie knew that all the stuff Shari bought her cost more than twenty dollars.

The first night, Cassie made over three hundred dollars. She had been scared, but she was also happy to have made so much money, and so fast! Shari showed her where to go and who to talk to to buy more crack.

Shari styled Cassie's hair as a grown-up would wear it. Shari picked out clothes for her that someone older would wear. If she was going to pass for seventeen, she had to look seventeen, Shari said. In fact, Cassie did not look like she was twelve years old. In her new clothes, men blew kisses at her and whistled when she walked by. Everyone believed that she and Shari were sisters. They were always together.

Like Cassie, Shari had been born in Texas. Unlike Cassie, Shari did not know her father because her mother left him and moved to Seattle when Shari was small. Like Cassie, Shari's mother kicked her out of the house when she was twelve. Like Cassie, Shari started selling drugs in order to take care of herself—"to raise myself," she said. She had a son who lived with her aunt. Her son's father was in prison.

"Cassie, never tell anyone how old you are, because they'll try to take advantage of you," Shari said again. Listening to her was like listening to her mother during their mother-daughter talks. But Shari's concerns were more concrete than Helen's. Helen had talked about life; Shari talked about survival.

Cassie did not tell anyone that she was twelve and she practiced what she would say if anyone questioned her: My name is Kendra. I'm seventeen years old. I'm Shari's little sister and I just moved here from California.

* * *

She missed her mother. She called her, but when her mother answered, Cassie sat silently crying while Helen said hello over and over. Afterward Cassie sat with the phone in her lap, playing over again in her mind, as if it were on a tape, all that had happened between her and her mother. Her mother had so often told her, "Never turn your back on the people you love," but that was exactly what she had done to Cassie. She had said, "Cassie, a person should deny you only once. Never give him the chance to do it again." Did that go for Helen too? Should Cassie never give her mother the chance to deny her again? Cassie wished she had not skipped school that day, and wished too that her mom had listened to her when she said she had done it only once. Everything happened so fast that night; Cassie wished she could do it all over, but slow it down so her mother could hear her.

* * *

Selling drugs was part of her life now. Some nights she would make five or six hundred dollars. Shari made more because she bought more. Shari told her, "Cassie, always spend your money on drugs first. Then you can buy clothes and the other shit you want. But buy the drugs first. If you have drugs, you'll always have money."

It had been over a month since Cassie had seen anyone in her family. She went to their school to see her sisters. They wanted to know where she'd been, what she had been doing, how she got those clothes, where she got the money to buy them. Keisha asked if she was selling her body.

No, not her body. Drugs, Cassie told her.

Drugs?

Yeah. Drugs.

Cassie was hurt that Keisha could think she was a ho. Don't they think any more of me than that? She was angry but she was also happy to see Keisha and Yvette and to hear about what was going on with her mother, so she did not let her anger show. She gave them each twenty dollars so they could eat something besides school lunches. She told them she'd bring them each twenty-five dollars a week from now on, but they couldn't tell Mom. The girls agreed.

* * *

That night Shari told her more about herself. When she was twelve her mother kicked her out of the house after Shari told her that her boyfriend— her mother's boyfriend—had touched her. Her mother did not believe her, or didn't want to. That's why, Shari told Cassie, I will never let anything happen to you. I've been through a lot with men.

Once she met a man who was much older than she was, and he took her to California and made her sell her body. He beat her, he burned her with cigarettes, sometimes he locked her in the trunk of his car, and he kept all the money she earned. But she had a regular who gave her a lot of money one time, almost a thousand dollars, and instead of going back to her pimp she got on a bus for Seattle. For a long time she was afraid that he would come up to Seattle and find her, but she never saw him again.

Cassie, she said, I know it's hard for you to be away from home, but you'll be okay. I'll be there for you. I'll take care of you. But don't trust any of these men you meet, Cassie. If they knew how old you are, some of them would try to turn you out, just like they did me.

Shari was so open with her that Cassie told her what Anthony had done to Keisha. Shari asked, Did your mom believe her? When Cassie said yes, Shari began to cry. Cassie hugged her and said she would never leave her, that Shari was her sister and that everything would work out for them. Cassie felt that they were taking care of each other. We have to stick together, Shari said, and Cassie nodded yes. She felt that Shari really was like a sister to her.

* * *

On the street, a guy named Rashif was hitting on her. Not really hitting on her, but teasing her, paying attention to her. Cassie was enjoying it but was also a little afraid. She could tell he knew she was young because he asked her who she was here with. My sister Shari, Cassie said.

Shari? Shari's your sister?

Yeah. My big sister.

Shari's my homegirl. Where's she at?

There, in the store. Here she comes.

Rashif wasn't lying. Shari was as happy to see him as he was to see her. He'd just been released from prison and this was the first time they'd seen each other in a while. He was dealing again and he and Shari agreed to hook up later. In the meantime, he asked about her little sis.

She's just makin' her money. You know, she's my sis.

So who's your man? Rashif asked Cassie.

I don't have no man.

As fine as you are, you don't have a man? She ain't got a man, Shari?

What did she say? She don't have no man. For real. She's my sis. I watch out for her.

So what's up, Little Mama? You gonna give me your number?

I don't have no number.

Give him the number to our room, Shari said.

Cassie did. And Rashif gave her his number.

So when you gonna call me, Baby?

You call me first.

Oh, so that's how it is. Okay, no problem.

We're gonna hit you up tonight, Shari said.

Yeah, I'm poppin'. But now let me get away from here. I'll see you later, Baby, he said to Cassie.

He's all about money, Shari said, and he's cool. Before Cassie could say anything, Shari said, Naw, he's my homeboy. He's hella cool. He's sweet, too. That's the kind of guy you should mess with.

They stayed downtown until they had sold their last packet.

That night while they ate junk food and watched movies in their room, Shari told Cassie to be sure not to lose Rashif's number because they were going to start buying from him. He would give them a good deal, she said.

Cassie asked her how old Rashif was.

Gotta be about twenty-two. But he's cool. Trust me. He's all about money, but he's not about no funny shit. He likes you, Cassie. We're gonna get a hella good deal on the goods now.

They were asleep when Rashif called. Cassie answered. It was one o'clock. Rashif apologized for calling so late. Time just got away from him, but he wanted to call because he had said he would. He asked what she and Shari were doing tomorrow.

Same as today, Cassie said, but they needed some goods. We're out.

Rashif told her to call him as soon as she woke up. And he told her to have sweet dreams.

* * *

In the morning Cassie called him and they agreed to hook up in an hour. She also agreed to go to a movie with him. Shari was more excited than Cassie about her going out with Rashif and said they'd have to find her some clothes to wear, something cute.

When Rashif came over, Cassie thought he looked even better than he had the day before. He had light skin and a body that could be in a magazine. He had the softest, sweetest voice and his smile would disperse the gloom from the unhappiest of people. They talked for a while and then Shari showed some money and Rashif began to pull out packages.

He and Cassie agreed that he would pick her up at seven-thirty. She walked him to his car. He had a white four-door on chrome wheels and with black windows. It was nice.

Back in the room, Shari was ecstatic. Rashif had given them extra goods without even saying anything, proof that he really dug Cassie. She and Cassie went downtown to make some of their money back and to get Cassie something to wear tonight.

*   *   *

Cassie was wearing a long black skirt slit up the side of her leg. She wore a red V-neck blouse that revealed her cleavage, black fishnet pantyhose, and a pair of black suede pumps. She opened the door.

Rashif looked at her. "Damn, Baby, you look good."

"You take care of my sis!" Shari called out from the room as Rashif and Cassie walked out to his car. "And, Cassie, you call me!"

In the car, Cassie found it hard to make small talk. Rashif would say something but she didn't know how to follow up on it, to make it into a conversation. He asked her if she was afraid. When she denied it, he asked her if she had ever been on a date before. She admitted she had not. Ever had a boyfriend? No.

Rashif could not believe she had never had a boyfriend.

"So you mean to tell me you're the big V?"

"The V. Yeah, I'm the V."

"How old did you say you are?"

"Seventeen. I'll be eighteen in January."

"So you just turned seventeen."

"Yeah."

All kinds of things were going through her mind. Does he think I'm lying? How can he tell that I'm nervous? What does he think we're going to do? I hope he doesn't try anything. She had taken fifty dollars with her, more than enough to get a taxi back to the motel if she had to. But she didn't know if she would be able to run in her pumps.

In the theater they sat in the center of a middle row. They talked through the advertisements and the trailers, but then the movie started and Rashif leaned close to her and put his arm around her and whispered, "Relax, I won't bite you. Why are you shaking? Come here. I'll keep you warm." And he began to massage her neck. He whispered, "You're so tender," but Cassie did not understand what he meant. She had never heard anybody call a person "tender" before. She had only heard people say that steak was tender. She gave one of those half smiles that could mean anything.

Walking back to the car after the movie, they talked about business things. Then Rashif asked her if she liked being out with him.

"It was nice," Cassie said. She asked if she could use his phone to page Shari.

"Sure," he said, then asked, "Why are you so quiet?"

"I don't know."

"What do you like?"

"What do you mean? Like what?"

"Like what kind of music, food, men, cats or dogs—what kinds of things interest you?"

Shari called. She was up on Third Street by the park. Cassie said they would be up there in about ten minutes. On the way, Rashif assured her that he was for real, that he was only about money, like she was. He asked if he could kiss her. Seeing her hesitate, he told her she didn't have to if she didn't feel comfortable. Maybe next time. She agreed on next time.

*   *   *

It was two months before Cassie slept with Rashif. Even then she wouldn't—couldn't—have sex with him. There was kissing and touching, but there was no intercourse. Rashif could see she was scared and finally he asked her if she wanted him to stop. She did, and he did, and soon they were asleep.

In the past, after a date he would take her back to the room she shared with Shari and then he would return to his mother's house where he was living until he got a stake together. When Cassie agreed to spend the night with him, he rented a room in the same motel she lived in. After that night they saw each other every day. Rashif no longer charged her for goods and they pooled their money. Even though he had much more than she, he never made her feel small or as though what she contributed did not matter.

Rashif taught Cassie how to buy, cook, cut, weigh, and package to sell. He delivered his goods only at night, and if he was buying or selling more than a thousand dollars' worth, he would not allow Cassie to go with him. He told her that if something were to go wrong, he did not want her to be part of it. Cassie trusted him and did not question his decisions. If he was out making a delivery, she would wait for him to call, telling her, "Baby, it's cool. I'll be there in a minute." She became known as Rashif's girl. She'd be on the street and she'd hear people say, "That's Rashif's girl." It was as though she did not have a name of her own, but she didn't mind.

*   *   *

She had told her sisters that she would see them every week at school, but she had not kept her word. Occasionally she would call their house when she was certain Helen wasn't home. She had not spoken with her mother since Helen kicked her out. Still, she would sometimes call late at night just to hear Helen answer the phone, but she never said anything back.

One night when Helen was at work, Cassie and Rashif went over to her family's house. Rashif had not met Cassie's sisters. Before going, while Rashif was out making a delivery, Cassie called Keisha and Yvette and got them to promise they wouldn't say anything about her age when Rashif was there.

She and Rashif stopped by the mall on the way over. She bought two pair of shoes for each of her sisters and got each of them an outfit that she knew was popular with schoolgirls.

Keisha asked to talk with Cassie alone and they went upstairs. Keisha blamed herself for Cassie's leaving home. If it hadn't been for what happened with Anthony, Keisha said, Cassie would still be here. But that had thrown everything out of kilter for their family. Mom really wanted Cassie to come home.

Cassie said the problem with Anthony had nothing to do with her leaving. She began to cry. She thought about Keisha and Yvette all the time, she said, but she couldn't come home. What if mom got angry and kicked her out again? She couldn't stand that.

"Keisha, I really do. I think about you guys all the time, and every time I think about coming back, or even calling, I think about that night and how everything went down. Mama wouldn't even let me tell her, Keisha. I only skipped school that one time. She wouldn't even let me talk. She always told me that she wanted her children to be able to talk to her about anything, but she wouldn't even let me talk."

"I know, Cassie."

"Keisha, I got to go. You call me if y'all need anything. You're not the reason I can't come back, so don't worry about that."

On the way back to the motel, Rashif asked when he was going to be able to meet her mom.

* * *

This time when her mother answered, Cassie said, "Hey, Mom." It had been seven and a half months since she last talked to her mother.

"Cassie, is that you?"

"Yeah, Mom. How you doin'?"

"Where are you? Where have you been? Who are you with? When are you coming home?"

"Mom, I'm fine."

"What do you mean, you're fine?"

"I'm fine. Don't worry about me."

"What the hell do you mean, don't worry about you? Don't worry about my twelve-year-old daughter? I don't know if you're dead or alive, but you're gon' tell me don't worry about you?"

"Mom, I'm really fine."

"And what do you think you're doing, bringing these clothes and shit over here to Keisha and Yvette? Don't be bringing that drug money over this way, you hear?"

"I just called to see how you were doin.'"

"We're doin' fine—"

"I'll talk to you later. Bye."

Cassie had hoped her mother would tell her that she loved her. Since she left home only Rashif had said those words to her: I love you. She needed someone to talk to, to dump this stuff on. She couldn't talk to Rashif about it because she had lied to him about her age, and one of the reasons her mother was being so mean to her was that she was only twelve years old. She didn't want to talk to Shari because Shari had her own problems now and Cassie didn't want to worry her with hers. Shari was in a relationship that wasn't going well. Cassie suspected that her new boyfriend was beating her.

Then it came to her. Pray, she thought. You should pray. But she didn't want Rashif to hear her. I'll pray in the bathroom, she told herself. Just thinking about it gave her peace. She would take a bath and bring the radio in the bathroom with her so Rashif wouldn't think she was talking to herself.

"Baby, I'm going to get in the tub."

"Why are you taking the radio?"

"I'm going to be in there for a while and I need some music."

She reminded God who she was.

God, it's me, Cassie. I haven't talked to you in a long time. I know what I'm doing out here is wrong, but, God, you know why I'm doing it. God, I have to talk to someone and you told me in your Bible that you will always listen to me.

God, I need your help. Ever since Mama kicked me out, I haven't known what to do. Ever since that night, things have not been the same with me. God, I took everything she told me to heart. I believed in her. I trusted her. She was my hero. But all the time she talked to me, she was hiding so much stuff from me. Why did she do that? I thought I knew everything, but I didn't know nothing about these streets.

God, I want to go home, but I just can't. She told me from her own mouth, "Never give them the chance to hurt you again." God, I can't go back.

God, what's going to happen to me if I keep selling drugs? You told me that you knew me before I was even born, and you knew this was going to happen to me. God, what's going to happen? Will I get rich? Will I stay with Rashif forever? What's going to happen to me out here? Is this what you want for my life? Is this how it's supposed to be? God, what's going to happen to me? I was a good kid. I only skipped school one time. You know I wasn't a bad kid. Except for that one time, I went to school every day and I went to church on Sundays. Why did this happen to me?

God, you've got to help me. You said you would always be there for me, no matter what. God, where were you when Mom kicked me out? Where are you now?

"Baby, are you alive?" Rashif called. "You've been in there over an hour."

"Yeah, I'll be out in five minutes. God, I got to go. I'm sorry for skipping school. I knew it was wrong. I'll talk to you later."

*   *   *

They spent Christmas at Rashif's mother's house. His stepfather was there as well as his brother and sister and aunt and uncle and a lot of cousins. Everybody exchanged gifts and sat around and talked and laughed and ate. Cassie enjoyed herself but missed her mother's cooking. After dinner she went into one of the bedrooms and called Keisha and Yvette to let them know she hadn't forgotten them and to tell them she'd bring their gifts by another time. When her mother answered the phone, Cassie became tongue-tied. She didn't know what to say. Finally, she said, "Merry Christmas, Mom."

"Hey, Cassie, how you doin'?"

"I'm doing fine, Mom. I wanted to come and give Keisha and Yvette their gifts."

"Well, why don't you?"

"Because I'm with my boyfriend. I want him to come too."

"Bring him."

"Mom, will you please not say anything about my age? I'll be in and out fast—"

"Cassie, I won't lie for you, but I won't say anything. I'll go to my bedroom. But your sisters really want to see you. They've been talking about you all morning."

"Okay, Mom, I'll be there in an hour or so. Please don't say anything."

"I won't."

"All right. I'll be there."

Cassie was surprised that Helen had been so friendly. She had been afraid that her mom would go off on her again. When she told Rashif her family was expecting them, he was surprised but agreeable. He wanted to meet Cassie's mother. On the way to her mom's house, Cassie was so nervous she thought she was going to be sick. She could hardly breathe.

Helen opened the door even before Cassie knocked. They hugged and then Cassie introduced Helen and Rashif to each other. Each said, "Nice to meet you" and then Helen went upstairs to her bedroom. There was nothing rude or disrespectful in the way she excused herself, and Cassie did not think Rashif was put out.

Cassie gave her sisters their gifts, plus fifty dollars. Both of them were pleased.

Keisha gave Cassie a box that she said was from Mama. Inside were pajamas, a Bible and a card. Before she left, Cassie gave Keisha a card to give to Helen. On the card she wrote, "Mom, you know my heart. If things could only go back to the way they used to be." Cassie folded five hundred dollars into the envelope with the card.

They were only halfway back to the motel when Rashif's cell phone sounded. Cassie answered. It was Helen.

"You can come back and get this drug money. I don't want this shit."

"That's your Christmas gift, Mom."

"I don't want it!"

"Then rip it up, 'cause I don't want it either."

"Cassie, I'm not playing with you."

"Mom, I'm not playing with you. You can get yourself something nice or pay some bills with it. I don't know—do whatever you want."

"Was she trippin' on the money?" Rashif asked after Cassie put the phone away.

"Yeah."

"My mom did that at first too. She'll get used to it."

"I know."

Back in their room, Cassie read the card Helen had given her. In it, Helen had written that she prayed for her youngest every day, asking God to watch over her. She said that when Cassie got past whatever she was going through, she would be welcome to come home again. She berated Cassie for making her sisters suffer with worry for the life she was leading. She warned her daughter that people who sell drugs end up dead or in prison. She asked Cassie to think about the dream she had had of going to college, telling her that she would not get there by selling drugs. She said again that if Cassie gave up selling drugs, she could come home.

* * *

It was Cassie's thirteenth birthday, although as far as Rashif knew, it was her eighteenth. They were going to go to a club with Shari and her boyfriend, Benjamin. But first she and Shari went shopping for new outfits. Watching Cassie try on a dress, Shari noted that Cassie's hips had gotten larger and asked if Rashif had been hitting on her more often since she had gained some weight.

"We haven't done anything yet," Cassie said.

"Stop lying, Cassie."

"For real. We haven't done anything. I would have told you."

"When you gonna give him some?"

"I don't know, girl. I'm scared."

"Cassie, you crazy. I didn't know that. Y'all haven't done anything?"

"Well, yeah, we kiss and stuff, but I'm just scared. I ain't ready for all that. You know I would have told you."

"Girl, we gon' have to start talking more."

It was good spending the day with Shari again, just the two of them. Since Cassie had been with Rashif, and Shari with Benjamin, the two girls hadn't had much time together.

Cassie had never been to a club before and she had never had a drink. She and Shari each sipped one through the evening while Rashif and Benjamin knocked back drink after drink. When they danced, Rashif's hands were all over her. During one dance, it was as if they were having foreplay right there on the floor. Rashif was drunk and both he and Cassie were sweating freely and her make-up felt heavy on her face. She was having a wonderful time, but she had had enough. Rashif wanted another drink, but Cassie wanted to leave. Shari drove.

Even before they got in the car, Rashif was kissing her. Benjamin sat in front with Shari, Rashif and Cassie in the back. "My baby is eighteen years old," Rashif said. Cassie and Shari caught each other's eye in the mirror and smiled. Rashif began to rub Cassie's leg.

In their room, Rashif fell back on the bed and Cassie undressed him. Then she took a shower. When she got into bed Rashif was insistent. Cassie knew she would go through with it, but she was frightened. Her body was shaking. She was so uninformed that afterward she didn't know why she was bleeding.

* * *

She called Shari the next day.

"Shari, I humped Rashif."

"What? Y'all had sex?"

"Yes."

"Last night? Was it good?"

"What do you mean, was it good? That shit hurt."

"Oh, yeah. That was your first. Were you trippin'?"

"Hell yeah, because that shit was hurting."

"What did Rashif say? He loves you, girl. He waited all this time for you to give it up."

"I know. He just walked me through everything, but I could tell he was getting annoyed with me because I kept moving away from him."

"So what happened? Why did you decide to do it? How did it happen?"

"He was just hella horny and I had just got out of the shower and we started kissing and all that touching shit, and then he asked me if I was ready."

"And you said yes?"

"Yeah."

"Where's he at now?"

"Went to make a run and get some baggies for the goods. But, girl, let me jump in the shower before he gets back. We got to do some more runs."

"All right. I'll talk to you later."

Love and Understanding

"Baby, what's wrong?"

"Mama trippin' with me, you trippin' with me—'Do this,' 'Do that,' 'When?' 'Why?' 'Where?'—and I'm fuckin' pregnant! I don't know what to do, Rashif."

"Cassie, I'm sorry. You've just been acting so different lately."

"I'm scared, Rashif. What am I going to do? I can't even tell my mother."

"Baby, I know. I'm sorry."

"You're all happy and shit. You can tell your family. I can't tell mine. I can't handle this shit, Rashif."

"Cassie, I'm sorry. I'm going to be there for you and the baby. Trust me."

"See? That's what I mean. You just fucking know that I'm gonna have the baby. Rashif, you don't understand."

*   *   *

Keisha called to ask Cassie to buy her some new shoes. Nike had just put them in the stores and everybody was getting them. Cassie said she would get her a pair. There must have been something in her voice because Keisha asked, "What were you doing when I called?"

"Just arguing with Rashif."

"Why? What happened?"

"Why? Because he doesn't understand that I'm too scared to tell y'all that I'm pregnant like he can tell his family."

"Cassie, are you pregnant?"

"Yeah."

That was how it got out to her family. She hadn't intended to tell Keisha. It just came out of her mouth because she was angry with Rashif. Now she said, "Tell mama I'm pregnant, okay? So I don't have to tell her and listen to her yell and scream."

"Are you for real, Cassie?"

"Yeah, I'm for real. I'll come by the house tomorrow to bring you your shoes. I'll call you before I come over."

"All right, Cassie."

"All right. Talk to you later, Keisha."

She couldn't believe she had told Keisha. Plus, she had asked her to tell mom. Well, mama would find out one way or another. Cassie was thinking now that she would have the baby. She knew Rashif loved her, but she also feared that he would leave her once he learned that she was only thirteen years old.

* * *

"Cassie, I need to talk to you." It was her mother.

"What's going on, Mom?"

"Cassie, what are you going to do with a baby? You're just a damn baby yourself."

"Rashif's gonna help me—"

"Cassie, don't be stupid. Rashif ain't gonna help you. He's gon' be runnin' up behind some other little girl, tryin' to get in her panties just like he got in yours, telling her everything he told you. That boy ain't no different from the rest of these no-good men."

"No, Mama. Rashif's gonna help me. He's a good man."

"Cassie, you keep on believing that if you want to. That's what all them dogs say. Then they don't do shit."

"Rashif will be there for me, Mama."

"Lies and promises, Cassie. Lies and promises. You keep on believin' it. But you're fuckin' up your life. You need to think about your own self and what you want out of life."

"What should I do, Mom? He's been the only person here for me. Him and Shari. They were here when you put me out. If they were gonna leave, they would have already been gone. So what should I do, Mom?"

There was a long silence. Cassie heard something that made her think Helen was having trouble breathing. Then she heard sniffling and then Helen's voice came again, calm now.

"Cassie, I don't know what you should do. I just want what's best for you, that's all. I know those people have been there for you, and I'd be wrong to tell you that they don't care about you. You know better than I do if they care about you or not. Cassie, I'm not going to tell you to kill your baby if you really want that baby. I don't know what you should do, but I do know that you need to figure out fast what it is you want to do, because you ain't got time to be wasting. Cassie, I'm sorry this is happening to you. I'm sorry you have to make such a hard choice at your age. I am sorry."

Tears built up behind the lids of Cassie's eyes, then spilled over. It had been more than a year since she and her mother had been able to talk. The thought, She cares about me, ran through Cassie's mind.

"Mom, part of me wants to have the baby and part of me doesn't want to. But if I decide to have it, I want you to be there. I need your help. I want you to go to the doctor's with me. I want to be able to call you in the middle of the night and tell you how I'm feeling. I want things to go back to how they were, or how you told me you always wanted them to be between you and your children. If I have this baby, I want you to be a part of its life."

"Cassie, I'll be there for you if you decide to have this baby. And if you decide not to have the baby, I'll still be there for you. But I can't make the decision for you. You have to make that choice. If you feel that Rashif is gonna be there for you, then okay. But whatever you choose, I'm gonna be there for you."

"For real, Mom?"

"Yes, Cassie. I love you and I want you to come home, but I understand if you don't want to. I understand why it's hard for you. You're right, I taught you never to go back, and, yes, that's just what I meant. I was not telling you something just to be talking. Cassie, you were like my right hand. I taught you everything. You were my baby. I never wanted to hurt you or set a bad example for you. I taught you everything I thought you needed to know and I taught you to be strong. I held back a lot about the streets from you, but I didn't want you to experience any of that, and I didn't think you would. I wish I could go back and change everything about that night. I made a terrible mistake by putting you out of the house. I admit that, Cassie, and I'm truly sorry. I'm sorry I didn't listen to you that night. I let my anger get in the way. I'm sorry I kicked you out, Cassie. I lie awake at night and think about you and wonder if you're okay. But all we can do now is go forward. I know the pain won't go away overnight, but I love you, Cassie, and I needed to say what I just said. I'm sorry it took me this long to say it all to you."

Cassie was overwhelmed by what she was feeling. Her mother had said everything she could have wished her to say. It could not have been better if she had written a script and given it to Helen to recite. But she couldn't find words to tell her mother what she felt. All she could say was, "Mama, I love you," which was a lot, but did not seem nearly enough.

"Cassie, I love you too. You make sure you let me know what you decide to do. If you can't call and tell me, write me and I'll understand."

"Okay, Mom, I'll call you. I love you." Those last three words she could not say enough times. She wanted to say them until she exhausted herself.

"I love you too, Baby. Good night."

*   *   *

Cassie had grown to love Rashif. For a long time she was not sure, and she questioned whether what she felt for him was really love, but now she was certain she loved him. And he made it clear to her how much he loved her, bragging about her to his friends and to Shari, and of course Shari told Cassie, "Rashif cares about you and that baby. That's all he talks about."

Cassie decided to keep the baby. It would be the first grandchild for both of their families.

*   *   *

Rashif told her about his life before he met her. He had wanted to marry his high school sweetheart, but she was unfaithful to him while he was away at college, so he had ended his relationship with her. He had always wanted his own family, and now, with Cassie, he would have one. Cassie felt that she was the most important person in his life. But she was afraid of what his reaction would be when he found out how old she was. She wanted to tell him, but she kept putting it off.

Jane, Rashif's mother, found an apartment for them in the south end. Cassie suggested Shari move in with them. By now Rashif knew about Benjamin's beating Shari. He agreed that Shari could stay with them, but was worried that Benjamin would come after her and that Cassie might get hurt simply because she was there. That's how things happened sometimes. He said that if anything happened to Cassie, he would hurt Benjamin. Shari did not move in with them.

*   *   *

Rashif liked Helen the first time he met her, and after the third or fourth time he and Cassie visited, Helen began to warm to him. She told Cassie that she believed Rashif was one of the few men who would stick around after getting a girl pregnant. Helen and Jane shopped for baby clothes together.

When Cassie delivered, Rashif, Helen and Jane were all in the room with her. Jane videotaped everything. At five in the morning, Cassie had an eight-pound, six-ounce girl. She had light red coloring and jet black hair, long fingers and oval eyes. Although Cassie had wanted a son, she fell instantly in love with her daughter. She named her Cherice.

*   *   *

They had just sat down to have dinner in a nice restaurant when Cassie excused herself to use the restroom. There she prayed to God to give her the strength to tell Rashif. She asked Him to help Rashif understand and to keep him from leaving her. He deserves to know, Cassie said. Helen had told her exactly that, and told her, too, that she should be honest with him.

Back at the table, pretending to look over the menu, Cassie tried to think of a way to say what she had to say. A dozen possibilities ran through her head, but she couldn't decide on one. Her right leg began to shake; she couldn't stop it. The corner of her mouth twitched. Her finger tapped on the table. She felt the need to tell him *now*. She drew a breath, put her menu down, looked at Rashif sitting across from her, and said it.

He didn't believe her. He told her to quit playing. He asked her if she had decided what she wanted to eat.

She stared at him. She couldn't say any more.

His face changed. His eyes took on a squint. He flattened his hands on the table. He was paying attention. Keeping his voice low, he leaned toward her and asked what she meant.

She repeated herself. She was only thirteen. She was sorry for having lied to him, but she was telling him the truth now.

How could she have lied to him? he asked. He thought she loved him.

She assured him that she did love him, and told him again that she was sorry.

He didn't believe it. That meant she was only twelve when…. He couldn't believe it. Why hadn't her mother said something to him? He told her again to stop playing with him.

Her mom hadn't said anything because she thought Cassie should be the one to tell him. Cassie said she wasn't playing.

He could go to jail for shit like this, he said. What about the hospital? Did she lie there too? Why hadn't anybody said anything to him? What about Shari? What about Keisha? What the fuck is going on?

All she could say was that she was sorry, that she hadn't wanted to lose him.

He had trusted her, he said. And she had lied to him. How could she lie to him? What was he going to tell his family? What would he tell his daughter? What was he supposed to do?

She was so ashamed. She returned to the restroom. She asked God again to help Rashif understand. She loved him and hadn't meant to hurt him, but because she did love him she hadn't been able to tell him earlier, and so she did hurt him. She was afraid he would leave her. And what about their daughter?

After ten or fifteen minutes, she heard Rashif say that he needed to go in to talk to his girlfriend, would you check to see if anyone else was in there? Cassie heard the restroom door open and close and then a woman said he could go in. The door opened again. Then there were footsteps and a tap on the door of her stall and Rashif asked her to open up and she did.

She couldn't talk through her tears. She kept trying to apologize again, but she couldn't get past her sobbing.

Rashif said she didn't have to talk. He knew this was as hard for her as it was for him, but they could work through it. He assured her that he loved her. "Look at me, Cassie. I love you." And finally she could tell him that she loved him too.

* * *

When they went to her mother's house to pick up Cherise, Helen looked at them and asked, "Y'all ain't fighting, are you?"

"She just told me how old she is," Rashif said.

"So what's the problem?"

"Cassie's been lying to me for more—"

"I know she's been lying to you and I don't agree with her lying to you, and that is why I told her to tell you. But there is no sense in y'all's getting upset and walking out on each other. Y'all need to work through this. Y'all just need to talk. What about this baby?"

"I know," Rashif said. "I don't plan on leaving her or my daughter, but I just can't believe this. I love Cassie. I would never lie to her or betray her. Those are two things I would never do. I love them both so much, but what am I going to do? How am I going to tell my family? I wanted to marry her. I got her pregnant on purpose. That way I knew we'd be together forever. I'm so sorry. I don't know what I'd do if this was Cherise and she was with somebody as old as I am."

Cassie had never seen this much emotion come out of Rashif before.

And she had not known that he wanted to marry her or that he purposely impregnated her. When they first met, when she told him she was seventeen, she could not have imagined all that would happen and that two years later she would be where she was now. This was like something you saw on TV. She sat silently, turning toward her mother when she spoke and toward Rashif when he spoke. She didn't know what to say to either of them.

Rashif was saying, "Cassie, I love you too much to walk away from you. You're all I have ever wanted in a woman—in a girl—and you have given me a beautiful daughter. We can get through this. It's just going to take some time."

Helen hugged her. "Cassie, you did the right thing by telling him. I'm proud of you."

Driving home, Rashif asked her what the last grade was that she completed.

"Sixth grade."

"You need to go back to school."

"I know."

That night she couldn't sleep. She lay in bed, staring at the ceiling. She needed to be reassured that it wasn't over between her and Rashif. She didn't blame him for being upset, but if she had not lied to him at the beginning, they would never have gotten together. Cherise would not have been born. She rolled over on her side to face him and saw that his eyes were open; he couldn't sleep either. She said there was something else she needed to tell him: Shari was not her sister. She was like a sister, but she was not her sister.

"How long have you known her, Cassie?"

"A month—at the most, two—before I met you."

"How did y'all meet?"

"We met at the bus stop the night mama kicked me out."

"Why didn't you tell me this before?"

"Because she was like my sister. She took me in when I didn't have nothing or nobody."

"So you were with her when she was out there selling her ass?"

"No, Rashif. She did that years ago."

"You never…. Never mind, you were a virgin."

"Don't ask me anything like that, Rashif."

"You're right. I'm sorry."

"Yeah, whatever."

"How did you keep it all together? I mean everything, not just Shari. Were you scared?"

"Yeah, I was scared. Especially when I was pregnant. Especially the last part of the pregnancy."

"Baby, I couldn't even tell. I mean you were a very well-developed twelve-year-old."

Both of them laughed.

"Cassie, is there anything else? Because I can't handle too much more."

* * *

Cassie started school again, entering the seventh grade a few days after her fourteenth birthday. Sleep was a problem for the parents of an infant daughter, and then there was Rashif's schedule. He continued to make his runs at night as he always had, but that meant getting to bed at four in the morning and then getting up at seven to drive Cassie to school. Often Cassie waited up for him, unable to sleep until she knew he was safe at home.

* * *

Here my journal entries concerning Cassie's life before she came to Ash Meadow end. I have little information on the ensuing three years. Her manuscript mentions that soon after she returned to school Rashif bought her a car, but provides no more of how their relationship changed or of her relationship with her mother. Finally her manuscript also ends.

Cassie told me she stopped writing because she no longer had access to a computer after she was transferred from Serpent Cottage. When I suggested she write in longhand, then transfer it to a computer when she was able, she made a face and I didn't press her. I think now that she stopped writing when she did because her emotions connected to what happened following the period recounted in her writing were still too raw for her to confront. She was estranged from her mother and she was no longer with Rashif. It was almost as though the life that began when her mother threw her out and ended with her going to prison had never been, as though that life had happened to somebody else, and this one, the life she was living now, began the day she was sentenced.

In the System

I had been in California for a week, attending the funeral of my favorite uncle. Afterward, visiting my sister and some of my cousins whom I had not seen in decades, I had the sense of completeness that family provides, especially when brought together in grief. It had been so long since I had felt this that I had forgotten it until now. Back in Seattle, doing one of the dull but necessary things in life—in fact, while shopping at a Safeway—I thought,

There are holes, open seams, in a life away from family. Anything can get in; the potential for peril is always there. But you can get out, too. The chance to apprehend the world unrestrained by family is always there.

When I left for California, I had a girl on my caseload who was in on a drug charge. This was her second offense. I had known her a year and a half earlier when she was locked up the first time. She had had a second child since I saw her last. This child was the result of irresponsibility on her and the father's part, or perhaps only on his part. She was very naïve. Her first child was the result of having been raped. It was her only experience of sex, if rape can be considered sex, until she met the man who fathered her second child.

Because she already knew me, she trusted me more than she trusted other staff, and because I knew her, I knew, too, where her sorrow lay and what her limitations were, and I thought I could help her. But when I came back to work she was gone, exchanged for a girl from another cottage.

According to staff at Peacock Cottage, this girl, Cassandra Martin, had told one of her peers, "I'll murder your face into the ground." She had also tried to intimidate staff and had a desk calendar with the home phone numbers of some of them written on it and had written derogatory comments about staff on it as well. I brought her into the office for our first talk.

She was a large, physically imposing young woman. She was an inch or two short of six feet and was overweight, as many girls at Ash Meadow were, owing to enforced idleness and a tendency to find comfort in food, but she walked without the slouch that signaled depression. She was comfortable with language; many of the kids we got could not express themselves accurately and sometimes said things they did not mean because they were unable to say what they did mean.

When I met her, she was not quite nineteen and had been in Ash Meadow for two years. She had a daughter who lived with her, Cassandra's, mother. Cassandra did not intend to sell crack again. She did not regret having sold it—"What was I supposed to do? I had a daughter to raise"—but she did not want to return to prison. What she wanted, she said, *all* she wanted, was to raise her daughter.

In the staff office during this, our first meeting, I asked her what she had meant when she told the other girl, "I'll murder your face into the ground."

She didn't know what I was talking about.

"According to staff at Peacock, you told another girl, 'I'll murder your face into the ground.'"

"I didn't say that. Who said I said that?"

"One of the staff. I don't know which one."

"I didn't say it. I don't even know what it means."

"Then why are you here, Cassandra?"

"I got caught selling drugs. I just told you."

"I mean why did your cottage send you to maximum security?"

"I don't know."

"Nobody told you?"

"All they told me was that I could be taken as intimidating because I'm African American and I'm big-built and I'm outspoken."

I felt myself staring at her.

"Peacock staff said that?"

"Yeah. I didn't try to intimidate anybody and I didn't threaten anybody. But I can't change what I am. If I see something I think is wrong, I'm gonna say something about it."

"You were large and African American and presumably outspoken before. Why are they sending you to us now?"

Peacock had a new staff member, a transfer from another cottage, a small, blonde woman only a few years older than Cassandra. Cassandra thought she may have frightened her once when she disagreed with something the woman said. Also, there were a couple of girls in Peacock who didn't like Cassandra. It may have been one of them who accused her of saying "I'll murder your face into the ground."

"Okay. You had a desk calendar. Peacock says you wrote some stuff on it that was staff-bashing, and that you had some of staff's personal phone numbers on it."

"I didn't do any staff-bashing. The only things I wrote on it were things staff told me they thought I should do to improve myself. And I didn't have anybody's phone number. How would I even know staff's personal phone numbers?"

"So you didn't know this was going to happen to you? You had no warning? Nobody told you that if you didn't shape up, if you didn't do something different from what you were doing, they were going to send you to max?"

"Nobody said anything like that to me. I was at my job at the commissary and somebody from the cottage called and said I had to come down there right away. And when I got there they told me they were sending me to Wolf and I should get ready. They had already taken everything out of my room."

Large tears crept from the corners of her eyes but she did not wipe them away. Her voice did not change as she cried. I wondered if she even knew she was crying. I handed her a box of tissues and she thanked me, but then set it on the desk beside her chair without taking one out of it.

I locked her in her room and returned to the office to look through the papers on her that Peacock had sent us. Her most recent competency report, dated three weeks ago, said she had almost completed her GED and held two jobs on campus. It called her a leader among Peacock's residents. It described a young woman who had turned her life around. So what happened?

I called her case manager at Peacock. She said she did not know what happened. She had been on her weekend when Cassandra was transferred to us. It was a complete surprise to her. She would have opposed it, had she been there. The cottage director had not been there either.

The desk calendar was not with the materials Peacock had sent. Neither was it in the box of belongings Cassandra had been permitted to take with her. I called Peacock back and asked them to send it. (It took six weeks and half a dozen phone calls before Peacock sent it to me. There were no phone numbers on it. There was nothing on it that I or any of the other staff I showed it to considered staff-bashing. I talked to Jan, our cottage director, about Cassandra and showed her the calendar. We agreed that at least some of the staff at Peacock, for reasons we did not know, appeared bent on destroying this girl. Her jobs, her high status in the cottage—all were taken from her in a moment, and she was placed in maximum security without any explanation that made sense either to her or to us.)

I told Jan that I could not figure out why Peacock had sent Cassandra to us; there was nothing in the supporting documentation that explained her transfer. Jan called her into her office and talked with her for close to an hour. She told me after Cassandra went back to her room that a lot of that time was spent just sitting with her while she cried. "We're just going to have to accept that she's here, even if we don't know why," Jan said. "That goes for Cassandra, too."

A couple of months later Cassandra was gone, transferred to Whale Cottage. Caroline Bloodworth was her case manager there. We had a history, Caroline and I. I had worked at Whale at one time, and Caroline had driven me out. I do not know even now what she had against me, but she did what she could to get me out of Whale, and she succeeded. That had been more than a year earlier. Now, ten days after Cassandra moved, Caroline called me. Did I think Peacock staff were justified in sending Cassandra to maximum security?

I didn't know how to respond. I didn't trust Caroline not to twist whatever I might say in order to use it against Cassandra, or against me. But before I could say anything, Caroline said, "I hate to say anything about other staff, but I think they framed this girl."

I said, "I think you're right."

Actually, Caroline loved to badmouth other staff, and now Peacock had provided her an opportunity. I found it interesting that she and I could be allies, but here we were. It showed, I thought, what people who were otherwise antagonists could do when they had a common concern.

*   *   *

Woodbyrne, one of our sister institutions, began accepting girls. This was a first. Until now, of all the juvenile prisons in Washington, only Ash Meadow had female residents. Jan learned from Kathleen Foreman, her supervisor, that Cassandra would be one of the first girls transferred. The issue of Cassandra's transfer had come up once before, when she was still with us and Headquarters had just announced that Woodbyrne would soon be taking up to twenty girls. Although Kathleen had wanted to transfer Cassandra, Jan had talked her into allowing Cassandra to remain at ash Meadow until she was eligible to go to a group home, so she could stay near her daughter. But now all bets were off. Cassandra was going to Woodbyrne.

Kathleen told Jan to get Cassandra to buy into it because it was inevitable. Why me? Jan asked. I'm not Whale's cottage director. No, but you have a good relationship with Cassandra; she doesn't trust anyone at Whale. She's scheduled to leave next week.

But she didn't go. Her exit physical revealed that she had ovarian cysts. She needed surgery and care afterward that Woodbyrne couldn't provide.

She had the surgery and when she had recovered, she was transferred to a group home only a few miles from where her mother and her daughter lived. She called me shortly before she left Ash Meadow and told me she wouldn't forget me. She said she had finally gotten her GED. A few weeks earlier she had been accused of stealing a sweatshirt from the commissary where she had been working again, and again she lost her job there. But at her GED graduation ceremony, the girl who actually stole the shirt confessed in front of everyone and apologized to her.

She said she had run into Danielle Priest at Administration. Danielle had spent her entire career at Ash Meadow in Peacock Cottage and was considered one of the anchors in a cottage that had never been able to establish its own direction. (At least this was how it seemed to outsiders.) At Administration, Danielle told Cassandra she regretted not opposing her transfer to maximum security. But Cassandra had hurt her, and she was angry, and without entirely understanding her own motives, Danielle had gone along with the other staff when she could have used her influence to keep Cassandra in Peacock. She had been hurt, Danielle said, because she had wanted to be close to Cassandra and Cassandra had pushed her away.

"I didn't push her away," Cassandra said. "She was making it sound important that her husband was black, and I didn't care what color her husband was. I thought she was being stupid for even talking about his color."

I asked her how she had been able to manage her life until things finally came together for her—getting her GED, her transfer to a group home where she could see her daughter every week, her exoneration from the accusation of theft, Danielle's apology to her. I thought she might say she discovered something inside herself that gave her the strength to persevere.

"God," she said.

* * *

Cassandra had been gone a week when I saw Caroline at a psychiatry team meeting both of us were attending. After the meeting she told me what Cassandra's life had been like at Whale. She had been recognized again for her maturity and leadership, had earned a high level, and had gotten her commissary job back. But then Kathleen accused her of having tried to intimidate the woman from Woodbyrne who had come to interview her by telling the woman she would go off if she was selected to go there. Again she was stripped of all her privileges and placed on Tables. It was Anna, Whale's new cottage director, who did this to her, under Kathleen's direction. Then Kathleen went on vacation.

In her absence, Caroline persuaded Anna to call Woodbyrne. The woman who had interviewed Cassandra said she had not tried to intimidate her and had not threatened to go off: Cassandra was turned down because she needed surgery. Even so, Anna did not give her back her level, although she did allow her off Tables.

"It's bad enough when they treat staff like this—and they do—but there's no excuse for treating kids like that," Caroline said.

On the way back to my cottage I reminded myself of what Caroline had done to me. Was she saying now that she was not responsible for my being forced to leave Whale, that it was all the administration's doing? Or was she talking only about Cassandra and Kathleen and Anna? I decided to believe what she told me about Cassandra's problems with Kathleen and Anna, but not what she may have been implying about mine with her.

Over the next seven months, Cassandra and I talked only occasionally. She would call me from the group home to fill me in on her life. She had a part-time job in a nursing home and she was taking business classes at a technical college. She liked both, but if nursing-home work paid decently, she would have liked to stay with that. She was having a minor problem with a couple of the staff at the group home, but it was nothing serious: they treated her as though she were a kid, but she wasn't a kid anymore. These little girls—

meaning the group home staff—expected her to respond to them as if she had no experience of the hard side of life.

She said she saw her daughter every week when her mother brought her to the group home, or she got a pass to visit her at her mother's house. It was as good an arrangement as Cassandra could hope for, given that she was still in the system.

*   *   *

Then she was back at Ash Meadow. At first I didn't believe it. I had talked with her only three days earlier. She had been optimistic; she was keeping up with her classes and was looking forward to graduating in three months. But a staff from Whale called and said someone had seen her on campus. I traced her to Serpent Cottage, another girls' unit, and talked with Jake Gorman, Serpent's supervisor. Jake said she had been forty minutes late in getting back to the group home one day and had refused to take a urinalysis when all the other girls were taking them. She did take it the next day, but the results were not back yet.

I went over to Serpent that evening when I got off shift. Cassandra said she had been eight minutes late, not forty. She had a pass that was good until four p.m. and she got back at four-oh-eight. Her case manager said she was due back at three-thirty, regardless of what the pass said. Cassandra said she did not refuse a UA; she just couldn't pee. The staff giving the UAs agreed to wait, but then she went home and Cassandra forgot about it until the next morning. She believed they simply wanted to get rid of her. Her case manager told her she could return to the group home in three months. Of course, she wouldn't be able to complete her business course.

Why did they want her out of the group home? It was the old story: she challenged them. She was almost twenty years old. She had a six-year-old daughter and had supported her or contributed to her support by legal and illegal means all of the girl's life. The group home staff wanted Cassandra to behave as a child herself, but it was too late; she had not been a child in years.

I visited her again a few days later. Rashif intended to move to Arizona, she said, and wanted to take Cherice with him. His argument was that Cassandra, in prison again, could not provide child support payments to him or her mother—the two together had been raising Cherice. Cassandra had been paying six hundred dollars a month toward Cherice's support and she had twenty-two hundred dollars left in her account. The group home had not transferred her money to Ash Meadow, so she did not have access to it, but when it did, she would be able to resume her support payments, at least for a few months. She asked me to call Rashif to try to talk him out of taking the girl.

I refused. I told her she had to go through Jake, her current case manager. I advised her also to talk to an attorney. There was one available to her, to all the kids who were locked up, and I thought highly of him.

She knew him, but she didn't want to talk to either him or Jake because she didn't want other people in her business, she said.

I said that as her friend I was tempted to call, but that in my role here at Ash Meadow, I couldn't insert myself into her and Jake's relationship, even if she didn't know Jake well enough to trust him yet. She thought for a minute or two about what I'd said, then said, "That's probably wise." But she was hurt. (As it happened, Rashif did not go to Arizona.)

A couple of days later, with Jake's approval, I brought Cassandra a copy of *The Shiloh Renewal* by Joan Woodruff and one of Strunk and White's *Elements of Style*, the former because it was about someone close to her in age and was inspiring, the latter because she had mentioned wanting to write a book about what she had been through in her life. She hoped it would keep other girls from following the path she had taken.

I continued to visit her at Serpent once a week or so. She was using a cottage computer to write her book and she seemed to be writing with ease. She read Natalie Cole's autobiography and was especially impressed by her struggle with drug addiction. Cassandra had never used drugs, she said—I believed her—and she had been contemptuous of those who did. She still regarded drug use as something a person did to herself, but now she was reconsidering her attitude toward addicts.

She told me that Jake was getting pressure from other staff at Serpent to treat her less favorably than he was. But he felt that she was an adult who behaved responsibly and he should treat her as an adult.

The group home informed her, after three months, that they weren't ready to have her back. They didn't set another date for reconsideration, but they also didn't reject her altogether. Because they didn't simply reject her, no other group home could consider her; that was how the system worked.

She requested a transfer to Woodbyrne. She wasn't able to see her daughter anyway, she said, because her mother was too busy to drive her out to Ash Meadow. Also, Woodbyrne had a contract with the Department of Natural Resources: its residents fought fires during the season and were paid firefighters' wages when they were on a fire. Cassandra, nearly broke now, needed to earn some money so she could continue to contribute to Cherice's upkeep and, hopefully, put away something for when she got out. All of this was in her mind when she wrote her request. Woodbyrne said they would take her.

Several of the staff in Serpent criticized her for her "power play." Cassandra did not understand what they meant—she wasn't trying to get over on anybody, she wasn't trying to dominate anyone. But I knew what they meant, though they themselves might disagree. There was a contradiction in the way staff treated residents. We encouraged them to gain control over their lives, but when they showed that they were doing that, we—many of us, especially younger staff—accused them of initiating a power struggle with us. Cassandra's experience at Ash Meadow and at the group home could be seen as her repeatedly getting caught in this bit of institutional hypocrisy.

Before she left, Jan talked to her about the way she presented herself. It was easy enough to say that some of those in authority had abused their power over her, but certainly Cassandra had provided them the opportunity to do it. It was a question of her attitude. No one, no kid or adult, wants to appear foolish, and Cassandra's willingness to argue for what she believed was right, her willingness to challenge staff if she disagreed with their policies, only made her vulnerable to whatever response they wanted to make. The lesson she should take away from her experience was this: Don't push unless you are able to protect yourself when staff pushes back.

*   *   *

She wrote me from Woodbyrne and, after I got permission from Woodbyrne and Ash Meadow, we talked regularly on the phone.

A girl at Woodbyrne hanged herself, but was revived. Then two other girls tried to kill themselves. In one of her letters, it was apparent that Cassandra was upset, and during one of our phone calls, she was close to hysteria.

She called me five days later. A friend of hers at Woodbyrne, someone she had known at Ash Meadow, had tried to strangle herself by tying a sheet to a sink and then around her neck. She didn't succeed but it was a genuine attempt, not just a gesture.

Cassandra said she felt as if she was the last advocate for change at Woodbyrne. I hadn't known she was advocating anything. One thing she wanted was for the staff to get training in suicide prevention. They were not prepared psychologically to deal with girls who were suicidal, even though there had been girls at Woodbyrne for over a year. Six of the eleven staff in the cottage where Cassandra lived had quit since the rash of suicide attempts began. The remaining staff "just don't listen," she said, although the administrators had invited her to talk with them. They had listened to her express her fears and offer suggestions about how to train staff, then asked her to hang on (pun intended? Whose pun was it? Theirs or hers?) a while longer, as though she had a choice.

I asked her if she felt that she herself was in danger. "I don't want to answer that," she said.

I talked with her again a week and a half later. She had just returned to Woodbyrne after eight days fighting a forest fire. She was enjoying what she was doing. Her training, as hard as it had been physically, was nothing compared to what was actually required in fighting a fire. For the first couple of days she didn't think she would last, but she had lasted, and while her body was still tired and sore, she felt really good. She expected to be called out for another fire soon. She asked me to call her in a few days in case she was still at Woodbyrne; it was my turn to call.

*   *   *

When I came in to work I found a message from Cassandra taped to my in-box, asking me to call her ASAP.

At first she was reluctant to talk. Finally she told me she'd been fired from her job on the fire crew. There had been some joking between another girl and a staff member that included some sexual teasing, and Cassandra had laughed. This happened at night in camp during a fire. Cassandra said that apparently the other girl said she was going to drug the staff member, but Cassandra had not heard that part, and her laughter, along with the girl's comment, was considered a safety/security problem.

She wanted out of Woodbyrne. She said she was going to hang herself. I asked her if she intended staff to find her so that she wouldn't die. She didn't know. I asked if she had talked with anybody else about it. She had talked with her mother.

"What did she say?"

"She wasn't pleased about it, but she said I should do what I have to do."

The superintendent was going to talk with her tomorrow, she said. She had written him, complaining about Woodbyrne's seemingly inadequate response to the recent suicide attempts. She would hang herself after they talked. She couldn't imagine his saying anything that would convince her not to. The other time she talked with him, he just put her off. She was crying; she felt hopeless.

We talked until she stopped crying, and then we hung up. I immediately called Woodbyrne back to talk with a staff member. I was put through to Cassandra's case manager and told him what she had said about hanging herself.

He was angry. She was manipulative, he said. She had been fired for inciting her peers. As he went on, it became apparent that the incitement he was talking about was Cassandra's complaining about things she didn't like, but it was worrisome because the "incitement" was at night, in camp, with only two staff to monitor a crew of ten or twelve girls. He continued for twenty minutes or more, not giving me a chance to break in. I was concerned that every minute he did not act to ensure Cassandra's safety was a minute in which she could decide not to wait, but to hang herself now. Finally he thanked me for informing him of Cassandra's threat.

I had suspected that she wanted me to tell someone so that she would be prevented from killing herself, but still get the satisfaction of having made the plan and gotten staff to respond. I was wrong. Three days later I received a letter from her telling me that she was "upset and let down" by my reporting our conversation to her staff. But after struggling through rewrite after rewrite of her letter, she finally concluded that I was simply doing my job. "I pray that's what it was because, Jerry, I've shared some pretty intimate things with you and I trust you a lot."

I called. I told her, yes, it was my job, but it was more than that. How could I live with myself if I allowed her to hang herself and she died?

"Mm hmm," she said.

"And when I asked you if you intended to actually kill yourself, you said you didn't know."

"I wasn't going to kill myself."

"We had a boy here once who did not intend to kill himself, only to strangle himself a little to get high. But he panicked and he fell and he broke his neck. Just because you intend not to die doesn't mean you won't die."

"Mm hmm. I wouldn't have made a mistake. My mistake was in telling somebody. Well, I'm over it. I only have four months till my release. I can just sit here and be quiet for that long."

"Did the superintendent ever talk with you?"

"Yes."

"What did he say?"

"He said they were making changes and I should be patient."

"Just what you wanted to hear."

She laughed.

"Okay, Cassandra."

"Will you call me soon? I have to watch my money now that I don't have a job."

"I'll call you next week."

I did, and after that call, I called her once or twice a month until, on her twenty-first birthday, she was released.

Prison Without End

Ash Meadow's rule was that staff and former residents could not see each other for two years following a resident's release; the administrators recognized that a personal relationship could result from the institutional one. The regulation could be waived if the staff's supervisor authorized it. I asked for and Jan granted me a waiver to visit Cassandra. She and Cherice shared a flat with a former inmate of the women's prison at Purdy and her daughter. Their apartment was in a sedate neighborhood in the north end of Seattle, walking distance from an elementary school. Cassandra was in a good situation.

It was obvious that the housemate, Ruth, was having a hard time. She was anxious, seemingly about everything. She could not be still. She talked incessantly, if not to Cassandra, then on the phone. Often, apologetically, she interrupted Cassandra's and my conversation to ask about bus schedules, the telephone bill, prices at one supermarket as against another, and whatever else she had happened to fasten on at the moment.

I asked Cassandra if Ruth was using. Cassandra hadn't seen her use, and they both knew that if either of them was caught using, the apartment manager would assume both were and evict them. Cassandra had told Ruth that if she caught her using, she would turn her in to her parole officer. Cassandra did not want to lose what she had because Ruth could not stay clean.

I met Ruth's daughter only once, a girl around Cherice's age, and saw Ruth twice before they disappeared. Cassandra did not know where they went but was glad Ruth was gone. Ruth had presented a danger, plus Cassandra liked having the apartment for just herself and Cherice.

When Cassandra was released from prison, Richard Stern, the attorney who had the contract with the Juvenile Rehabilitation Administration to represent kids in state institutions, hired her part time to do some clerical work. Celia Barney, one of Ash Meadow's administrators, learned of this and accused Richard of being unprofessional in hiring a former inmate. Richard told Cassandra that he hadn't done anything illegal and, as he was his own boss, he couldn't be fired, but he intended to present the issue to a panel of his law firm's overseers to get their opinion. He himself didn't see anything wrong in his having hired Cassandra. (Neither did the overseers.)

It looked like bad things were starting to converge on Cassandra's life as they had before. Her mother had loaned her a car, but was saying now that she wanted it back. Helen, who had argued against Cassandra's taking custody of Cherice, was saying too that Cherice should live with her again or, alternatively, that both Cassandra and Cherice should live with her. But Cassandra liked where she lived. Cherice was attending a good school and their neighborhood was safe.

Although she did not know yet if she would have to leave her job with Richard, Cassandra decided to look for another job. She found one in a hotel about a mile from her apartment. She would work in the laundry on graveyard shift on some days, and on other days she would work the front desk on evening shift. Helen would pick up Cherice at school on days when Cassandra couldn't be home.

Once I gave Cassandra money to cover some of her bills. She was learning not only about the cost of living on the civilian economy, but about which stores to shop at and what to do when your bus doesn't arrive. She must have felt some of the anxiety Ruth had experienced, but she didn't disintegrate as Ruth had.

*   *   *

She had been out for several months when she was arrested on an outstanding warrant. She called me from the jail in Kent, a satellite of the one in Seattle. She hadn't known there was a warrant out for her and she didn't know what it was for. She asked me to bail her out. I drove to Kent and was told by the officer at the desk that Cassandra had been transferred to Seattle where she would be arraigned in the morning; she was en route as we spoke, the officer said. I asked the officer to get word to her, if she could, that I had come and wanted her to call me. The officer assured me that she would let Cassandra know, but I knew she wouldn't. I asked only because I didn't know what else to do. I went home.

When, six weeks later, I finally heard from Cassandra again, she told me that she hadn't been moved to Seattle until the following day and hadn't been arraigned until three days later. She had served a thirty-day sentence for parking violations dating back to before she went to Ash Meadow. That's what the warrant was for: parking tickets. She was already in Ash Meadow when it was issued. But the judge was uninterested in explanations.

In the thirty days she was in jail, she lost her job, she lost her apartment, and her mother reclaimed her car and took Cherice back to live with her. Cassandra was living with her sister Keisha and trying to find work. She wasn't optimistic. She couldn't get Helen's car back because Helen needed it to get Cherice to and from school. Cassandra would have liked to have her daughter live with her again, but there wasn't enough room in Keisha's apartment for even one more person, much less two. Yes, her mother's offer to live with her was still good, but no, she couldn't.

I didn't see Cassandra again. She called occasionally. I asked for her phone number a couple of times and she gave it to me—it was a different number each time—but when I called, no one answered and no voice mail or answering machine came on.

* * *

It had been more than a year since I had heard from her when she called for what would be the last time. She just wanted to check in, she said. She wanted to stay in touch. I don't know what made me ask this—I meant it only as a flip question during a lull in the conversation; her life with men other than Rashif had never been a subject of our talks—but I said, "How's your love life?"

She began to cry. She had had an abortion only a month earlier. She couldn't support another child and her relationship with its father was over. She said she was sorry for crying; she hadn't even known she felt so bad until I asked. She asked if it would be all right if she called me back in a few minutes. I said that would be fine. She didn't call back. I didn't have her phone number and she hadn't told me where she was staying.

* * *

Cami Lessing, who had worked with us in Wolf Cottage and then transferred to the adult parole system, called me at work. There were some new warrants out on Cassandra Martin: identity theft, credit card fraud, check forgery. Cami knew I had taken an interest in Cassandra and thought I would want to know.

I remembered Cassandra telling me after she had been out for a few months that she could understand how someone would be tempted to forge a signature on a check—that's how badly off she was then. Not that she would do it, she said. I had talked with her only three months earlier. Perhaps she had called to ask me to loan her some money. If she had been hitting me up, I hadn't detected it.

She had worked hard at low-wage jobs, none of them paying enough to allow her even to sustain herself and her daughter without her mother's help. But it was the criminal justice system that put an end to her hope of living a life within the law. That was how I saw it. I was angry.

She must have been desperate. Now, presumably, she was living underground, trying to avoid looking conspicuous, trying to avoid arrest. She was probably using a false name. She used one before she came to Ash Meadow.

II

Marcus Bellows
A Feral Child

I used to facilitate a treatment group called Alternatives to Violence. There were many groups with that name in prisons for juveniles throughout the country, but I had invented this one. My idea was that if kids understood how having been a victim of violence had influenced their thinking and behavior, they might be less eager to visit it on someone else. I originally designed the group to run for eight weeks—this was when I worked in Swan Cottage, a unit for older boys, mostly gang kids or wannabes—but after a few cycles I began to see how domestic violence related to gang violence, and how warfare could be understood as a kind of gang violence that nations practice, and the duration of the group eventually extended to twelve and then to sixteen weeks.

In Swan Cottage I accepted as many as ten kids in each group, but when I transferred to Wolf, our maximum security unit, I limited the number of kids to six or seven. I reduced the number of kids I was willing to try to manage, even with another counselor assisting me, because we had so many kids with ADD or other mental health problems that I didn't know how they would interact, sitting together for an hour. In both cottages, the criteria for acceptance—after word of the group got around, I always had more applicants than I could accommodate—included a kid's having committed a crime of violence or a crime that might have resulted in violence, such as residential burglary. The group met once a week following supper and clean-up details, while the other kids in the cottage were locked in their rooms.

In late April we got a new kid in the unit, Marcus Bellows, whose arrival coincided with the start of a new group. Usually I preferred to observe a new kid for a couple of weeks before even considering him for the group, but I talked with Marcus a little and found him thoughtful, and, perhaps also because he was on my caseload, I decided to include him. Watching his interaction with other kids in the group would give me the opportunity to learn something about him that I might otherwise miss.

Old Life, New World

The kids lined up at the door and when they had quieted, I said, "Let's go," and we went outside and down the porch steps to the classroom that was set at the edge of the recreation yard behind the cottage. Bernie, assisting me, led, and the kids followed single-file, I behind them. Marcus was last in line. When he got to the door of the classroom, the others already inside, he stopped. "You first," he said.

"No, go on in," I said.

"Age before beauty."

Bernie had come back to the doorway and I saw him tensing. I said, "Go on in, Marcus. Kids first."

"You go. I've got your back." He was smiling. I did not think the smile concealed anything malevolent. This was either a test of power or he wanted to ingratiate himself with me.

"Okay." I stepped inside. Marcus followed me and Bernie followed him. Marcus took a seat behind the other kids who sat in the first row in a semi-circle. I asked him to sit in front with the others and they scooted their desks to make room for him and he moved his desk into the opening they left.

We had had a number of kids who did not like to have people behind them; they had been jumped—"stolen on," in the parlance—or had seen someone else jumped from behind, and I thought Marcus might be like them. On the other hand, he had not objected to Bernie's being behind him at the door. I thought again that he might be playing a power game with me. Perhaps that, or perhaps it was only that he did not want other kids behind him. Perhaps he only wanted my attention.

He was tall for a fourteen-year-old, about six feet, and was very thin and had large, bony hands that swelled out from wrists that looked too narrow to support them. He had a quick, broad grin that he flashed at me but not at the other kids, whom he mostly seemed content to listen to on this first day. When he did give his opinion, it was as though he had thought about the topic before and, seemingly off the top of his head, said something worth considering.

Many kids, especially the gang kids, were careful about disagreeing with other kids, afraid to cause a problem that would reverberate in the cottage later, or to touch on something that might resonate with something from the past. The gang kids knew: everything has a context; everybody has a history.

Some kids, including gang kids but not limited to them, did not know how to disagree with someone without attacking him. They could not say, "I disagree with you," but had to preface whatever point they wanted to make with "You're a fool" or "That's stupid" or "That's weak." These kids wanted to win their point and some of them were prepared to fight for it. I paid special attention to these kids and imposed rules—we called them "group norms"—that prohibited this kind of offensiveness and tried to teach the kids in the group to say, simply, "I disagree with you and this is why...."

Marcus, like the other gang kids, avoided alluding to past events that the other kids might know about, and he did not feel he had verbally to destroy his opponent in order to make himself heard, but he would retaliate in kind if a kid called him weak or a fool, saying, "You're the fool," or "We'll see who's weak," the latter carrying the implication that he would test the kid later when staff wasn't watching. Marcus' problem, even if he did not see it as a problem except when he got caught, was that he hit other kids, though he did not do this during a group session. For most of his time in Wolf Cottage, he saw his hitting other kids as giving them something they deserved.

During the first session of Alternatives to Violence, the group defined "violence." Someone wanted to look it up in a dictionary, but I didn't allow it; I wanted them collectively to come up with a definition that we could refer back to over the course of the group. I wanted them to distinguish between violence to the person and violence to property, and between physical violence and emotional violence (which was worse? That question was always good for a discussion) as well as between legal and illegal violence.

I asked questions: if you slam your hand down on your desk, is that an act of violence? Is the violence done to your hand or to the desk, or both? Does violence have to result in damage before we can consider it violence? If someone drives a car into a group of people, is that the same as a car, driverless, rolling down a hill and smashing into pedestrians?

Most kids felt that violence done to them by police was legal because judges always back up the police, whereas when kids do the same kind of violence, it is illegal because police arrest them and judges sentence them. Kids agreed, even if they had to acknowledge that they agreed with the police and the courts, that what youth gangs did to one another was often illegal, but what else could you do? Did this mean retaliation was moral? In what context? The context of the gang or the context of the mainstream of society? If a nation is attacked by another nation, or if a key political figure is assassinated by agents of another country, does this justify going to war against that other country? Is war legal? What if one country says its soldiers are engaged in military operations, but the country against whom these operations are being conducted says no, those soldiers are not soldiers engaged in military activity, but are criminals conducting criminal activity and, if captured, will be treated as criminals rather than as soldiers?

Some kids came away from this first session claiming their head hurt. Marcus was one of these: back in the cottage, he told me, "My brain hurts." They wanted to be told what was the right answer after they made their guesses; they wanted to be told what they were supposed to do, how they were supposed to think, even if they didn't like it. They were thirteen or fourteen or fifteen years old, and many of them hadn't been in a school except to sell drugs since they were eleven, or eight, or even seven. I was challenging them to think analytically and they wanted to please me, but were frustrated.

One of the group norms was confidentiality, meaning that what was said during group could not be repeated out of group. The purpose of this norm was to encourage kids to be truthful, to allow themselves to be vulnerable. The problem with this norm was that while it promoted openness and trust, sometimes I got a mix of kids who, for particular reasons, would have been foolish to trust one another.

Once, after the group had been going for three or four weeks, I saw Marcus punch Durrell in the stomach as the kids were filing out of the classroom. I punished Marcus, of course, confining him to his room for the rest of the evening and most of the next day, and placing him on Tables status, meaning he wouldn't be allowed to take recreation with the other kids for several days. Then I took Durrell into the staff office and asked what was going on. Why had Marcus hit him? Durrell said he hadn't done anything to Marcus to cause him to hit him, but he had known Marcus on the outs, and they had fought once and Durrell had beaten him down, so that was probably why Marcus hit him—because other kids knew Durrell had beaten him and Marcus wanted to prove that he was strong. It wasn't the first time Marcus had hit him, it was only the first time staff had seen it. Marcus had been hitting Oren too. Had Durrell hit Marcus since he had come to Wolf Cottage? No. He could have, he said, but he didn't want to get in trouble with staff.

The response was too slick.

"You know I'm going to talk with Marcus, too," I said.

"I know."

"Do you want to change anything you said? Are you sure you haven't hit him when staff wasn't looking?"

"I'm sure."

I put Durrell in his room and went and got Oren and brought him into the office. He was a year or so older than Marcus, almost as tall, and heavier. His weight was well proportioned and he was a fair athlete, while Marcus avoided basketball and football. I knew enough about Marcus now to know that he did not know how to play team games and was afraid of other kids laughing at him if he screwed up.

I, and other staff, wondered why Oren was in prison. Unlike most of the boys we had, Oren was still attending school when he was arrested, and he tested at the educational level standard for a fifteen-year-old. He spoke well, by which I mean he spoke grammatically and he didn't elide his words with the affectation of a gangbanger. He did not claim gang membership, but said he knew some gang kids. This was smart of him, to take a position that would allow him some of the other kids' regard because of his knowledge and connections, but at the same time let him escape the stigma of false-claiming, the pretense that he was a member of a gang when he wasn't. He did not appear to be an angry kid, which made him almost unique among the boys we had, and he seemed not to have a problem with doing what staff wanted him to do. I don't remember now what crime he had committed to get locked up, but it could not have been too serious: he was in Ash Meadow for only a few months before he was paroled.

I told Oren that Durrell had said Marcus had been hitting them when staff wasn't watching. Oren said it was true. Had Oren hit Marcus? He had hit Marcus back a couple of times, hoping Marcus would stop if he saw he couldn't bully him, but Marcus hadn't stopped. Oren said he had tried to befriend Marcus when he realized that returning his punches wasn't going to convince Marcus of anything, but that hadn't worked either. Like Durrell, Oren said he could defend himself, but didn't want to get in trouble with staff.

I asked Oren if Marcus had hit anyone aside from himself and Durrell. Not that he knew of.

"Then why does he hit you?"

"I have no idea," Oren said. Then he said that Marcus had exposed himself to him in the zone and on another occasion had asked Oren to go into the head with him to have sex. I asked Oren if anyone else had witnessed this and he said no.

I returned him to his room and got Marcus and took him into the office. He admitted to hitting Durrell when he thought staff would not see him. Why? Because Durrell was a false-claimer; he claimed to be a member of a Blood set, but he wasn't. Durrell's brother was, but Durrell wasn't. Marcus himself was a Blood, so he knew. Durrell was trying to ride on his brother's shirttails.

"Coattails," I said. I wondered where he had heard that old expression, even if he had gotten it wrong. He must have been listening to *some* things the older people in his family had said.

I told him what Durrell had said about beating him down. I told him because I believed Durrell, at least about his history with Marcus, and I intended to tell Marcus to drop it, to let go of his wanting revenge. I did not believe Marcus was hitting Durrell because Durrell was false-claiming. But I didn't say all of this. Immediately as I said Durrell had told me he'd beaten Marcus down, Marcus' mouth dropped open and his eyes widened in what appeared to be genuine incredulousness.

"He said that?"

"Yes," I said.

"It was the other way around. See, that's what I mean about him being a liar. He's been saying that to everybody. *I* beat *him* down."

"So one of you is lying to me."

"One of us is, but it isn't me."

"So if I went and got Durrell and brought him in here, with you here, what would he say?"

"I don't know what he'd say, but if he said anything but what I said, he'd be lying."

"So if I bring Durrell in here, would you give me your commitment not to assault him, no matter what he says? You'll have your chance to say your side."

Marcus said he wouldn't assault Durrell.

Bernie was on the floor, waiting for me to wrap it up so we could get the kids out of their rooms for rec. I asked him to bring Durrell back to the office, and to get a commitment from him not to assault Marcus. If Durrell refused to commit, leave him in his room.

When Durrell came in, I reminded him and Marcus that they had committed themselves not to assault each other. Then I asked Durrell to tell Marcus what he had told me.

Durrell spoke so softly as to be barely audible. He looked at the floor rather than at Marcus or me. Marcus was grinning without mercy.

I said Marcus had told me that the opposite was true, that he had beaten you up.

"Be honest," Marcus said.

Durrell said something I couldn't hear. I asked him to say it again.

"What Marcus said is true," he said.

"Uh huh," Marcus said. He laughed.

"Why did you lie?" I asked.

"I don't know," Durrell said. He had not looked up from the floor since he sat down.

"All right. You can go. Tell Bernie I said to put you in your room."

He left the office. Through the window I saw Bernie stand up. I pointed to the zone where Durrell's room was and Bernie nodded.

"There's more to talk about," I told Marcus, "but I don't have time now. You know you've got twenty-four OP. We'll talk tomorrow if I have time. But for now, you need to give me your word that you'll leave Durrell alone. And that you'll stop hitting Oren."

"Oren? Did Durrell tell you I hit Oren?"

"Doesn't matter who told me. Other kids have seen you do it too."

"Just because they say they saw me doesn't mean I did it."

"If you haven't been hitting him, it should be easy for you not to."

"All right. I won't hit him, or Durrell. Is Durrell getting consequences too?" "Consequences" was the word we used instead of punishment.

"For lying to me? You bet. Not as much as you, but he'll lose something."

Marcus looked pleased. I locked him in his room and Bernie and I got the kids out while Layton monitored the floor. I hadn't yet found out why Marcus hit Oren, but I was pretty sure I knew.

*   *   *

The next day Marcus hit a kid at school. He said Casey hit him first but I did not buy that, especially as other kids had seen them and the kids' stories were consistent. Then Marcus said he hadn't meant to hit Casey, but Casey had bucked up to him and he, Marcus, had responded by putting his hands up and accidentally making contact with him. I pointed out that he "made contact" enough to raise a welt over Casey's eye and that Casey was the smallest kid in the cottage, while Marcus was the largest—the tallest anyway.

I told him that if he didn't curb his aggressiveness, he would find himself in Elk Grove or The Rivers when he turned fifteen. He said he didn't care that much and I said I didn't believe him, that I knew him well enough to know that he did care what happened to him. Suddenly he said he would change, he would commit himself not to be aggressive and he would sign a contract committing himself not to be aggressive. I told him to write up a contract and I would review it with him. I believed he was serious and would try to honor his word. Whether or not he would be successful was another story.

In the evening, after the other kids were locked in their rooms, I got Marcus out and took him into the office. I told him what Oren had said and asked him if it was true. Had he exposed his penis to Oren? Marcus was angry, as I had expected him to be, or at least to show himself to be, and he said no, he had not. He seemed to be telling the truth—his eyes met mine, but without aggression—but I had been deceived before and I didn't allow myself to form an opinion. Why would Oren lie? I asked.

"You know why," Marcus said.

He meant that Oren knew Marcus was a sex offender. Ever since another boy had accidentally been permitted to see a cottage document indicating this, there had been rumors about Marcus, and several of the kids had found ways to victimize him, although all were physically afraid of him.

"Is Oren one of the kids who targets you because of your crime?"

"No. Not until now."

"Then why do you hit him?"

"I haven't. Not since I told you I wouldn't."

"Okay. Then why did you used to hit him?"

"I hate him."

He hated Oren because Oren was rich, or his grandmother was, and Oren boasted about her giving him money. She even took him to the Caribbean with her once, and said she would take him to Africa when he got out of prison. Oren didn't know anything about gangs, but acted as if he did, Marcus said, whereas Marcus did know because he had grown up in a gang and with drugs and not having any money. Oren was claiming knowledge he didn't have, pretending to know about things he didn't know about, and at the same time trying to make Marcus feel small because he, Oren, had a grandmother who could do things for him. Marcus said he wished he hadn't made a commitment not to hit Oren, because, thinking about him now, he was so angry that he wanted to beat him into the ground.

* * *

At the next meeting of Alternatives to Violence, we talked about why some burglars defecate on the carpet or on a bed in the houses they burglarize. The standard explanation, I said, is that the burglar's fear of being caught loosens his bowels so that he has to dump. But that doesn't explain why he dumps on the carpet or on the bed instead of in the toilet.

Half of the kids said they had done this, or something like it. If they couldn't steal something in a burglary, they wanted to destroy it because they didn't want the owners to enjoy it. They hated people more privileged than themselves; at least they hated the idea that there were such people.

Marcus didn't share their feelings, although he said he understood them. Once, on Christmas Eve a year or so before he came to Ash Meadow, he and another boy broke into a house and took everything they found under the tree. When they unwrapped the gifts, they discovered that almost everything they had stolen were toys for small children. Feeling ashamed, Marcus returned his share to the family the next day—Christmas Day. (His cohort felt bad too, but not bad enough to give up his part of the loot.) Even though the homeowners turned Marcus in to the police and he had to spend some time in detention, he did not regret returning the gifts; he did not want to deprive a child of his Christmas, he said.

Shame

Marcus' father disappeared when Marcus was seven. His mother told him his dad was away on a business trip. For the next seven years Marcus waited for him to return. Eventually his mother brought another man into the house and Marcus came to regard him as his stepfather. Marcus liked him well enough, but continued to miss his father who wrote to him but never said when he would be coming home. A few months before Marcus was locked up, his mother and his stepfather broke up and his stepfather moved out of the house. Marcus didn't feel one way or another about his stepfather's leaving, he said. Then, when Marcus had been with us for about three months, his mother told him in a telephone conversation that his father had returned and they were going to try to live together as a family again. Then she gave the phone to Marcus' father.

Marcus seemed in a daze when he got off the phone. He didn't know what to think. He hadn't expected ever to see his father again, yet here he was, he had just talked to him. His dad and his mother would be coming to visit. Marcus didn't know if he felt glad or not.

*   *   *

On my recommendation, we placed Marcus on an In-and-Out program because he continued to be assaultive. At rec in the asphalted yard behind the cottage, he hit Linsey Lopez with a ball during a battleball game. The problem was that they were on the same team. He said she hit him in the head with a ball first, so he turned and hit her—twice. Then she picked up a plastic bowling pin they were using as a goal to defend herself, and then both she and Marcus began talking trash, threatening each other.

Dick got between them and Bernie escorted Marcus into the cottage and I locked him in his room. Then Dick brought Linsey in and locked her in her room.

After we got the rest of the kids inside and locked them down, I took David Banks, a recent arrival from county detention, into the staff office to do an inventory of the clothing he had brought with him. Dick went into Zone 2, Bernie behind him, to tell Marcus he had twenty-four OP. Hearing this, Marcus tried to push past him to get out of his room, but Bernie shoved him back and he and Dick hemmed Marcus up.

In the office, out of sight and hearing range of Marcus' room, I happened to look out the window into the day area. Clare, one of our newer staff, was at the desk across the floor. I saw her suddenly raise her head and turn toward Zone 2. She stood up, started toward the zone, came back, went into the zone, and then returned to the desk in a hurry. From somewhere, she took out a brush and began to brush her hair. I took David out of the office, pointed at a chair in the day area and told him to sit there. I told Clare to watch him and went into the zone, Clare handing me a set of leg shackles she took from the bottom drawer of the desk as I ran past her.

When I arrived at Marcus' room, Dick was handcuffing him and Bernie had immobilized his legs. Dick told me to call Security. I handed Bernie the shackles, went back out and called to Clare, asking if she had already called Security. My shout startled her and she jerked and turned and got the radio. I went back to Marcus' room. All through his struggling with Dick and Bernie he had been yelling that he was going to get Linsey; now he was yelling about getting staff. But it was obvious that Dick and Bernie had him under their control and I left, got David, and returned with him to the staff office to finish his inventory as Security arrived to take Marcus to Central Isolation.[1]

The next day I asked Marcus what was in his mind that caused him to push Dick. He said he wanted to get out of his room so he would have space to box. He intended to hit Dick, go out on the floor where he heard some kids, hit some of them, and wait for Security to arrive to take him down. He hadn't anticipated Bernie moving so fast. He said he started thinking about the consequences to himself if he succeeded in doing what he intended, but then he pushed that thinking out of his mind.

There weren't any kids on the floor, I said.

He said he heard kids on the floor. He heard David's voice.

I told him David was in the office with me and nobody was on the floor but staff.

I said it wasn't Linsey who hit him with the ball. I didn't know who had thrown it, but it hadn't come from where Linsey was playing.

He didn't believe that. Also, he said, other kids had laughed when she hit him, so he had to take off on her.

And you wanted to hit the kids you thought you heard on the floor because they had laughed at you.

That's right.

*　*　*

This is how I thought about Marcus at this point: When he was very young—he said he was "bad," beating up other kids even when he was in preschool—he had the shit beaten out of him, probably more than once. Now he was afraid of getting jumped, so he targeted kids he thought were likely to attack him, thinking if he could get them before they got him, or at least make them fear him, he would be safe. He was ashamed of something, possibly of having been sexually abused at some time, possibly of having been beaten down—he admitted the latter had happened to him several times just within the last two years, that is, since he had joined his gang, and that his OG had once punched him square in the forehead and knocked him out of the chair he was sitting in, to teach him not to trust *anyone*, his OG said— so he was determined to avoid re-experiencing that shame if he could, and this made him the more determined to dominate those who might visit it on him.

Of course, other kids, like Oren and Durrell, sensed where his buttons were and pressed them. And others, like Casey, seeing how Oren riled Marcus, imitated Oren and made Marcus feel his back was to the wall. After all, if Casey, a kid with an IQ of sixty, could get over on Marcus, who couldn't? But the other kids didn't want to fight him because they *did* think about the consequences if staff caught them fighting—well, maybe Casey didn't. Still, they pressed Marcus' buttons to get him to go off so he would get in trouble.

I ran all of this by Marcus—his fear and his trying to keep other kids by whom he felt threatened at bay.

"Right on the dot," he said. He admitted that he was afraid of a lot of things, including someone stealing on him, coming up behind him and hitting him when he was not aware. When he acknowledged that he used anger and intimidation to keep people away from him, I told him that I thought he had been beaten badly at some time in his life.

"How did you know?" he asked.

I knew because that was what he wanted to do to others. A lot of times people try to re-experience bad things that were done to them, either by setting themselves up to be the victim again, or to be the victimizer.

He asked if I could see it on him.

"Do you mean can I see it in your face or in the way you move, something like that?"

He nodded. I had been walking him to his room after talking with him in the staff office, and when I asked this last question he was already inside.

"No," I said. "It was all just something I assumed because I've known so many kids these things have happened to—not to diminish what you've gone through."

He came back to the doorway and put his head between the door and the jamb. "Crush my head," he said.

"I'm not going to crush your head."

He laughed but he didn't move his head. I pushed him so that he staggered back three or four feet. As I locked his door, I listened for his laugh again, but it didn't come.

The Opposite of the Golden Rule

I was talking with Marcus in the staff office, my back to the window looking onto the day area, when he said suddenly, "That's him, man!" I had no idea what he was talking about; he had been about to answer a question I had asked about his relationship to his gang set. He began breathing hard, his jaw muscles working. I turned and saw a kid who had just been transferred into the cottage facing us from the other side of the window, his chest pumped up, gesturing with his hands, saying something unintelligible behind the glass. I turned back to Marcus who was rising from his chair. I stood up with him. He tried to walk around me, but I pushed him back. He tried again—he wasn't looking at me, but past my shoulder—and this time I slipped behind him and put a full nelson on him and held him until Bill from Security, who was still in the cottage after moving the new kid in, came into the office. We put Marcus in the quiet room appended to the office and then we went out and put the new kid in Room 16.

Afterward I went and talked to Marcus. He said the new kid, Jeremiah Court, had stabbed the father of one of Marcus' homies because he, the father, had burned Jeremiah in a drug deal. Marcus' set had sworn to kill Jeremiah. Marcus said Durrell also had had problems with Jeremiah and Durrell had beaten him up when they were in detention.

Layton and I talked with Durrell and Jeremiah separately. Durrell said Jeremiah was his worst enemy for personal rather than gang reasons. He said Jeremiah instigated problems between Durrell and his family, and that he beat Jeremiah up on the outs. The issue between Marcus and Jeremiah was a gang thing, and Jeremiah had already said, before he got put in his room, that he was going to beat Marcus down.

Jeremiah said he had a problem with Durrell and another problem with Marcus. He said that when he was in the day area he stood up "to stand my ground" when he saw Marcus moving toward the door from inside the office. He was lying. He was already on his feet when I saw him, before Marcus got out of his chair. Jeremiah denied he was in a gang, saying, "I don't bang." He was lying here, too. I told him he talked like a gangbanger, alluding to his saying he wanted to stand his ground. He smiled and said, "No comment."

He was afraid that Marcus would jump him; he said that if Marcus was as tough as his reputation made him out to be, he would have to jump Marcus first, before Marcus could hurt him.

Jeremiah had been transferred to us from Dolphin, the boys' mental health unit, because he intentionally hit another kid with a soccer ball. We kept him overnight, locked in his room, and sent him back to Dolphin in the morning.

*   *   *

I asked Marcus if he remembered me telling him that people often did to others what had been done to them. "Kind of the opposite of the Golden Rule," I said.

Marcus said he had been thinking about that.

I asked if anyone had done to him what he later did to his victim.

He made himself smile. It was hard to look at him. His lips were twisted and seemed to have swelled. His entire face seemed to have swelled and the skin had reddened. His eyes shined with tears that he refused to release. He shook his head no.

"All right." I would wait, and if he did not bring it up, I would ask him again some other time.

I said now, "Are you unhappy, Marcus?"

He said he did not remember ever in his life being happy.

*   *   *

I talked with Marcus and his parents after their visit one Sunday. I had not met Marcus' father before. I was struck by how alike they looked, father and son, considering that Mr. Bellows was older and heavier. But he moved with the fluidity of an athlete, while Marcus was clearly not an athlete. I looked for signs of bitterness on Mr. Bellows' face, but I saw nothing that spoke of prison.

Both parents were concerned about Marcus and said they were committed to doing what they could for him. I told them that they presented Marcus with an unusual situation: it was rare for a father to be absent from a child's life and then to come back into it. I had experience with only one other case that at all resembled this one. In that case, the father was able to re-establish himself in his son's life. Their relationship was difficult for a long time, but perseverance by both eventually resulted in the boy's giving up gang life, finishing high school and then going on to a university. I emphasized how hard it was for them to start up their relationship again and then to maintain it, and said that it required some re-evaluation of themselves as well as their expectations of each other.

Mr. Bellows watched me as I spoke. I had learned that when Marcus looked at me without expression he was not blanking out, but was absorbing what I said and would think about it later. Mr. Bellows stared at me now with the same open look I had grown accustomed to seeing on Marcus' face.

After a while, Marcus' parents and I decided to talk alone and I asked Marcus to go out to the day area and have one of the staff there lock him in his room—he was on an In-and-Out program again. I watched from the office as he approached Dick. I waved to Dick when he turned toward me and then he and Marcus disappeared into Zone 2.

Marcus' mother said he was doing better now than he had in years, in terms of controlling his anger. And he was reading and writing better than he ever did. But some of the things Marcus had revealed surprised them—assaults he had done on the outside that neither of them had known about, and his fantasies, even now, of retaliating against kids who he felt had wronged him. They saw the world, and Marcus, as being caught up in a war between Good and Bad. Sometimes Marcus won a battle against Bad and sometimes he lost, but they did see improvement.

I asked them if they could remember Marcus' having been abused in any way when he was small. They could not. I asked this question to try to detect any indication of guilt or shame in their response as much as to prod them to search their memories, but nothing in their reply led me to think either of them had abused their son. They did not appear at all defensive.

Mr. Bellows described Marcus as intellectually less capable than other kids his age when he was small, and feeling estranged as he watched his age group advance through the education system, leaving him behind. He started attaching himself to older boys who were socially marginal, Mrs. Bellows said. (Marcus' co-offender was an older boy who was considered by the social workers in detention to be mentally disabled. Their victim, also older than Marcus, had the mind of a ten-year-old, according to the social worker who evaluated Marcus before he came to Ash Meadow. All three boys had been friends. Marcus and his co-offender—Marcus said it was the older boy's idea—forced the other boy to fellate them.)

I asked Marcus how he could say on one day that he was going to let God do His work on his behalf, and that he was going to avoid people who want to goad him to fight, but on the next day try to assault David.

Marcus said David used to be down, but he wasn't now. He said he knew where David was weak. David had once been in a gang, but he had chosen to get jumped out. What Marcus meant when he said David was weak was that David didn't have the heart for gang life anymore.

I told him this did not explain why he had gone after David.

Marcus said then that David had threatened him and at the same time Marcus saw two other kids walking over who, he had been told, intended to jump him. So he decided to strike first.

I gave him the assignment to describe, in writing, four incidents in which he assaulted or tried to assault someone. With each description, he was to tell me what led up to the incident, who said what, and how he, Marcus, felt just before, during, and after the incident.

Who Owns Your Life?

Suppose, I said, two kids get in a fight. Let's name them Ernie and Morley. Morley says something or does something that pisses Ernie off, and Ernie hits Morley and then they fight.

Now suppose Ernie is not really pissed off, but hits Morley anyway because a third person—maybe another kid, maybe an adult—has told him to. We'll name this person Scott. Maybe Scott is not even at the place where the fight happens, but he's told Ernie to look for a chance to beat up Morley, and then do it. In both cases, kids are fighting, but are the contexts the same?

We were in Alternatives to Violence, one of the last sessions.

Now, I said, suppose Morley says something and Ernie gets pissed off, takes out a gun and kills Morley. Would we call that a fight? No. What would we call it? Murder, okay. Suppose Ernie has been told by Scott, who is not present, to kill Morley. Is that still murder? Who is the murderer, or who are the murderers? Who is more likely to get caught, Ernie or Scott, the shooter or the person who ordered him to shoot?

Now suppose we have the same situation, but with this change: whereas before Ernie was told by Scott that the reason for killing Morley is to send a message to Morley's gang to stay out of the territory controlled by Ernie's and Scott's gang, or maybe Ernie was told that the reason is to retaliate for something Morley's gang did, what's going on now is that while Ernie is told the same thing by Scott, the truth is that the real reason for Scott's wanting Morley killed is that Scott wants Morley's girlfriend and Morley is in the way. Is this situation the same as the one where Ernie kills Morley for revenge, or the one where he does it on impulse, or the one where the two kids fight?

You should know that in almost every situation here at Ash Meadow when we've had a problem between gangs, it has begun over a girl—because of jealousy or because a boy has disrespected her and another boy feels he has to stand up for her. But the issue takes the form of a gang problem when one boy misrepresents to his homies what is really going on, maybe because he doesn't think he can handle the other boy alone and doesn't want to admit this, or maybe because he's afraid of retaliation by the other boy's set.

So now I want you to imagine that you are Ernie, you are the shooter and you're shooting Morley because someone you respect has told you to— or maybe you don't respect him, but you think you have to do what he tells you to do anyway. But in any case if only one person is going to go to prison, it's going to be you, and it may not even be for the reason you've been told, and I'd like you to ask yourself: Whose life am I living? Am I living my own life or someone else's? Who owns my life?

You don't have to answer now, but I want you to think about this.

* * *

Marcus said he was afraid he wouldn't be able to live up to staff's, and also his mother's, expectations for him. He recognized he'd made a lot of progress toward controlling his anger, and he'd found a way to brush off most of other kids' attempts to belittle him or otherwise put him down, but his impulse was still to respond with intimidation. He asked me to arrange for him to see a psychiatrist for his anxiety, but I had referred him to the psychiatry team months before and they had declined to see him. I told him I was working on getting him transferred to Crane Cottage.

He said then that he hated being in Wolf. He had had no idea it would be as bad as it had been for him. Everything he had done on the outs to earn respect from his homies had no value here. He said he had no friends here, but was surrounded by enemies. He kept saying, "The things I've done … the things I've done…," meaning the things he had done for his homies.

He felt they had betrayed his love for them. Not one had written or contacted his mother to send a message of regards. When Marcus was getting ready for his trial, he called a nineteen-year-old homeboy and asked him to testify on his behalf. But the homeboy refused, saying, "They already got one fool. No sense making it two."

He had done plenty for his set. They had relied on his craziness, his fearlessness. Once, they were jacked of their money by some older kids who had guns and ordered them to get down on the floor. Marcus' homies did as they were told, but Marcus did not get on the floor with them. He handed over his money but did not lie down with his homies who had earned his contempt for being so obedient.

He had told me only about 50 percent of what had happened to him, he said. He had been really traumatized by some of it. He used that word, "traumatized," which he had probably heard me use.

I told him he could tell me more whenever he was ready. I had come to believe that, whether or not he had been abused when he was very young, he had probably been used sexually by a member of his own set, or perhaps raped by another set.[2]

*   *   *

Marcus got twenty-four hours off program for threatening Johnny Kerwood who was his friend, perhaps his only friend in the cottage. It was ostensibly over some candy that Johnny had promised to give him, but then had eaten himself.

Marcus said he would like to beat Johnny up so he would "feel what I'm feeling." He felt worse than if Johnny had beaten him up, he said, but he wasn't going to retaliate because even though Johnny had betrayed him, he still liked Johnny.

*   *   *

He was looking forward to going to Crane, although he wasn't counting on it. At Crane, he would begin the treatment program for sex offenders. Also, once he was out of maximum security, he would attend school on upper campus. Like the other kids in Wolf, he went to school in the classroom behind the cottage. Upper campus would give him the opportunity to meet other kids; it would also be a test to see how well he could integrate himself into their society.

I asked him to try to anticipate what might happen at school to get him in trouble. He said girls might try to manipulate him into intimidating someone or hitting someone by saying something like, "Marcus, you know what so and so said? He said blah blah blah."

"Girls like boys who are tough," Marcus said, and they would want to see how tough he was.

I asked him what he would do if they tried to manipulate him like that.

"Tell them to take it somewhere else," he said.

*   *   *

Marcus' mother told me again that she felt Marcus was doing better. I agreed, even though he was off program again. Somehow he had found a way to defuse his anger, sometimes anyway. One thing that helped, I thought, was that I modified his treatment: for every perfect day—a day without a demerit—I took him outside to shoot hoops during quiet time. Still, he often fronted, assuming the pose and demeanor of a gangster, when other kids were around. Although I sometimes called him on it, to let him know that I knew what he was doing, he did not usually break off. It was easy to imagine how this pose could lead to trouble if another kid wanted to challenge him. Wolf did not currently have kids who were rivals of Marcus' gang. In their absence, he was doing well.

*　*　*

Marcus talked about the problems he had had in school on the outside before he stopped going. In fourth and fifth grades, he wasn't permitted to be in a classroom with other kids because he was so aggressive, but met one-on-one with his teacher. Finally, in sixth grade, he was allowed back in class. But he got angry with a girl and told her she smelled like a fish. He was yanked from class for making "inappropriate sexual comments." He said—and I thought this was probably true, given his age and the fact that he had had little socialization with other children, and almost no contact with kids in school for two years—he had had no idea he had made a sexual comment; she *did* smell like a fish.

This memory was important to him—I could see the hurt on his face, the way the muscles in his cheeks and around his mouth twisted as he forced himself not to cry—and he did not let go of it, but went through it again. In the fourth grade, he said, his teacher and the principal had told him that if he was good this year, if his behavior was good, he could rejoin his class next year. So he had made himself be good, and it was hard for him, it took some effort. And then next year came and they still wouldn't let him go back to regular school, but said he had to be good for another year. So he was good for a second year, and finally they let him go to the sixth grade in a real class-room, and then this thing with the girl happened.

He hadn't been able to stand the thought of spending another two years or one year or whatever in a classroom with only his teacher, so he didn't go back to school after that, at least until he was imprisoned, but preferred to be out on the street. What education he got, he said, he got from the older boys in his set, once he joined it.

We were just conversing now. Actually, I hardly spoke because Marcus kept talking, checking my face now and then to be sure I was still listening, and then going on, one subject after another. He had missed his father terribly during the years he was gone. His mother kept telling him his dad was away on a business trip, but he was in prison. He was gone for six and a half years. Marcus was weeping as he told me this. He couldn't trust his parents entirely now, he said. They had lied to him and allowed him to hope, even when they knew there was no hope. Even though his dad was eventually released, there were all those years…

As we were talking, Jan came into the office and told us Marcus would be transferring to Crane tomorrow; the administration had just approved the move. Marcus put his head on his knees and said, "Thank the Lord, thank the Lord." Jan stared at him.

*　*　*

A month after Marcus moved to Crane Cottage, he grabbed the arm of a girl at school and tried to persuade her to touch his penis. She became hysterical, explaining to her staff later that the incident had caused her to flash on something that had happened to her before she came to Ash Meadow. Marcus did this only a day after his mother called me to thank me for helping her son, telling me that only I and, to a lesser degree, Layton seemed really to care for Marcus when he was in Wolf Cottage.

When Marcus was sent back to his cottage from school after the incident, Debra, his counselor at Crane, called me and filled me in on what had happened. Then she asked if Marcus had done anything like this when he was in Wolf. Had he shown anger or aggressiveness toward girls? Her cottage director was angry, Debra said; he had not wanted to accept Marcus into Crane's program, he had had another kid from another cottage in mind to fill the slot, and he believed I had lied to get him to take Marcus. I told her Marcus' aggression had been directed toward boys, except for one occasion when he thought a girl had hit him with a ball.

Marcus was transferred to Elk Grove, a sister institution, two days later. He left this note with Debra to give to me.

To Jerry
From Marcus Bellows

Dear Jerry
    I want you to know that you were there for me when no one trusted me. I could not have made it this far if it was not for you. This is a big achievement for me. You showed me things and how to do them.
    To some people they think I am a failure but me, when I look back over my life this [is] the most I have ever accomplished, and you are a large part of it.
    I would like you to keep in touch with me when I go to Elk Grove. I want to keep achieving my goals in life.
    When we had the staff talks, I told you things that were so dear to me and you accepted them and gave me feed back I would have gotten from my father if he was there.
    I hope you don't feel that I've let you down. I will continue to accomplish my goals. We have come too far just to let something like this stop us. I want to learn and do more.
    Not just a staff but one of my best friends in the world, Jerry Gold.

A Confluence of Things

Marcus' case manager at Elk Grove allowed him to call me shortly after he had settled in. He said he was doing all right, but there was a lot of gang activity there and he'd already been in a couple of fights. He'd been sent to Elk Grove instead of The Rivers, the institution for the most difficult boys, because Elk Grove had a superior mental health program, which all of us who knew him at Ash Meadow agreed he needed. But he said now that he had not been placed in the mental health unit. Before he hung up I asked him to connect me with his staff again. The counselor said Marcus was too aggressive to be placed in the mental health lodge—Elk Grove used the term "lodge" instead of "cottage"—but once he stopped fighting he would be eligible. Marcus had to decide for himself how he wanted to spend the next few years.

A year or so later, I was at Elk Grove for a conference and inquired about Marcus. He was in the mental health program now and was doing well. Not so his co-offender who had been sent to The Rivers originally, but then was transferred to Elk Grove when staff realized how disturbed he was. Like Marcus, he had been taunted and belittled by other kids in his lodge but, unlike Marcus, he had been too afraid to assault anyone physically, until finally he did. Until then, he had not known how powerful he was—he weighed close to three hundred pounds—but now that he understood he could put fear in the eyes of other kids, he did.

Two years after the conference I had the occasion to call Marcus' parole officer about a matter concerning another boy. Having wrapped up the business I called about, I asked about Marcus. He was in school, the officer said. An alternative high school but, still, a school. His UAs were clean, he had a girlfriend, he seemed to have dropped his gang affiliation. His parents were doing okay. Both were working, his father at a shitty job, but at least he was working. You never knew, of course, but the parole officer did not expect any problems from Marcus.

And, of course, you never knew what turned a kid around. Certainly it was a confluence of things, but you liked to think that something you did or said was one of those things, and maybe it was even true.

III

Reggie Greene
A Sister's Love

I had not heard anything about Reggie in years, so I was surprised when Jan told me he had called Herman. I was surprised again when she said he was doing well, he was married, had a couple of kids and was enrolled at a community college. I had thought Reggie would be dead by now, or in prison. And he had called Herman. If he were going to call any of us, it would be Herman. I had worked for Herman as I now worked for Jan, and Reggie had been on my caseload the last time he was at Ash Meadow.

When I met him he was in mid-adolescence. He did not have anything going for him that I looked for when I was trying to decide whether or not to invest my hope in a kid. He did not have an able parent. His father was doing life without parole and his mother was in a wheelchair, paralyzed in an auto accident. She couldn't catch him when he ran away after he did something wrong, he told me. There apparently was no one in the world other than his sisters who loved him without qualification, and they, I thought, were powerless to influence him. He was not someone I could imagine sticking to the straight-and-narrow.

He did not seem to be able to go without marijuana for long, provided it was available to him. There was a four-month period following his sister Stecia's murder, he said (though this may have been a lie), of which he had no memory because he had smoked almost constantly every day. In Ash Meadow, marijuana was not available and he was forced to deal with himself.

He was a committed gangster, although he insisted his gang, the Black Gangster Disciples, was an "organization" akin to the Mafia rather than a gang like the Crips or the Bloods. Once, he told me, he was being chased by three Crips when the thought came to him that he was a BGD and he should not run from Crips but stand his ground, regardless of what might happen. He stopped and waited for the first one to reach him. Reggie hit him and knocked him down and then waited for the others, but they ran off. Another time he shot a kid. I suspected that he had shot others, but he didn't mention them to me. Once a homie invited him to come along on a drive-by. Reggie almost did it because he wanted to avenge Stecia's murder on someone—he didn't care who. But he had the opportunity to have sex that night, so he begged off. His homie understood: you don't pass up sex with a girl that pretty; there will be other drive-bys. The shooting went wrong and the shooters killed a seven-year-old girl instead of her mother whom they had gone after. Reggie's homie had driven the car. He received the shortest sentence of the boys involved: twenty years.

Love and Loss

Reggie and two of his sisters were at their grandparents' home in California when their grandmother received the phone call about the accident and her daughter's paralysis. When she told Reggie, he made himself believe that it wasn't true, and even though he knew it was true, he kept this knowledge out of his thoughts until he saw his mother again. Instead of going home after their vacation, he and his sisters stayed on to live with their grandparents.

One night while their grandmother was away at a church retreat, their grandfather took a little girl who was staying with the family, a toddler whose mother was also at the retreat, into his bedroom to sleep with him. When Reggie and his sisters heard the little girl crying, they knew what was going on. His sisters told Reggie that their grandfather had done the same thing to them. Reggie wanted to go into the other bedroom and sock his grandfather, but the girls talked him out of it. He was barely nine. Even so, he stayed awake all night to protect his sisters in case his grandfather came for them.

When their grandmother and the little girl's mother returned the next day, the kids told them what happened. The women began yelling and punching the kids' grandfather and the toddler's mother called the police. Waiting for the police to arrive, the girls told their grandmother that what their grandfather had done to the little girl he had also done to them. Their grandmother was beating her husband again when the police arrived. Despite what his grandfather had done, Reggie felt bad for him when he saw him in handcuffs. He felt, too, that he had betrayed his grandfather by telling on him. Worse, when the police told Reggie and his sisters that they would have to go to the police station, he had the sense that he was about to lose both them and his grandmother. Later, as a teenager, he would say that he could not get over the feeling that if he allowed himself to love someone, he would lose her. He traced the beginning of his chronic anger to being taken away from his family.

Foster care was bad. The kids were separated, each going to a different home. For the first time in his life, Reggie felt completely alone. What he hated most was that the foster children in the home had to eat in a separate room from the one in which the foster parents and their biological children ate. He felt like an animal in a cage with other animals. He was angry and he fought with the other kids. Because of his aggressiveness, he had to stay back when the other kids went on outings.

After six months he and his sisters were reunited and sent back to Seattle by the California authorities. His family—sisters, cousins, aunts, everybody except his mother—were all at the airport to meet them. He had not seen his mother in three years. When he asked one of his older sisters where his mom was, she told him she was at home because her wheelchair wouldn't fit in the car. Even then he could not persuade himself that his mother was paralyzed, but thought that his sister was lying to him.

On the drive home he talked silently to himself, telling himself that what he knew was true was not true. When the car pulled up in front of the house, he stopped talking. He was frightened. He was the last to get out of the car. He walked inside and there his mother was, and he began to cry and then she began to cry. He cried because he could no longer deny her condition; she cried because she hadn't seen him in so long and he had changed.

*   *   *

He was in the third grade and on the honor role and he was popular with the other kids at school. His mother was proud of him and he was proud of himself.

Two years later he had stopped studying and had eschewed his popularity at school in order to gain status with some of his cousins and the kids they hung around with. They introduced him to the Black Gangster Disciples and to marijuana. That year, too, he got in trouble with the law for the first time. He and one of his cousins beat up a boy who claimed to be a Crip, but the case was dismissed for lack of evidence. A year later, when he was twelve, he began dealing and using marijuana regularly. He was suspended from school for bringing drugs and a weapon to the campus.

He gained a reputation with the police for theft and assault. At a party attended by both Crips and BGD, some of the Crips began throwing gang signs. Reggie gathered together the other BGD and called one of the enemy over. He came, but Reggie could see from the way he moved that he was afraid. Reggie said, "What are you and your Crab homeboys doin' at this party?"

"Cuz, why you disrespectin' us like that?" the other boy said.

"I ain't no cuz, and don't be screamin' that bullshit here. This is a G party," Reggie said.

"Cuz, you be trippin.'"

Reggie hit him and he went down. Reggie followed him to the floor, hitting him again. Reggie's girlfriend tried to get him to stop, but he wouldn't. The kids from both gangs were fighting now and stopped only when somebody said someone had called the police. Everybody left and Reggie went home feeling that his side had won. He felt good because he thought he had made a name for himself. He called one of his cousins and told him what had happened and his cousin came over and they got high together.

* * *

Reggie's mother was worried that he was smoking too much weed. One day she told him they were going to visit his father. They would stay overnight in a trailer at the prison. Though they had talked on the phone, Reggie hadn't seen his father in years and believed his mother had arranged the visit so his father could reprimand him for smoking.

When Reggie saw him, he gave his father the obligatory hug but afterward tried to avoid him. If his dad walked into the kitchen, Reggie went into the living room; if he came into the living room, Reggie went into the kitchen. Finally his father called him into the living room. He smiled and said how much Reggie had grown; he was even bigger than in the photos his mother had sent. His dad asked if Reggie had started having sex yet. Reggie said he had. "How many times?" his dad asked. "I don't know," Reggie said. His dad asked if Reggie used a rubber. Reggie said he did, but he was lying. He thought his dad knew that he was lying, so he admitted that he had not used a rubber. He felt weird talking about sex with his father.

After a while his father asked him if he ever used drugs. Reggie said yes. What kind? Only bud, Reggie said. His father grinned and said, "Smoke some weed with your dad."

Reggie refused, unsure about what would come next.

"You can smoke weed with your homies, but not with me?" his father said.

Reggie said that wasn't it, he just didn't have any.

"Don't worry about that. Do you want to smoke some or not?"

"Yes."

His dad pulled a bag out of his pocket and took out a joint and handed it to Reggie. Reggie lit it and took a hit and passed it to his father.

"I can tell you ain't no rookie at this," his dad said.

They passed the joint back and forth a couple of times and then they went into the kitchen where Reggie's mother was preparing dinner and his dad told him to give the joint to her. Reggie hesitated and his mother said, "Boy, give me that joint." Reggie felt weird again. He had never smoked with either of his parents, but here he was, smoking with both of them. His mother said, "From now on, if you want to smoke weed, just ask me," but both she and his father told him they didn't want him even experimenting with heroin or cocaine.

*   *   *

After Reggie and his mother returned home, he started smoking with her and was soon getting high with her every day. He began buying from her and selling the weed to his friends. Even so, he was losing money because he was smoking so much, not only with his mom, but also with his friends. Finally he arranged with his mother to take over her business. He told her the police were watching the house because she was bound to her wheelchair and her clientele had to come to her, but if he was selling, he could sell in the street, away from the house. He knew he was manipulating her, but he wanted some independence and he wanted money. He once robbed another dealer and bought some clothes with the money he got, but he didn't want to rely on robberies as a source of income.

Soon he was making twice what his mother had made. He sometimes took in a thousand dollars in a day, rarely less than five hundred. He had earned respect from other kids and he felt like he was king of the world. He was almost thirteen.

One of his cousins was selling crack. Reggie was drawn to him because he had a good-looking girlfriend, a couple of cars, jewelry, and a lot more money than Reggie had. He started hanging out with his cousin, learning how he did things. They would go to a mall to buy clothes, but also to meet girls. Reggie found that girls were attracted to him and he enjoyed the power he discovered he had over them. But, dealing crack, he had also attracted more attention from the police and he was arrested and charged with a number of offenses, including theft and possession of stolen property. He was not convicted of any of these charges and came away from the courtroom believing the law would never be able to convict him, although he knew the police would continue to watch him.

After a concert one night, Reggie was in the parking lot with a group of BGDs when they confronted some Crips. One from each group began arguing with the other and when the BGD hit the Crip and other BGDs joined in to stomp him, the other Crips went for their guns and began shooting. In the melee, Reggie found himself holding somebody's gun and he pointed it at the first person he saw who was wearing blue and fired. He didn't stop shooting until he emptied the magazine. When he was finished, he stood for a moment, shocked at what he had done, then ran until he found his cousin standing by his car. They both hopped in and took off. Reggie didn't know if he had shot anybody or not.

On another night they went to a party where they smoked weed with two girls who agreed to spend the night with them. On the way to his cousin's house, they saw a boy on the sidewalk who, Reggie's cousin said, owed him money. His cousin stopped the car, got out and confronted the boy. The boy pushed him, and Reggie, seeing this, popped the trunk release and got out and ran to the rear of the car and grabbed a gun out of the trunk. Later he remembered the girls' yelling at him, "Leave it alone! Your cousin can handle it himself!" but at the time what they were saying didn't register.

Reggie shouted at his cousin to move and, seeing that Reggie had a gun, his cousin jumped out of the way. The other boy started to run. Reggie fired and the kid fell to the ground. When Reggie thought about it later, he was sure he saw the bullet strike the boy in the back. His cousin went through the kid's pockets but didn't find anything. In frustration, he kicked the kid and the kid groaned. Until then Reggie thought he was dead. Then his cousin felt in the kid's socks and in one of them he found a roll of money. Reggie and his cousin ran back to the car. All Reggie could think about as he ran was the look on the kid's face when he saw that Reggie had a gun.

In the car, the girls screamed at the two boys, at Reggie particularly, telling him he was crazy, but he was so high on weed and adrenalin that he thought they were praising him. As they drove they saw the lights of a patrol car behind them and he could see how frightened the girls were. Then he realized that he was still holding the gun and he felt himself panicking too. The patrol car drove past and they calmed down. On another occasion they might have laughed at themselves, at the silliness of their fear or from relief, but they were all still too scared to laugh.

At his cousin's house, Reggie went around to the back and hid the gun in a thick shrub. Then he went inside. Everyone was staring at him.

"What the fuck you lookin' at?" he said. He meant his tone to be playful but he wasn't sure it came out that way.

"You crazy, Reggie!" "You crazy, niggah!" the girls said.

"I had to help my cousin," Reggie said.

He pulled out some weed and rolled a couple of joints.

"All that excitement brought my high down," he said, but that wasn't it. He was still high from the party, but he wanted to be even higher.

They smoked the weed and drank some beer they found in the refrig-
erator. They were still smoking when there was a knock on the door. Reggie's
first thought was that it was the police and that they had surrounded the
house. Everybody was looking for a place to hide when the door opened.
Reggie thought it was over for them—they were going to prison. But it was
only one of his cousin's clients. His cousin sold him some crack and he left.
This time he and his cousin and the girls did break up laughing, and in a
minute they were talking and getting high again.

"You shoulda seen your face!" his cousin laughed.

"Me! I thought you were gonna jump out the window! And what kinda
people you sellin' to? What kinda man just walks into another man's house?"

"Well, he did knock."

Which sent them again into a sphere of laughter.

After a while his cousin and his girl went into a bedroom. Reggie's girl
said she was tired and they went into another bedroom and had sex.

*   *   *

On his first day in the eighth grade Reggie went to school high. He made
some new friends, all of them either BGDs or Bloods. (BGDs and Bloods
considered themselves related, akin to cousins, as opposed to Crips who were
the enemies of both.) At the beginning of the second week, he met a girl
downtown named Meika who was in a gang. She didn't go to school, but
spent her days selling dope. Reggie had given his business back to his mother
a few months before finishing the seventh grade; it had taken up so much of
his time that he was attending school only sporadically and he was afraid of
failing. But now Meika offered to set him up again and even gave him some
dope to get started. He sold it all in less than half an hour, making seven
hundred dollars. He bought more from one of his cousins who also showed
him how to cut it. Within a week he had his own small clientele and was selling every day.

He quit going to school. His mother found out and Reggie left home
after a terrible argument with her. He ran into Meika and she told him about
a place that sold fake IDs. Twenty minutes later he had one.

For almost a year he lived in motels, supporting himself by selling crack.
He gained a reputation among the BGD as a dealer and as someone who
wasn't afraid to use violence. Then he was arrested and charged with possession with the intent to distribute a controlled substance. His lawyer told him
he could expect to get up to thirty-nine weeks in prison. He called his mother
for the first time in months. She said she was glad he was locked up because
now she could sleep at night instead of lying awake, worrying about him.

Reggie yelled at her over the phone, angry that she would not do anything for him. He pleaded guilty and was sent to Ash Meadow.

His sister Sacha was there. He hadn't even known she'd been arrested. She had only a few weeks remaining of her sentence when he arrived. The day she left she gave him some advice: get treatment for his marijuana addiction; don't get in any fights; do what staff tell you to do.

Approaching the end of the fifth month of his sentence, Reggie went into an eight-week, residential treatment program on campus. He told himself that he was going to learn how to manage his addiction, but he knew, too, that when he got out he was going to use again and that he was going to sell again, although he intended to be smarter about selling. He passed the treatment program.

Because he passed, he had to serve only seven months instead of nine, plus he was given a five-day home leave. On the bus home, he realized how happy he was to be able to see his family again. Except for Sacha, he hadn't seen them in over a year. Also on the bus was a kid he had known in school who gave him some weed. When one of his sisters picked him up at the station, he gave it to her because he knew he would have to undergo a urinanalysis when he returned to Ash Meadow.

After talking with his mother and sisters for a while, he grew bored and called one of his cousins and asked him to come and get him. Except for his first hours at home, he spent all of his leave with his cousins and homeboys, but he neither drank nor smoked weed.

He was saying his goodbyes to his family and packing to return to Ash Meadow when Michael, his case manager, called to tell him that Ash Meadow had extended his home leave for twelve more days, when his sentence would be up. All he had to do was return to Ash Meadow twelve days from now and he would be officially released from custody. Reggie was overjoyed. He thanked Michael and left immediately to tell his homies. He found them at the park where they hung out. They were smoking weed and he asked for a hit. He said he would smoke for only one day and then he would drink vinegar to flush out his system for the next eleven.

After a few days he was selling crack again. While he did not use crack— he had never used crack and, like many dealers, he was contemptuous of those who did—he had not stopped smoking marijuana since that first hit on the day his home leave was extended. He did not return to Ash Meadow, even thought he knew there would be a warrant out for him. When eventually he landed on my caseload, he told me he didn't know why he decided not to go back. He may have been afraid of his UA coming back dirty, but he wasn't sure.

I thought that he was afraid of disappointing Herman by having a dirty UA. It was Herman, our cottage director, who had arranged for Reggie's home leave and its extension. It was Herman who had gotten Reggie his minimum sentence after he passed his drug-treatment program. In the few months that Reggie had been at Ash Meadow, Herman had become as near to a father as Reggie had ever had.

They had much in common. Both were aggressive and resorted to bullying if they believed it would get them what they wanted. Both were angry, though Herman's anger took a greater racial cast than Reggie's. Both were ambitious, Reggie's ambitions focused on winning respect on the street and making money, Herman's on gaining power and recognition within the Juvenile Rehabilitation Administration and various social and political organizations in which he was a member, and making money. Each had his own vices but only one of Reggie's—marijuana—was illegal. Both knew violence. Herman, as an adolescent, had been in a gang and boasted still that he had been his gang's "warlord." He had been a boxer, an infantryman in Viet Nam, and a homicide detective later in his life.

When Reggie had a problem in the cottage, it was Herman he went to rather than his case manager. Herman regarded Reggie as, if not quite a son, a young man very near to being his son, very near, I think, to being himself. I want to say this about Herman, and then I'll move on: for all of his faults—and he had many, among them a kind of insecurity regarding his relationship with his staff that resulted in repeated attempts to intimidate us, which in turn invoked the resentment of some of us toward him—when it came to children, I have never met anyone, at least in the United States, more generous of heart.

* * *

After five or six months Reggie was arrested again for possession with intent to distribute. He pleaded guilty and was returned to Ash Meadow. He spent a month in maximum security, then was transferred back to Swan Cottage. Michael was angry with him. Herman, as Reggie had anticipated, was disappointed. Coming from Herman, disappointment was worse than anger.

Reggie decided to change himself. He had gotten two years on his second offense and he was already tired of being locked up. He felt old.

A few months after Reggie came back to Swan, Herman told him he'd been watching him and thought he was ready for another chance. Did Reggie feel ready? He did. Within days he found himself in a group home not far from where his mother lived. He met a lot of kids there that he'd known on the outside. He began going to NA meetings, but looked down on people who couldn't manage their marijuana use. After a while, though, he came to feel that some of what they said about themselves was also true of him. He attended a public high school, and kids there offered him drugs, but he told them he couldn't, and he didn't.

He had been in the group home for three months when he got a call from his mother. She was crying so hard that she had to keep going back over what she had already said in order to say it clearly enough that he could understand it. His sister Stecia had been killed. That was all Reggie could take in. After talking for ten minutes or more, all he retained was that Stecia had been murdered. He put the phone down and ran to his room. As he had done when he learned of his mother's accident, he told himself that it hadn't happened, that Stecia was fine and the phone call had been a mistake. He started to cry, but knew that if he cried he would have to acknowledge that there was something worth crying about, so he forced himself to stop.

He returned to the day area, intending to ask one of the staff for permission to call his mother back, but she had called again and the staff simply handed Reggie the phone. He asked his mother what happened. Stecia was the witness to a murder, his mother said. She saw one boy shoot another over some money, and then he shot her. She begged him not to kill her, telling him she had two children and was pregnant, but he shot her anyway, five times, in the head and the back.

Reggie dropped into a chair beside the phone. He asked his mother how she knew all of this. The boy had told his homies, she said. And Reggie's aunt, who was affiliated with that Crip set, told her. Reggie still couldn't force himself to accept that Stecia was dead. He asked who identified the body. His aunt did, his mother said.

Reggie told her to give one of the staff whatever information he asked for so that Reggie could go to the funeral. He handed the phone to the staff nearest him and went back to his room.

After a while Reggie's counselor came in and asked him if he was all right. Reggie asked him to leave.

He didn't want to go to school the next day but staff told him he had to. At school a kid he knew offered him some weed and this time he took it. He was high the whole day. It felt good not to think about his sister. But when he was in his room at the group home again, he could not keep from thinking about her.

On the drive to Stecia's funeral, he fought himself to try to make himself believe that Stecia was dead. When he walked into the funeral home and saw his family, he began to cry. He had smoked weed with his cousins before the service, but even the weed and his mind's persistent denial that Stecia was dead could not remove the agony he was in. He kept thinking that he was to blame because he had been locked up, so was not there to help her. Later, when he told me about her and how she died, he still blamed himself for her death.

When it was time to view her body he broke down. He said later that he cried more that day than he ever had. When he thought about her a year and two years later, he thought about a white coffin with a white skirt hemmed around with pink ribbon.

Following the funeral, he and the staff member escorting him went back to the group home. It was already late when they left the funeral home, and the insistence of the staff on stopping for a hamburger made it even later before they got on the road. When they arrived, Reggie went straight to his room and to bed.

The next morning he was told he would have to take a UA. He forced himself to drink water all day, but by evening when he took the UA, he had stopped caring about getting caught. The test result came back a week later and he was placed on restriction: he could leave the group home to go to school and to work—he had gotten a job in a restaurant—but he had to return to the group home immediately after he got out of school or off shift. Staff knew his schedule and the schedules of the buses he would take.

One day he went to work but they needed him for only half the shift. He called a girl he knew from school and she picked him up. They hooked up with his homeboys in a nearby park and he smoked weed with them and drank and started thinking about not going back to the group home. By the time he was due back, he had made up his mind.

Two weeks later he was arrested again and again charged with possession with intent to distribute. He was sent back to Ash Meadow, first to maximum security, then to Swan where he was placed on my caseload.

A Distorter and a Fabricator

If Herman had asked me, I would have told him that I didn't want Reggie. Everyone knew that Herman had a special feeling for him. Michael warned me that, regardless of what Herman may say, he would be the one to decide what would happen with Reggie. The case manager was there only because a resident was required to have one.

Michael was right, at least at first. Reggie was back with us less than a week when he was suspended from school for having demeaned a particular girl, as well as girls generally, at a school assembly. When I came in that afternoon to start my shift, Reggie had just been sent back to the cottage and was in his room. Herman was pacing between his office and the staff desk that sat at the edge of the living room. When he saw me, he said, "You're going to have to do something about your kid. He really fucked up." Then, before I could say anything, he went down to Reggie's room. I don't know what he said or what Reggie said, but Herman decided that, contrary to the cottage rule about pulling at least some of a resident's privileges if he was suspended from school, Reggie would be confined to the cottage only until school was out for the day—less that an hour from now—and then he could go outside to shoot hoops if he wanted. He would also be permitted to go to a social— a party—that evening at one of the other cottages.

When staff at the girls' cottage next to ours saw Reggie shooting baskets, they were livid. One of them called and berated me for allowing Reggie out of the cottage after he had alluded to girls as bitches in front of the entire student body. I could not break in and when she demanded to speak to the cottage director, I was happy to transfer her.

I could see Herman talking with her through the open door of his office. He sat at his desk and listened attentively and when he spoke, he spoke quietly. He was not trying to convince her of anything. Afterward, he came out of his office and said, "Reggie won't be able to go to the social. Are you taking kids to the gym tonight?"

"I was going to, unless something comes up."

"Well, you'd better leave him back. He's restricted to the cottage until Sunday night. He can go to chapel services Sunday night, but he can't talk to any girls until we sort this out. You'll have to tell him. I'm leaving for the day."

"Oh, thanks."

He laughed. He always laughed when he screwed you. At least when he screwed me. But when he screwed you, it was always in small ways. Among the dozen other cottage directors, he was known as the only one who always stood up for his staff, who never criticized or belittled them to others. This was really quite a lot to say about one of your own. It showed a kind of grudging admiration for someone who was often difficult to like, as well as a view of oneself that was not complimentary.

Soon after I got Reggie on my caseload, he complained about me to Herman. I had told him he couldn't wear his jewelry any more—his gold necklace, his watch with the gold-plated band, his rhinestone ring—because it sent a message to other kids that crime pays.

"It does," he said.

"Then why are you locked up?"

"That's just me. Maybe I won't be caught next time. Maybe I'll learn how to do it better. Maybe I'll do something different."

"Maybe. But in the meantime I don't want you influencing other kids. Do you want to be responsible for them spending their lives in prison?"

"That's on them."

"It's on you, too, if you wear that stuff. Besides, it's ugly."

"What!"

"Just kidding. But you can't wear it."

The next day he told me that Herman said I was the best staff on campus. Reggie's eyes were wide, as if he were in awe.

"Why did he say that?"

"I don't know. That's what he said."

"I mean, what did you say that he was responding to?"

"I said I wanted another staff because you just didn't get it."

"Oh. Well, that's nice."

"And he said you're the right one for me 'cause you're the best one on campus. One of the best. No, he said 'the best.'"

I thought about asking why Herman thought so, but I didn't ask. Later, I thought about asking Herman why he said it, but I didn't ask him either. It's possible that, believing Reggie would pass his comment on to me, Herman wanted to do what he could to keep me from getting discouraged because he knew that other staff would resist working with Reggie. It's possible, too, that he wanted to keep Reggie from getting discouraged, for the same reason.

Staff did not like Reggie. They considered him a problem, and one made worse by Herman's interference. When Reggie was punished by the loss of some of his privileges, such as staying up later than most of the other kids or visiting a friend at another cottage, Herman would reduce the length of the restriction from seven days to three. When Reggie was confined to the cottage for the weekend because he had not turned in a school assignment on time on Friday, Herman declared that as soon as Reggie completed the assignment, he could go outside; Reggie was done by lunchtime on Saturday. Staff's view was that Reggie needed to meet our expectations of behavior just as other kids did. Herman's view was that there was a lot going on in Reggie's head and we needed to work with him.

What most bothered a number of the staff were Reggie's lying and his manipulation of other kids to get what he wanted. We discovered that kids had been exchanging their meds with one another. Then we learned that Reggie had been the one to initiate the exchange. Almost half the cottage was involved. When Rob, the cottage supervisor, called him into his office and confronted him with what other kids were saying, Reggie continued to deny his culpability. "I put that on my dead sister," he said.

A few days later, when it was clear that we were not going to back down, and when even Herman became convinced of Reggie's guilt, he admitted to having worked out the plan on who would exchange what med with whom, and what his own share of the transaction would be. Rob was enraged. He said to Reggie: "You swore on your dead sister! Your dead sister! Your sister who you said you loved so much!"

"I never did," Reggie said.

"Bullshit! I was standing right here when you said it. I know what I heard. And you know you said it."

"I didn't."

"You said, 'I put that on my dead sister.'"

"I said, 'I *fut* that on my sister.' I didn't say 'I *put* that on my sister.'"

"You're going down to your room. Now. You're down for twenty-four."

Herman was discouraged and did not intervene. I was not discouraged and I was not angry. I expected kids to lie. I was pleased when they didn't and punished them when they did, if I caught them at it. But I expected them to lie no less than I expected adults to lie to try to get themselves out of a jam, and police and prosecutors to lie to try to trick somebody into revealing himself. But I was surprised at Reggie's use of his sister in this way. Kids would say, to try to persuade you that they were being honest, "I put that on my mother!" and sometimes they meant it, sometimes they were telling the truth. But sometimes they weren't. Considering how intensely Reggie loved his sisters, and they him, for him to say "I put that on my dead sister" was to betray his memory of her.

I told him this. "You want to be respected as a man, but you do something like this. This is something a little kid does. You knew you were deceiving Rob, regardless of what you actually said. And what does it say about your respect for Stecia's memory?"

He seemed genuinely to feel bad. "I already thought about that. I can't say anything good about myself for what I did to my sister. I'm not going to lie anymore if I get caught doing something."

"What about just not doing something where you have to worry about getting caught?"

"That's not my life, Jerry."

"Remember that paper I asked you to write about Martin Luther King and Malcolm X?"

"I turned that in. I know I did."

"Relax. I have it. I just want to ask you about something you wrote. You said you didn't see yourself emulating either of them. My question is: Why not? You're ambitious. You have leadership qualities. You can organize people. Why not use your abilities to do something good for people? Or to help them do something good for themselves?"

He shook his head. "They both got killed. I'd rather get killed for doing something bad. If that happens, I know I deserve it."

I thought about that for a while. Finally I said, "You're in Youth Group, right?"

He nodded.

"And you're one of the senior members. The other kids trust you, right?"

He considered my question, finally conceding, "Yeah, in some ways. I'm pretty sure they do."

"So when Grant or Herman or somebody hears about something going on on campus—gang kids talking about jumping someone, say—you're one of the kids they send to try to talk them out of it, right? Right?"

He nodded. He knew what was coming. I could see it in the reluctant smile forming at the corners of his mouth.

"So you're already doing something good. Right? If I'm wrong, tell me how."

"It's not the same thing."

"How is it not?"

"It's not something I could do on the outs."

"Nobody's asking you to. They're just asking you to do what's possible here. So how is that different from what Martin Luther King or Malcolm X did?"

"They got killed. They crossed the wrong people."

"Are you going to let fear tell you what to do with your life, Reggie? You haven't when you've done bad things. And you're more likely to get killed doing some of the things you've done than trying to be like Martin Luther King."

"Are you going to make me write a paper on this?"

"No. You understand what we've been talking about."

*   *   *

We had a rule that kids could talk on the phone only with members of their immediate family. Reggie claimed to have fathered a child with June, the girl he'd had sex with instead of going with his homies on the drive-by in which they killed the seven-year-old girl. June was raising the boy with the help of her mother, he said. I allowed him to talk with her. But I and other staff were suspicious, and I asked Reggie which hospital June had gone to to have her baby. He didn't know but said he would ask her; he had been locked up when she had it. He showed me photos of his son.

When he gave me the name of the hospital a few days later, I said, "You know I'm going to call them."

"I know. I got nothing to hide." When I laughed, he laughed too.

The records clerk at the hospital confirmed that June had checked in on the day Reggie said she had. The symptoms the clerk read off indicated that June was having a miscarriage, but nowhere in the chart was the word "miscarriage" used, and it was not clear that the fetus had been lost.

But Reggie said now that June told him that she had had a miscarriage.

Then where had this baby come from—the one whose photos Reggie had?

Reggie shrugged. June said it was his, but he didn't know if it was. He was afraid it wasn't his, but how was he to know?

If this was a hoax, it was one that required more time than I had to spend on exposing it. Other staff, while still suspicious, were also willing to drop the matter.

It was a hoax. June had, in fact, been pregnant with Reggie's child, but she miscarried. She went to the hospital to try to stop the miscarriage, but she was too late. The photos were of her sister's son. I learned all of this several months after we transferred Reggie to another group home. He had confided in the chaplain who told me when she calculated that there would be no consequences for him if I found out. He had confided in her because June had broken up with him and he needed someone to talk to.

* * *

The cottage had a student government whose mission it was to present kids' concerns to staff, to propose changes in cottage procedure, and to plan for such events as socials and football games between cottages. It was time for student elections and Reggie was running for cottage president. He was certain he would win because he had the gang vote and, he believed, the votes of those kids he had intimidated enough not to vote for someone else. He understood that the vote was by secret ballot, but he didn't understand how this worked. When I explained it, he was aghast and argued that it wasn't fair to have a vote where nobody knew how anybody else voted. I said it was fair and that was how we were going to do it—we were going to do it just like the grown-ups do.

Even with the secret ballot, it looked like Reggie had won, until I counted the ballots and found that there were more ballots than voters. The discrepancy was widened when one boy said he hadn't voted. Another boy said he had voted twice but hadn't known he was not supposed to.

Over Reggie's objections I announced that I was throwing the vote out; there would be another one. This time each voter, instead of tossing his ballot in a hat, would hand me a single piece of paper with the name of the person he had voted for written on it, and folded so no one else could see it.

Reggie lost by a single vote to a kid who was not in a gang. He could not believe it. In fact, he said exactly that. "I can't believe I didn't win." He demanded to count the ballots himself, which I allowed him to do while I watched. Then he counted the number of gang kids. Not all of them had voted for him. He was stunned by their disloyalty. He was doubly frustrated because he didn't know who had voted for him and who had not. He asked me what adults did in a situation like this. He was sincere in wanting to know; voting by secret ballot was not in his experience.[1]

"Accept it," I said.

A few days later I asked him how he was handling his loss. He still didn't think it was fair, he said, but there was nothing he could do about it.

*   *   *

The kids were frustrated, and we staff were too. They had almost no opportunity to earn money so that they could have something to spend at the student store. There were a number of jobs for kids on campus, but girls held almost all of them. Administrative and support staff preferred working with girls rather than boys; girls' anger usually took the form of depression and it was far easier to deal with a sad girl than with a boy who might go off on you. The administration allowed us to pay kids for doing certain jobs in the cottage—washing dishes, sweeping and mopping the kitchen floor, preparing and putting out the buckets of soapy water, scrub brushes, toilet brushes, dust rags, rubber gloves, etc., for the kids to clean their rooms and bathrooms. The kids who did these jobs earned fifty cents an hour, about two dollars a day. The other kids, those who vacuumed the living room carpet, cleaned the tables, swept and mopped the floor of the dining room, and picked up trash outside the cottage got nothing.

Each cottage had a small operational fund. At our weekly staff meeting, Herman said he thought it would be a good thing to use part of it to pay a kid to do a job that was currently unpaid. Staff agreed. Actually, Herman thought it would be good to create another job, that of "resident work supervisor," whose duties would include overseeing the performance of kids' work details and inspecting the results. Staff waited. Herman thought Reggie Greene would be the ideal resident to handle the job of resident work supervisor in that he had proven leadership abilities ("If you call intimidation leadership," one of the staff said. Herman pretended not to have heard) and the other kids respected him. Also, he'd earned his privileges back and he needed to be shown that staff had confidence in him ("I have confidence in him to make other kids give him their meds," another staff said. Herman appeared not to have heard).

"So what do you think?" Herman said. "Jerry, you're his staff."

"I think he'll start second-guessing staff and then, if he can get away with it, he'll block the flow of information between kids and staff by inserting himself between them and us. He'll tell them that if they want to talk to staff, they'll have to talk to him first. He'll work it so that he takes the place of student government."

"Hear, hear," one of the staff said.

"That's why you'll have to watch him," Herman said. "Don't let him do the things you just said."

"If we have to watch him, doesn't that show that we don't have confidence in him?" John Loring said. Herman did not respond.

"How much authority do I have over him?" I asked.

"You're his staff. You have a lot of authority."

The staff who said, "Hear, hear" now said, "Uh huh."

I said, "Uh huh."

"Michael, you'll have to supervise Reggie after breakfast and lunch."

"Herman, you know I don't have the time. I've got—" Michael began. Everybody except, perhaps, Herman knew that Michael liked to read a novel in the staff office while the kids cleaned up after meals.

"You've got the time," John, who worked with him, said.

"I'll have to reschedule some things—"

"Reschedule them," Herman said. Everybody except, perhaps, Herman knew Michael would let Reggie run the cottage during his shift. Everybody knew, too, that John would step in when Reggie threatened to go too far.

* * *

After supper, when half the cottage were locked in their rooms and the other half were doing clean-up details, Reggie and I and sometimes Stan, the other staff on evening shift, would sit on the plywood ping-pong table at the edge of the dining room and monitor the kids at work. I was straightforward with Reggie. I told him what I thought he might do and I explained what the consequences would be if he did it: I would block his getting any time off his maximum sentence. He asked if Herman would let me get away with that. I said Herman may disagree with me but he couldn't force me to change my recommendation and, when it came down to the administration's determining whether or not to give a kid less than his maximum sentence, the case manager's recommendation carried as much weight as the cottage director's. Reggie said he understood. He did not appear frustrated or angry. He just needed to understand what the rules were and whether and how much he could use them for his own ends.

After a few days I checked some of the details he had inspected. Everything looked good. The toilets and shower stalls were clean, the silverware had been wiped dry before being put in the drawer, trash baskets had been emptied. A week later, things were not as good. A couple of toilets had not been scrubbed and the silverware was wet. I felt under a bathroom sink. A toothbrush with a sharpened handle lay on the lip of the underside of the sink.

Stan and I locked the cottage down and searched rooms. We found nothing else that could reasonably be called a weapon. I showed the shank to Reggie. "From now on, if something like this is found in an area that you're supposed to be inspecting, we'll hold you responsible as well as the kid who put it there. Understood?"

"But I didn't put it there."

"I believe you. But one of the obligations of being a leader is taking responsibility for the welfare of everybody who relies on you. A lot of these kids rely on you to some extent, Reggie. Also, the fact that the shank was in the head when I looked shows that you haven't been doing your inspections diligently."

"When I tell them to clean the toilet better, or to sweep before they mop, they say 'What are you gonna do about it? You gonna tell staff?' They know I won't be a snitch. And you won't let me hit them. Can I give them demerits?"

"No, you can't give demerits. The other staff would never go for it and neither would I. But if you find a shank, you'd better snitch. The consequences are too great if you don't. Do you know what's going to happen to the kids who use the head where I found it? I'm going to call Rob and he's going to tell me to lock them down and keep them down until the kid who put it there confesses or until somebody else tells us who did it."

"Can you do that?"

"We've done it before. It works. As far as getting kids to do their details, tell them I'm going to check them after you do, so they'd better get them right."

"Michael doesn't check."

"He will after I inform Herman that I found a shank. Why do you think someone made it?"

Reggie shrugged. For him to show anything other than ignorance might indicate that he knew something he wasn't telling me.

"It might be anger," I said, "but more likely it's fear. He's afraid somebody is going to do something to him, so he made a weapon to protect himself. Which means that something is going on in the cottage that I, for one, don't know about. Which means, too, that when other kids find out that this guy has a shank, they'll start making shanks for themselves. That's not good, is it, Reggie?"

He shrugged again. He wouldn't look at me.

"Is it?"

"If you say so."

"I say so. It's not you he's afraid of, is it?"

"Me? Hell, no!"

"You need to convince me. Don't put it on your dead sister."

Now he looked at me. "He's got no reason to be afraid of me. Nobody does."

"Uh huh. Well, we'll let it go for now."

I called Rob and, as I thought he would, he told me to lock down Zone Four. I did, and explained to the kids whose rooms were in that zone what it would take for them to be allowed out of their rooms again.

* * *

Late one afternoon Reggie came back to the cottage after grief-and-loss counseling with the chaplain. The counseling was about his sister Stecia and his relationship with her both before and since her death. He asked to eat alone in his room.

When supper was over we sat on the ping-pong table as usual. Ordinarily we talked a little as we watched the kids doing their details, but this evening he was withdrawn. I often brought a Granny Smith apple to eat instead of the overly sweet desserts that the central kitchen sent down with our meals. Reggie had asked me so often for part of it that I had taken to bringing in two, one for each of us. I waited for him to ask for it, but he didn't. I noticed that he wasn't inspecting the details, but I decided not to say anything. When the details were done he asked to talk with me and we went into one of the offices.

After his sister's death, he said, he promised her that he would kill the boy who killed her. He promised also to finish his education and make a success of himself, as she had wanted him to do. But now he realized that he could not do both—he could not kill her murderer and become successful. The chaplain wanted him to write Stecia a letter in which he apologized to her for not being able to do it all. As he talked, he cried and I held his hand. It was larger than my own, and muscular, a boxer's hand like Herman's. The chaplain had asked him what Stecia would want for him, he said. I sat with him as he gave himself up to his grief.

That evening we had an AA/NA meeting in the cottage. Reggie talked about his dilemma, then told the other kids that he had decided not to kill the boy who killed his sister. Although he had promised his sister that he would kill him, he believed that she would not want him to because, if he did, it would mean the end of the possibility of his achieving legitimate success in his life. Also, if he killed that boy, the boy's family would suffer, and Reggie did not want anyone to go through what he was going through. He said he had decided to forgive the boy who had murdered his sister.

Later in my career at Ash Meadow I sometimes told kids this part of Reggie's story, of how he decided not to kill his sister's killer, and they would go "Whoo!" or they would listen in silence, just as the kids did in the AA/NA meeting Reggie spoke to. The kids I told the story to were always in awe. Occasionally a boy would say he didn't think he could do what Reggie did. They could not imagine someone having the strength and the compassion to do what Reggie did. I used to tell this story to present the idea of possibility to them, to let them know that sometimes even the hardest thing is possible.

*　*　*

Reggie's dark night of grief was not over. A few days after the AA/NA meeting, he told me he'd been irritable since his last talk with the chaplain, and he'd been having pains in his stomach. Two weeks later, after another grief-and-loss session, he said he had never felt so bad in his life. Staff had noticed that he had become whiny and that he taunted other kids when, before, he used to place himself apart from most of them. A couple of months earlier we had seen him as one of the more mature kids in the cottage, even if he wasn't the most trustworthy. Now it was as though he had become a small child again.

While the loss of Stecia was what Reggie most concentrated on in his sessions with the chaplain, he also began to think again about his mother's paralysis and his father's imprisonment and his grandfather's abuse of his sisters and what it all meant to him. He had realized, too, that in the last two years, six of his homies had been killed. He said that if he were on the outs he would beat somebody up to relieve the stress he felt.

Less than a week after he confided all of this, his mother told him that her closest friend had died in a house fire while trying to save her smallest children who, unknown to her, were already safe. She had been like an aunt to him, Reggie said. In fact, he had called her "auntie." She had taken care of him when he was younger and his mother could not. He asked if he could go to her funeral but then, before I could answer, he said never mind, he knew the administration would never approve it.

The pain in his stomach became chronic, but he learned to accommodate it as he did the other symptoms of depression. Two months after he said he didn't want to be a leader like Martin Luther king, Jr., or Malcolm X, he told me that, regardless of what he wanted, he had to be one because of his personality. He could be a leader for either good or ill, he said, but thought he should be a leader for the good.

A couple of weeks later he told me he was determined to be a success. He wanted people to remember him. He believed God had provided him Tony Hunter as an example of what could happen to him if he did not change. Tony Hunter was the kid who drove the killers of that seven-year-old girl. June had shown up just as Reggie was getting into the car with Tony. Reggie believed God had sent June to him that day. Only a girl as beautiful as June could have kept him from going with Tony.

* * *

Herman and I agreed that it was time to give Reggie another chance. I called group homes. There was only one bed available and that was in the town where his sister had been murdered. Reggie didn't want to go; he wanted to avoid the temptation to go after her killer. I was reluctant to send him because I didn't want him to lose what he had gained with us, but Herman insisted.

I drove him to the group home. He met a homie there and they talked about someone they knew who was doing time in another juvenile institution. Just before I left, Reggie said he would try his hardest to make a go of it. I did not see him again.

One day several months after he transferred, he left the group home and did not come back. I heard from another boy that Reggie had met a girl and had taken off with her. Herman believed it. I did not know what to think.

A year later Reggie called from Elk Grove, one of our sister institutions. His staff there had allowed him to make the call. He was doing two years now. Possession with intent to distribute. He had given himself up, he said. He had been pulled over because of a traffic violation. When the officer asked his name, Reggie gave him his real one. He had a fake ID, but he told the officer the name on the ID wasn't his. He told me he was just tired of being on the run. He wanted to do his time and get it over. He said he had run from the group home last time because it was just too hard being in the same town as Stecia's killer and not being able to do anything about it. He had started smoking weed again and then he met a girl and he ran away with her.

He asked to talk to Herman, but Herman wasn't around. We talked for a while longer and then his phone time was up and we said goodbye.

Three years later I was working in a girls' cottage. One of the girls on my caseload knew Reggie. In fact, he had called her at her group home when he was arrested on another drug charge. He was eighteen then and he was going to be charged as an adult. He asked her to post bond for him; it was a thousand dollars. As it happened, she had a job and had saved that much, but she couldn't get to the bank until the next day.

The following day she left work early, went to the bank and withdrew the money, and went to the courthouse. Reggie was gone; someone else had put up bail for him. But because she had left work without her group home's permission and then refused to account for the next several hours or tell the group home staff why she took a thousand dollars out of her account, she was sent back to Ash Meadow as an escape risk. She thought it was funny, the way life works, especially since I had known Reggie and now I knew her and I could laugh with her about some of the things he had done. She had really liked Reggie. He had had a legitimate job before he started dealing drugs again, but the people he worked for went out of business and then he couldn't find another job.

I did not hear anything more about Reggie until, seven years later, Jan told me about his call to Herman. Reggie was living in another city now, one where his old gang no longer had a presence. I knew this from the stories the kids we had from that area told me. So it was possible that Reggie had left his gang. And if he wasn't in a gang, maybe he wasn't selling drugs anymore. So maybe he was as he described himself to Herman—a respectable young man with ambition.

Reggie complained to me once that for all of his hard work to change himself, staff continued to look at him through the filter of their history with him. They still thought he was lying, that the change he presented to them was a façade. A few weeks after he left Ash Meadow for the last time, our chaplain told me that she didn't have a lot of hope for him, that the grief he was trying to manage would eventually overwhelm him as it had before. There was much he hadn't dealt with, and because his emotions had been numbed by marijuana, he had not had any significant breakthrough during the time he met with her.

Like the other staff in Swan Cottage, I remained suspicious of any progress Reggie appeared to have made. I never knew how much of the truth he was telling me, nor what was a distortion of the truth. I often did not know if he had fabricated something out of whole cloth. I could not see how his dishonesty would benefit him if he ever had the chance to live in an environment different from the one he grew up in. I tried to clue him in about other ways of looking at the world; not every other young man wanted to harm him.

But I was more hopeful than the chaplain. I thought it was likely, given Reggie's commitment to his sister Stecia, that he would not go after her murderer. That in itself was something; that in itself was a lot. And I thought it was possible that the restraint he imposed on himself to keep from doing what he so wanted to do would open other doors for him. But I thought, too, that he would do other things, and that the changes he may have made in himself to please Stecia and Herman would not be enough to keep him from serving more time. I saw him as spending a large part of his adult life locked up.

When Jan told me Reggie had called, I asked her to get his phone number for me. She didn't. She forgot, I'm sure. She was easily distracted in those days, fighting cancer and trying to find a way to retire, and I decided not to ask her again. If Reggie wanted to present himself to Herman as a young father with a loving wife and loving children and a bright future, that was all right with me. If he was truly as he said, and really had a wife and children and a promising future, that was all to the good. If he was not, and he did not, if it was all just another lie, I could live without knowing.

IV

Jamal Willson
The Lost Boy

The article in *The Seattle Times* said Jamal was serving adult time now on a weapons charge and had been indicted on a charge of car theft. It said that when Jamal was younger he was one of a group of boys who, out of boredom, beat to death a man they had never seen before. That was what the article was about—Jamal had helped to kill somebody and now he had committed other crimes. The article was not about the crimes but about the person who did them. Its tone was such that a reader would not feel much sympathy for Jamal—the headline was "Convicted of murder at 12, Killer Linked to Other Crimes"—but would feel instead that he was someone predestined to do bad things. There was also a subtext, something not immediately apparent in the article, but there for someone who might be looking for it. More about that later.

*   *   *

I remember Jamal as a young man who wanted to play college basketball. He was the best basketball player any of the staff had seen at Ash Meadow, the juvenile prison where I worked as a rehabilitation counselor in maximum security. I worked with a man who had coached college basketball, another who had played college ball, and occasionally one who had played pro ball in Europe. All were agreed that Jamal could play college ball and, were it not for his height—he was five nine—might even hope for a pro career. He said he wanted to go to community college when he left prison.

At Ash Meadow a woman who had been his teacher on the outside visited him once a month. She always brought lunch for Jamal and herself and she always brought a checked tablecloth that she spread over one of the metal tables bolted to the floor of the dining room in our cottage. She did not want him to forget how people eat on the outside, she said. She would stay for a couple of hours and they would talk and leisurely eat their lunch. If he was having trouble with math, she would tutor him after they ate.

When he first came to us, he refused to talk to his case manager because Dick was white. I asked Jamal once why he wouldn't talk with him and that's what he said: "Dick's white." I sensed no vitriol; there was only the fact of Dick's being white that led automatically to Jamal's refusal to talk with him.

A couple of things happened around the same time that I think led Jamal to change his mind. One was that Dick required him to participate in Aggression Replacement Training, a class I taught. It was a rigorous, demanding class that met three times a week for ten weeks. Unlike treatment groups in which a kid might get kudos just for attending and expressing an opinion, ART had inflexible standards; you met them and passed, or you did not and failed. In Washington State, there was a 24 percent greater likelihood that you would not re-offend if you graduated from ART than if you did not. I said all of this in my introductory remarks each time I taught the class.

I did not say that the statistics were skewed toward offenders who had committed nonviolent crimes. The authors of the study said that too few juveniles had committed violent crimes to allow evaluation. Some of the ART trainers who were aware of the study believed that the problem was not that there were too few violent offenders to make up a valid statistical category, but rather that there were so many who had re-offended that they would drag the success rate down if the full results of the study were taken into account. Implicit in this belief was the corollary belief that those who had committed violent acts wanted to commit others or could not keep themselves from committing them. The trainers and others who believed this had succumbed to despair or cynicism.

Though I, too, flirted with despair, I did not believe that kids who had committed violent crimes ached to do others, or that they necessarily would give in again to peer pressure or parental influence. My experience as a case manager of violent offenders in a gang cottage, in a girls' cottage, and in maximum security told me that almost all regretted the physical misery, or death, they had dealt other people. The regret could derive from a number of sources: from the consequences of the offense—that is, their incarceration; from fear of retaliation after their release from prison; from the sense that what they did was not only legally but morally wrong; or from their own agonizing over what they did, this distress often taking the form of nightmares in which they relived the crime or punished themselves for having done it, or even of reliving it as daydreams or flashbacks when they were awake. A girl told me once that she had not expected there to be so much blood; whenever she was alone she thought about what she had done. A boy was bothered because he had crossed a boundary that existed even in the milieu of violence in which he had lived, and felt he deserved more punishment than the sentence he had received; he, too, dwelled on his offense when he was alone in his room. Another girl, in dream after dream, was slain by the man she had helped murder.

Like most kids who enrolled in ART, Jamal did not like it at first. One of the reasons, at least in his case, was my style of teaching. I used stories and anecdotes to illustrate the points I was making. Unlike most kids, Jamal wanted simply to be told what he needed to know—he had no patience for my stories. I used them because I enjoyed telling stories, but also because I believed they would encourage kids to provide their own stories, parts of which they could use in role-play. Hardly any kid liked doing a role-play. You were up in front of the class and you were being evaluated by staff and by the other kids in the class. If you didn't get it right, you might have to do it again. They did a lot of it; two of the three hours we met each week were filled with role-play.

But by the fourth or fifth week, almost all kids, including Jamal, had begun to enjoy ART. Part of the reason, I think, was the camaraderie that developed between the students. This was encouraged by a kind of intimacy that came about from the vignettes they acted out in role-play. Most were autobiographical. Some were cathartic as well. In the middle of one role-play, a girl suddenly remembered having witnessed the murder of her cousin when she was small. His killers told her to forget what she had seen and so, afraid that they would come back and kill her too, she had forgotten—until this afternoon.

The second thing that may have induced Jamal to change his mind was the introduction of Blues in the Schools to our cottage. Blues in the Schools was a program put together by Curly Cook, a singer and guitarist who had played with a number of blues and rock bands over the years. Funded by grants, Curly and three or four other professional musicians came in several afternoons a week for four weeks to teach kids to play blues on guitar, bass, harmonica and drums as well as to sing and to compose their own songs.

The first session was given over largely to Curly's explaining what blues was about, how it was structured, and its history. The musicians behind him would demonstrate with riffs accompanying the topic Curly was talking about. At the end of the introduction, they broke out into an R & B number that had the kids moving. Jamal had not wanted to attend, had stood like a stele at the back of the room and, when the music started, had been reluctant to let himself go. But then his head started to move, and his shoulders, and in a minute he was stepping forward and back, forward and back, in a dance of his own invention. A girl, Sonia, yelled out, "Look at Jamal!" and he grinned in spite of himself.

Part of the way through both ART and Blues in the Schools, Jamal began talking to Dick. Throughout his first weeks in the cottage, Dick had insisted that Jamal meet with him at scheduled times even if Jamal refused to participate in their counseling sessions. Now Jamal began to talk about his life, his family, his relationships with other kids, the murder. When I asked him why he changed his mind about talking to Dick, he said he didn't know.

* * *

Although he had refused to talk to Dick because Dick was white, only one of the kids Jamal was closest to was black; the other two were white. Two of the three were girls. All were in for murder.

Five other kids in the cottage were also in for murder or manslaughter. One was a co-offender in the killing Jamal was part of; another was mentally unbalanced, alternating between anger and depression; a third was very young, and even then, immature for his age, emotionally and physically; the fourth, if he had gone before a judge in an urban county, may not have come here; certainly he would not have received a seven-year sentence; the fifth was so loaded when she killed the man she killed that, even now, though she could recall part of the episode, she did not remember the man dying. Of these five, none were black.

Though Jamal was cordial enough to all of them, even the one among them he did not like, he spent most of his free time, if he wasn't playing basketball, with the two girls and the boy I mentioned a moment ago. All, like Jamal, were bright, reading at high school senior or college level and doing math at their own freshman level or higher. The other boy, Michael, was exceptionally talented in math and science and we got him a volunteer tutor from the outside because he had gone beyond the ability or the desire of the school faculty to teach him.

While Jamal was probably the most coordinated kid in the cottage, at least for basketball, Michael's coordination was also well developed, having played baseball in school before he came to us. In basketball, he had a good eye for a shot from outside the key, but he was very short and could not get past his guard when he was under the basket. The two girls, Sonia and Caitlin, had played basketball before they were locked up, and Caitlin, later in her time at Ash Meadow, would be a starter on both the girls' and the boys' teams. Jamal would also play on the boys' team.

Three of these four kids came from single-parent families; Sonia was raised by her aunt and her grandmother. Only Jamal and Caitlin came from a background of poverty. (Of the other five in for killing a human being, four came from single-parent families; one had lived with both of his parents.

Two were middle class, judging by the income level of their parents; the others were poor.)

As an aside, let me point out that while readers may think a kid who kills somebody is difficult to deal with, in almost all cases, the opposite is true. In prison, kids who have killed usually become model inmates, probably because they know the prison will be their home for many years. Another reason is that they have time to reflect on their lives, on what happened to bring them to prison, on what it is possible for them to do there and what it is possible for them to do when they leave. I have not heard of a former resident—we called them residents, not inmates—convicted of murder who committed another after release, although a few kids who had served time for other offenses murdered someone later, and some who had served time for murder, like Jamal, committed a different felony some time after they got out.

Jamal and the two girls had something else in common besides basketball and their intelligence: all had been dependent, in one way or another, on another person who ultimately led them to murder. (Michael's case was unique. In order to conceal his identity, I won't go into it here.) In the girls' case—they had participated in the same killing—they were intensely loyal to each other in a relationship that extended back to when they were eight years old. Caitlin's mother, Linda, who had brought together several kids, including Caitlin and Sonia, to carry out the murder of her employer, had regularly beaten her, beginning as far back as Caitlin could remember, and probably even before her memories began, and it was out of fear as well as loyalty to her mother that Caitlin had joined in the killing. Sonia, her closest friend, had tried to escape out a window during the murder, but had been brought back by Linda who called to her: "You're not being a very good friend to Caitlin!"[1]

Several months before this killing, Jamal was hanging around with a group of boys who were drawn together by summer doldrums and the personality of the oldest among them. "He was crazy," Jamal said of this boy. "You never knew what he was going to do." He was big and he could lose control of himself in acts of violence. Once he beat another boy—not one of the group—so badly that some of the others thought he had killed him. Nobody tried to stop him; they walked away while he was still punching the unconscious youth. They were afraid of him; he could do the same to them. I asked Jamal why he hadn't just stopped hanging out with this kid. He didn't have an answer.

One night toward the end of summer, led by this older boy, the kids decided to beat up the next person they saw. The next person they saw they beat to death.

Something had happened to Jamal earlier in his life. Once, coming inside from recreation in the fenced yard behind the cottage, Michael pushed Jamal from behind. It was a kind of affectionate play, the way teenage boys do, equivalent to a boy mussing another boy's hair; Michael was laughing. Jamal spun around, his fist cocked, and looked from Michael to me, bewildered, barely able to restrain himself. He stepped forward, but did not take a second step as Michael backed away. I held my hand up and Jamal turned and continued into the cottage. I pulled Michael aside and explained to him what a startle reaction is and advised him not to touch Jamal again from behind. I had not seen this response from Jamal before, but I knew a startle reaction when I saw one. Whatever had happened to him had been intense.

* * *

Jamal had been in maximum security for almost a year when he transferred to Whale Cottage, another, less structured, unit.[2] He was doing well there but then, after a few months, was sent back to max along with a couple of other boys. The other boys had made a plan to escape; Jamal was returned to us because he knew about it, but hadn't told staff. Given the nature of his offense, he was held to a higher standard of behavior than the other kids in Whale who had known about the plan.

When he walked into the cottage with his bag of clothes and toiletries, I was going to say something cutting, but I saw the expression on his face and said only, "What happened?"

Tears started down his face and I told him to come over and sit by me as I finished a log entry at the staff desk. Other kids would be coming in from school soon and I wanted to spare him their questions, at least for now.

He said he heard about the escape plan the day before it was supposed to go down, and intended to tell staff when he had a chance to speak to one alone. He was going to do it at lunch, but by that time someone else had told and the cottage was locked down. I believed him. I had not known him to lie.

Dick came in, saw Jamal, and got that look on his face that he got when he was about to say something mean, but I shook my head and he said instead, "What happened?"

Jamal laughed and I said, "I asked exactly the same thing. Go on, tell him."

Dick also believed him. The question now was how to "rehabilitate" Jamal enough so that he would be able to transfer out of maximum security again. Dick thought Jamal was too passive. Except in basketball, where he dominated, he just went along, hoping nobody would notice him. I was not certain I agreed, but Dick was his case manager and knew him better than I did. Dick asked him what he thought would teach him to step up when he should. Jamal suggested he take Aggression Replacement Training again. I said that would be all right, I would be starting another class next week, but he would be bumping someone else who was already scheduled to be in it.

"What if he was your assistant? Could you handle that?"

"I can handle it, but what about Jamal? Could he handle it?" I turned to Jamal. "Kids would say things, you know. They'd say you were kissing staff's ass."

"Or worse," Dick said.

"Or worse," I agreed. "They'd want to piss you off, bring you down."

"I don't care what they say," Jamal said.

"Okay then," Dick said. He looked at me. "Okay?"

"Okay."

* * *

Durrell was the kid who devised the escape plan at Whale. When I heard this, I did not believe it. I did not see him as a leader; he was a kid who was regularly punked by tougher kids.[3] But this was what I knew of him when he was in max, before he went to his new cottage. In that cottage, he was able to manipulate younger, smaller kids, or kids less able to imagine consequences, into doing what he wanted. Four or five kids were involved, but only he and another, older boy, though one with limited intelligence, went to max. The staff at the other cottage thought they could work with the younger boys once Durrell was gone.

I felt sorry for him. I sensed something sad and unfillable in him that I think other kids sensed too. Like Jamal, something bad had happened to him at some time in his life, something worse than being punked. But where Jamal made himself work harder to overcome a setback, Durrell went into an often immobilizing depression. And where I felt sorry for him, some of the harder kids wanted to hurt him. While Jamal was not one to victimize him, he kept a distance from Durrell, as he did other kids he had no regard for.

This was Durrell's third time in max. The first time he stayed with us until he was released to parole. That time he was punked regularly by a kid who despised him because Durrell pretended to be something he wasn't: a committed gangster who claimed experience he didn't have. Paroled, he stole a car and was sent back to Ash Meadow and maximum security. This time he was targeted by a different kid, one who had known him on the outs and who had bullied him then too. Durrell earned his way out of max by exemplary behavior and eventually we paroled his latest nemesis.

It was during this period away from Wolf that he came up with his escape plan. It was not only a plan to escape. It involved overcoming and raping a female staff member and beating down the male staff she was working with and taking his keys. Conceptually, the kids could have taken the young woman's keys and locked the male staff in a room or tied him up and then escaped. And, of course, they wouldn't have had to rape the woman in order to get out of the cottage. As much as Durrell wanted to degrade women, he also hated gays; the male staff was gay and it was important to Durrell to hurt him.

With us again, he seemed to settle in, although we knew him well enough now to anticipate that he would try to do something. The something, as it turned out, was to persuade a couple of other kids to join with him to jump Jamal. We found out about this latest scheme during a meeting of staff and residents to discuss some minor changes in how we staff ran the cottage. Out of nowhere, one of the kids Durrell had recruited said that there was a plot to jump a kid and that Durrell was behind it. The boy did not say who the prospective victim was. Pressed by staff, Durrell admitted it was Jamal. It was obviously the first Jamal had heard of it: his eyes grew large and his mouth opened and he stared, as though in wonder, at Durrell.

Durrell said he had no good reason for wanting to attack Jamal, only that he didn't like him because Jamal acted as if he was better than everybody else. But what some of us staff thought was that Durrell resented the high regard Jamal enjoyed from other kids and wanted to bring him down. If he could do this, Durrell's thinking would be, he could then step into Jamal's place in the hierarchy the boys had established among themselves in the cottage.

Jamal began to laugh. Durrell looked embarrassed more than anything else, and tried to smile. Jamal continued to laugh, not to taunt Durrell, but seemingly at how ludicrous Durrell's plan was. Durrell was larger, taller and heavier, than Jamal, but everyone knew that if Jamal wanted to, he could damage Durrell easily. Jamal stood up. I moved closer to him and I saw Dick move in from my left. But Jamal only turned and, still laughing, said, "Jerry, lock me in," and started toward his room, I walking a couple of steps behind him, the laughter coming out of him almost uncontrolled. I asked him the next day what the laughter was about; it was how he dealt with his anger, he said.

His laughter, of course, was another humiliation for Durrell. We decided that he should be treated as dangerous and he was kept in his room except for head calls and showers until we transferred him to The Rivers, a sister institution, a few days later. The Rivers housed older boys or younger boys who were especially aggressive.

* * *

People, except for Durrell, liked Jamal because he was, in fact, so likeable. He was usually cheerful and he wanted to do well and he had the ability to do well. On his own, he had developed laughter as a technique for reducing his anger so as to stay out of trouble. He knew he would face an uphill fight when he got out—it would be difficult to find a job that paid decently, or to play college basketball. What if he attracted media attention? His talent and his smallness might well lead to that. How far would the media dig into his background? What would the college administration say when it learned he had served time for murder? For that matter, what would anyone say who didn't already know him?

And what were their lives like, those he knew, those who would be his models? I remember that his mother called once when we were monitoring his phone calls. We were monitoring them because we had learned that a girl in another cottage was calling him—a no-no—presumably taking advantage of that cottage staff's inattentiveness. He, of course, had not reported her. I listened on another phone during his conversation with his mother. Her language—the swearing, the rage that lay behind it—obviously embarrassed him. He reminded her that a staff member was listening, but it made no difference. He tried to smile, but it barely registered on his face and then it was gone, replaced by a kind of softness that I took as sympathy for her, this troubled woman, his mother.

* * *

I last saw him a few weeks before I myself left the institution. I had come in on one of my days off to see a concert performed by the kids in Blues in the Schools. Caitlin, who was on my caseload, was going to be on drums and I wanted to see her play for the last time. She would be transferring soon to the women's prison; she had turned eighteen. I had parked and was walking to the gym where the concert would be held when I heard "Jerry!"

He had gotten a little taller and his face a little fuller since he transferred out of Ash Meadow. He was five ten, or close to it. If wishing counted for anything, he might make five eleven; he was seventeen. He was in a group home now, getting ready to be paroled. He introduced me to his staff from the group home, a small woman with a wide smile. She had brought him in for a meeting or something relevant to his parole; I wasn't listening or maybe he wasn't explaining well. I suggested they try to catch part of the concert if they had time after the meeting; some of the kids Jamal had known here would be performing and he might like to see them again. His staff didn't think they would have time, but she'd see.

About halfway through the concert, Caitlin was sitting in front of me, having finished her piece, when Jamal and his staff came in and stood against the wall where they could see and listen. I tapped Caitlin on the shoulder and pointed. "It's Jamal!" she said. "Can I go and say hello to him?"

I accompanied her over to where they were standing and separated myself from them by a few feet while they talked. He asked about Sonia and Caitlin said she had already been transferred to Purdy and that she herself would be going any day. Michael had transferred to Elk Grove. It had been a while since Caitlin and Jamal had been together and they weren't as easy with each other as they had been, or perhaps the distance was there because they knew that, for better or worse, change was upon them and there was nothing they could do about it.

Jamal and his staff left after a few minutes. Caitlin went back to the cottage and after a few minutes during which I caught up on gossip with a counselor from another cottage with whom I used to work, I left too.

Although I did not see Jamal again, a couple of other staff heard from him. He intended to enroll in a community college near where he lived and try out for its basketball team, but meanwhile he was playing wherever he could find a game.

Then, that summer, someone said he was working in construction and hanging out with Derek Evans and Jessica Johnson who had hooked up with each other after they were released. I did not think this was a good thing, if it was true. I liked Derek—he, too, had been on my caseload—but both he and Jessica had psychological problems that would not be treated now that they were no longer incarcerated. They are two examples of kids released into civil society who have no job skills and an inferior education and whose mental instability precludes their making sound decisions. I expected both to drift back into drug use and, probably, dealing—it was what they knew. The staff who kept me informed about Jamal were also concerned for him.

Then I did not hear anything more about him until I read about him in the newspaper.

Everything has its context. Derek had served time for shooting a drug dealer who owed him money but refused to pay him. What Derek did not tell the judge or even his own lawyer was that the dealer had pulled a knife and was moving toward him when Derek shot him. Derek had not told this to anyone until he told me because it would have indicated that he had acted out of fear, and he needed to pretend that he had not been afraid. He had rather be known as a stone-cold shooter than as someone who panicked.

What drew Jamal into criminal activity after his release from the group home? Certainly his home life was not of the kind that would encourage him to persevere in the face of the obstacles life put before him, that would push him to go to college, play ball, graduate, get a white-collar job, live as though his life had always been like yours or mine. Perhaps he was lonely. Going home after having spent almost all of his adolescence in prison, who would he know but others who had gotten out around the same time he had? What kind of opportunity was available to him, a black adolescent with a prison record in a time of economic downturn? But I'm speculating: maybe he hadn't been laid off from his construction job when developers stopped building houses.

According to the newspaper article, he had fallen in with a man a few years older than him who taught him and other younger men how to steal cars. This was the first thing in the article that jumped out at me, for I remembered immediately his talking about the killing he helped do when he was twelve. Then, too, it was his attachment to someone older that had led him into trouble.

*   *   *

What are we to make of Jamal? We can tell ourselves that there is something immanent in Jamal that impels him to embrace the criminal life. But there is no way to confirm immanence as a cause of crime, at least in Jamal's case. We can look at his personal history and behavior and decide that Jamal is a bad person—an "evil" person, if you prefer—but we would have to skew our view of his history to conclude that. It is a matter of belief, of faith or ideology that takes us there.

Or we can say that Jamal's situation determined what would become of him. Here we are dealing with likelihood, the degree of probability that kids born into poverty and all the social and economic circumstances that attend it are more likely to find themselves engaging in criminal activity than kids born into affluence. But probability does not explain the individual case.

So we have the opportunity to choose the explanation we prefer: immanence—call it DNA, or call it a kind of evil that kids who commit crimes are born with—or the environment, social and economic, they are born into or fall into.

There was something else in the newspaper article that struck me—a kind of subtext—and that was the reporter's writing that Jamal had cooperated with the detectives investigating the murder and that he was now talking with those investigating a rash of car thefts. I wondered why the reporter wanted to set Jamal up. Surely the reporter knew that to say someone is "cooperating" or "talking" is to label him a snitch. Surely the reporter had seen in a movie or on television or read in a novel or had friends who had been in prison who had told him or knew because he himself had been in prison the peril an inmate who has been so labeled is in. Maybe he didn't like Jamal, or maybe he didn't like the idea of Jamal, of Jamal having killed someone and then having done something else. Maybe the reporter owed somebody something; everything is personal. There was no by-line.

V

Norah Joines
A Valley Girl in Bad Times

Broken Family, Broken Foster Family

She was barely thirteen when she did her crime and still two months shy of fourteen when she arrived at Wolf Cottage from county detention. She and another girl had assaulted their foster mother. Crystal, the other girl, testified against Norah and got a few months. Norah got six years. She had no prior record. She committed her offense in a county whose judges were notorious for meting out harsh sentences to juveniles.

I saw her for the first time when I went into Zone Three one morning to unlock the doors to the kids' rooms so they could go to school. She came out of Room Twelve and began talking to the girl coming out of Eleven as if she were continuing a conversation begun earlier. She didn't look at me.

"Are you Norah?"

"Yes." Her voice became uncertain and so small as to be almost inaudible. She herself was small, not much over five feet, and thin. She had large, oval eyes.

"I'm your case manager. My name is Jerry. We'll talk later."

Laurel, the girl in Room Eleven, who was also new to the cottage, was five six or seven and weighed around a hundred and eighty pounds. She had come to us after bombing out of another unit. That is, her behavior there warranted sending her to maximum security. I watched them walk out of the zone, Norah talking to Laurel from behind, Laurel's comments over her shoulder conveying that she had things to do other than listening to Norah.

*   *   *

It was Thursday. From the beginning, Thursday nights were the time for our talks. It was a relatively easy day for me. I came to work at two and stayed until I finished what I had to do sometime between ten and midnight.

112

Thursday was the last day of my week and I did not have to get out of bed the next day until my body told me to. Plus, Thursday afternoons were set aside for the cottage's weekly staff meeting which ran at least until dinnertime, and sometimes past dinner. During PC—"program committee," what our staff meetings were called—the kids were locked in their rooms until we took a break to give them head calls. As their bedtime was eight o'clock, on some Thursdays I saw them for only an hour before PC and an hour or two after supper.

The first time we talked, Norah described her mother as neglectful and alcoholic. She recalled one of her sisters breaking her mother's jaw in a fight with her. Norah, the youngest of three daughters, did not fight with her mother. Her mom was clean and sober now, Norah told me during one of our first talks. Holding down a job. She lived back east.

When she was six, Norah was raped by her mother's boyfriend. Her mother refused to believe her and accused her of lying when Norah told her. About six months before she got locked up, Norah said, she was raped by one of Geraldine's friends. Geraldine was her foster mother. Norah ran into this friend at a party Geraldine took her to.

Later in her seventh year, or perhaps at the beginning of her eighth—in talking about events in her past, Norah often would not remember when something occurred, or how long a period of time had elapsed between events; this was a characteristic that remained with her into adulthood—she went to live with her father, her mother having lost custody of her daughters because of her drinking and her neglect. But then Norah's dad had a stroke and had to go into a nursing home. That was when Norah went into foster care, going to live with Louise Keyes. She was with Louise only a short time when Louise passed her on to Geraldine, her twenty-three-year-old daughter.

Geraldine smoked weed and drank with Norah. She taught Norah to drive and sent her on errands even though she was too young to have a driver's license. When Norah told Geraldine that her friend had raped her, Geraldine got her brothers to beat the guy up, although they didn't beat him up badly enough, Norah said. After the beating, she saw him on the street and he asked her who those guys were who attacked him and Norah said she didn't know, and that was how she knew he had not been hurt badly enough; if he had, he would not be looking for them.

When Geraldine was angry with her, she would tell Norah, "I hope somebody kidnaps you and beats you and rapes you and kills you." She would say this to Crystal too, another girl for whom Geraldine was responsible. The two girls planned the assault against Geraldine, how they would get her alone, who would do what; it was not an impulsive act.

The three of them were shopping, going from store to store, when the girls assaulted Geraldine in the car. Geraldine was behind the steering wheel and couldn't move to defend herself. After the girls stopped hitting her, Norah ran out into the street and found a pay phone and called Guillermo, her boyfriend, and asked him to come and get her. She was standing in the street, waiting for him, when the police pulled up. There was still blood on her hands, even though she had wiped them on a rag and then on her clothes.

I asked her if she had intended to kill Geraldine; she had been convicted of first-degree assault and conspiracy to commit murder. No, she said, she just wanted to hurt her for saying those things to her. But when she saw what they were doing, how frightened Geraldine was and how badly hurt she was, Norah stopped and she made Crystal stop. That was when she called her boyfriend, Guillermo, to come and get her. She didn't know what else to do.

On your MAYSI, I said, you said you'd seen rapes and killings.

Yes, the gang she was in did that.

Had she participated in any of it?

No, she'd only seen them do it. Sometimes when there was a fight with another gang, she'd fight too, but she'd never killed anybody, or even tried to. No, she'd never raped or held anybody down so the boys could rape her. "I wouldn't," she said. I didn't know if she meant she had been told to do it but had refused, or that she had not been asked, but wouldn't do it if she had been.

*   *   *

The next time we talked, she asked if I wasn't afraid of being with kids who had murdered people or had done other terrible things. We were in the staff office, sitting so that we faced each other as we talked, but she wasn't looking at me. She was staring at her hands in her lap. Asking that question was obviously hard for her.

I said no, the nature of a kid's crime didn't frighten me. I didn't believe that because a person had done something terrible, she was always getting ready to do it again.

She said that when the judge sentenced her, he told her he was giving her the longest sentence he could because he wanted to protect society from her for as long as possible. She asked me if I thought she was evil. She did not look up from her hands. Her voice had that same unsure quality it had when we first met.

"No, Norah, you're not evil. The judge was probably angry with you and wanted to hurt you, and he did. I see you as having made a bad mistake, but I don't see you as evil."

She brought up Geraldine, saying she was a bad person, citing again some of the things Geraldine had done that she shouldn't have. She was trying to justify having assaulted her. Sometimes she had a difficult time believing she had actually done it. Yet she dreamed about it and had flashbacks of it. When she talked about it with me, she focused on the amount of blood that came from Geraldine's wounds; Norah hadn't expected there to be so much of it. She hadn't thought about blood at all before she attacked her.

The week before, I had asked her to write a short autobiography—to answer questions about her life that I had listed on a sheet of paper. She hadn't turned it in. I asked if she was having a tough time with some of the questions. She had just told me that after her mother's boyfriend raped her and she had gone to live with her father, she had thought about killing herself with his gun because she was so afraid that her attacker would get out of prison and come after her; he had threatened to kill her if she told anyone what he did to her.

She said she was having a hard time with the questions. She didn't like to think about her life, and the questions—not just the ones that evoked the memories of being raped and what happened after—made her think about things she wanted to forget.

You can refuse to think about them, I said, but that doesn't mean they'll go away. I said I thought she was very angry with her mother, that while she may care for her mom, she was also angry with her for having allowed her to be raped and then for having accused her of lying about it. I reminded her that she had told me that while her mother was always asking her if she loved her, the most Norah was able to say was "I care about you."

"You assaulted Geraldine out of anger at Geraldine, yes, but also out of anger at your mother. The anger about your mother is still there."

Norah didn't speak. Her eyelids began to swell, but she didn't allow herself to cry. She said Geraldine was really mean. Geraldine once told her to take the car to get a pack of cigarettes, then called the police to report her car stolen; Norah was arrested and spent the night in detention. Later she told me that a year or a year and a half ago, she had tried to commit suicide by overdosing on Valium because she felt so trapped in her life with Geraldine.

*   *   *

She had been dreaming about her father. She dreamed that he was dying and that she wouldn't be able to see him again. If he died, she said, she'd want to die too. He was the only person who had been there for her.

She kept trying to write about her life, but every time she got to the part about being taken away from her mother "and all the other things," she couldn't write about them. She couldn't write about herself beyond the time "when everything went bad." She believed people—her mother, her sisters— had left her because she'd been bad. She knew she was being unreasonably hard on herself but she couldn't help it. On the surface, she was a cheerful little girl, but beneath the cheery façade lay despair. She cried in bed at night, from sadness and from fear of losing her father.

* * *

I've written about this elsewhere: how Ash Meadow's superintendent assured Jan, our cottage director, and me that after forty-five days in maximum security, per Ash Meadow regulations, Norah would be transferred to another cottage where she would be under fewer restrictions, provided her behavior remained acceptable; how we passed that promise on to Norah; how, when the day came to transfer her, neither the superintendent nor any of the other administrators would sign the transfer papers; how neither the superintendent nor any other administrator would return our phone calls or emails; how, finally, two weeks after Norah had been scheduled to move, the superintendent told Jan that the administrators had decided that, owing to the severity of Norah's offense and the length of her sentence, she would have to spend the next five to six months in max; how Jan and I learned that it was only one administrator who objected to Norah's move—Celia Barney, who had never worked in a cottage but had made her career supervising the clerical staff; how I told Norah and how she broke down, asking, "Why are they doing this to me, Jerry? I've worked so hard. I've done everything they wanted me to do. Why won't they let me go?" and how I did not have an explanation.[1] No Ash Meadow resident had ever been kept in maximum security for such a long period; even kids in for first-degree murder had been transferred after three months unless their behavior warranted retaining them. In a cottage where kids averaged two to three demerits a week, Norah had gotten only one in all the time she had been with us.

Over the ensuing weeks, she grew depressed. She admitted she was depressed and said she was trying not to be. She knew the administration had singled her out for harsh treatment, but did not understand why. She asked again if any other resident had ever been treated this way and I told her again: No, none. And again she asked, "Why are they doing this to me?" and again all I could honestly say was "I don't know." I tried to persuade the chief psychiatrist to assign one of the psychiatric fellows to her, but he came up with one reason after another not to. He appeared to recognize that someone in the administration had something against Norah and he did not want to involve himself or his colleagues.

*   *   *

Guillermo's mother wrote Norah that Guillermo had been charged with armed robbery and assault. He was facing several years in prison. Norah was shaken, believing that he would get in more trouble after he was locked up because he wouldn't let anybody get away with disrespecting him.

She would never be happy, she said. Whenever something happened to make her happy, something else would happen to take her happiness away. She adored her father, but then he got sick, and now he was elderly. Her mother was so neglectful and so violent that she was someone to fear, or to take care of when she was drunk.

She had not mentioned her stepfather before, but now she told me that he was in prison for having raped a number of teenage girls. Norah was very small when he was arrested, not more than four or five. She was questioned by the police and answered honestly, as she had been taught to do. She believed now that her answers helped to send her stepfather to prison. Later, after her mother's boyfriend raped her, he went to the same prison her stepfather was in. She made a point of this, that the man who raped her was in the same prison her stepfather was in. She was ashamed of her stepfather, and the girls he hurt were about the age she was now, and she believed he belonged in prison where he couldn't hurt other girls, but he was her stepfather and she felt she had betrayed him. That was the word she used: betrayed. But she'd been taught to tell the truth, so she had. She didn't like people to know that her stepfather was a rapist; she had considered him her father when he was married to her mother.

*   *   *

I had been thinking for some time—since Norah's time in maximum security was extended—that we needed something to combat the hopelessness kids began to feel when they stayed more than a few weeks in max. Norah was not the only resident in this situation, though none had more time in Wolf than she. In many cases, other cottages refused to accept transfers from maximum security even when they had sent the kids to us in the first place; Wolf's program was designed to get a kid with a behavioral problem back on track within a month or two, after which the kid would be returned to his original cottage. But I had Norah in mind when I wrote a proposal for a program change. It allowed for an additional level, to be called "Honors Level," for residents who had accomplished certain things. They had to have been in Wolf for at least forty-five consecutive days. They had to have gone three consecutive weeks without a demerit. They had to have a B average or better in school. They must have earned the trust and confidence of staff.

And they had to provide a model of good behavior for other residents. In the two years I had worked in Wolf Cottage, only four residents, including Norah, would have qualified. I presented my proposal to PC. It was approved and Norah was elevated to Honors Level.

*   *   *

Dr. Nader, the superintendent, told Jan that after Norah had spent five or six months in Wolf from her date of admission, Wolf staff could determine her eligibility to be transferred to another cottage. This was a change in that he had said earlier that Norah would have to stay in max for five to six months in addition to the time she had already been with us.

"They finally decided to follow their own regulations," Jan said, even though the superintendent's latest decision had come several months late. Had they followed the regulations, Norah would have been transferred months earlier. But Jan had a way of making a bauble look like a gem. (For a long time I thought she did this in an effort to shore up her staff's morale, but later I came to believe that she needed to deceive herself in order to continue to work at Ash Meadow.) Trying to document Nader's commitment, she sent him an email telling him what she'd understood him to say at the meeting, and asking if her understanding was accurate. He didn't respond.

When I came in to work that afternoon, the morning staff told me that Norah had been so depressed that she had not gone to school. She got up, did her chores, and returned to her room. In the evening, after the other kids were locked in their rooms, I talked with her about life in general and joked with her about some of the other kids. Then I told her what Nader had said, but cautioned her not to count on anything.

"I know better than to count on anything. I've learned my lesson," she said.

As I was locking her in her room after our talk, she said, "I love you." I pretended I hadn't heard. Expressions of endearment between residents and staff were not permitted.

I trusted that I hadn't made a mistake in encouraging her to hope again. But she'd been so unhappy—I'd been afraid for her. In any event, we still had a couple of months before she could transfer.

*   *   *

At one point in her life, she lost her voice—I think this must have been after the first time she was raped; recall that the man who raped her threatened to kill her if she told anybody—and had to undergo therapy to learn to speak again. She was living with her father then. She listened to tapes that taught her how to pronounce words. I had wondered how she had acquired such a large vocabulary and why her pronunciation was so clear compared to that of other kids in Ash Meadow. "It was the tapes," she said. "I listened to them for a long time." Years, she thought, though later, when I finally obtained her complete file from county detention, or perhaps Ash Meadow's administration had been late in forwarding it, I learned that it was one year.

When she lived with her father she had money. He was rich, she said, because he had retired from Boeing. When she had money, she associated with other girls who had money and ignored the girls who did not. She demonstrated for me a kind of willfully silly, affected style of speech and gesture she had learned from older girls and from television. It reminded me of the Valley girl way of talking that I had heard sorority girls at the University of Washington use back in the Eighties. She lost all that—the status, the sense of privilege, the feeling of superiority—when her father had his stroke and she was no longer rich and had to go to live with Louise and Geraldine. She had been a pretty, intelligent, middle-class girl whose father appeared to have been a thoroughly decent man and whose mother was an alcoholic, abusive and neglectful, with a boyfriend who raped Norah. If fate had been a little less twisted, Norah might have been born to a different mother, and been, if not happy, at least less unhappy than she was.

* * *

I asked her once where, on a scale of one to ten, ten being most angry, she would place herself on a typical day. "Eight and a half," she said. "Sometimes six."

I was stunned. No other kid had ever said more than six unless he was primed to fight. But she was adamant. "I hate the world because it's treated me so bad."

* * *

She'd felt down and irritable most of the week without knowing why. She talked about how she often didn't know what she was feeling or thinking until long after she had stopped feeling particular emotions or thinking particular thoughts. But people—meaning staff—wanted to know what was going on with her, and when she said, "Nothing," they accused her of trying to hide something. It was frustrating.

She thought she might be feeling depressed because she was beginning her period. She was often "snappish" before and during. Guillermo knew to stay away from her when her period was starting. But she thought she might have been especially depressed this week because Layton, the cottage supervisor, with whom she was close, had been away in training. She told me not to go away for a week like Layton had, particularly if he was gone too.

She said she'd been skipping meals because the food here was so rich in calories. I made a mental note to start monitoring her food consumption. She was already too thin.

*   *   *

We had nothing special to talk about and just joked about boys. She said she'd had a dream in which she assaulted Daniel Lyons, one of the boys in the cottage, while Jan and I laughed. At one point during the fight Daniel wrapped his arms around her beneath her breasts and I yelled at him to watch where he put his hands. He apologized and then he and Norah resumed fighting, quitting only when they were tired. She wasn't upset by the dream. I knew that she and Daniel were attracted to each other, and that she saw me as her protector.

She gossiped about some of the other residents. Laurel, who had transferred out but had been sent back to us, had hit her a couple of times. Laurel would pretend to be stretching and would fling her arms out when Norah was walking out of the zone beside her, or when Norah stepped out of her room. I told her I would watch for it and would alert other staff to keep an eye on Laurel.

Norah gave me her feelings about staff. She liked Layton, Dick, Clare and me, but didn't trust some of the others. Jan and Bernie were all right, but she didn't feel close to them. She didn't like James or Gil or Frank, James because he joked too much at kids' expense, Gil because he was mean, and Frank because he didn't know what he was doing and made decisions without thinking.

*   *   *

I talked about Norah at the psychiatry team meeting for the first time. I said the reason for the referral was her depression. I reported that after she, and the cottage staff, had been led to believe that she would be transferred last December, the superintendent, or other administrators, changed his mind. This had the effect of throwing her into a sudden and, for the staff, frightening depression. I was looking at Don Martino, one of the administrators, when I said this. He shifted his eyes away from mine.

I had expected him to challenge me, but it was Dr. Williams, the psychiatry chief, who stopped me. He asked why I was referring Norah to them. I said again that Norah was depressed. Then Williams said she had probably been kept in maximum security because of the severity of her offense.

I said she had met Ash Meadow's requirements for transfer out of maximum security. By keeping her in max, the administration was in violation of its own regulations. I stood up and walked out of the room.

A couple of days later, I asked Norah about her depression. It wasn't as bad as it had been, she said, though she still wasn't able to sleep. I had asked the health center several times to send down some Benadryl for her, but they hadn't responded.

She asked if I thought she would ever leave Wolf Cottage. I said I hadn't heard anything to indicate she wouldn't.

She was worried about her father. She had left messages on his answering machine, but he hadn't returned her calls.

*   *   *

She had been withdrawn for several days. Every few months, she said, she felt she had to do something bad in order to release the anger that built up in her. Here at Ash Meadow she had handled this feeling by pulling into herself and sometimes crying. She knew her judgment was affected at times like this such that she stopped caring about the consequences of what she did.

I asked her if she had assaulted Geraldine when she felt like this. She didn't remember.

She said she stopped trusting people or regarding them with anything but contempt when she was small. Her ex-boyfriend was twenty or twenty-one when she started going out with him. She was ten.

Was she living with Geraldine then? Yes.

I asked her what kind of man goes out with a ten-year-old girl. She shrugged. I could have asked her what kind of foster mother allows her ten-year-old charge to go out with a twenty-year-old man, but I already knew Norah's feeling about Geraldine.

I asked if anything in particular had prompted her to re-evaluate her life, as apparently she'd been doing. Nothing she knew of; she'd just been doing it.

*   *   *

Jan said the administrators would be discussing Norah's transfer at their March 28 meeting. She handed me a sheet of paper with a list of questions on it and asked me to respond to them. Marty Biggs, a new administrator and Jan's immediate supervisor, would be pitching Norah's case for us and she wanted to give him something he could use against the other administrators' arguments. She didn't have a lot of confidence in him.

The questions asked for a summary of Norah's progress in Wolf Cottage.

I said she was an A student. She participated in several treatment groups and classes the cottage provided, including Victim Awareness, Grief-and-Loss, Drug-and-Alcohol Education, Alternatives to Violence and Aggression Replacement Training.

In one-on-one counseling, we dealt with the effects of her having been emotionally and sexually abused, and looked at how these experiences related to her anger and her offense. The loss of her father, and then her stepfather, and then her father's illness had presented issues of abandonment for her. Her relationships with men reflected these issues; she had shown a tendency to attach herself to older boys and men, some of which had exploited her. We discussed possibilities for her future, for after she left Wolf Cottage and then after she left Ash Meadow. She wanted to work in the social service field.

I said she suffered from depression and that she had attempted suicide before coming to Ash Meadow.

*   *   *

Jan told me that Marty would bring up Norah's transfer at the administrators' April 4 meeting instead of the one on March 28. He said the March 28 agenda was so full that she would have no chance of a hearing. This was Marty's way of extending Norah's time in max just a little bit more, Jan said.

I thought Marty was trying to ingratiate himself with the other administrators. From what I had seen of his interaction with them, they appeared to regard him as a lightweight.

*   *   *

Norah said some of the boys with whom she'd had relationships had hit her. She said she usually deserved it because she got mouthy with them and then they would hit her.

I asked her who had the right to determine that she deserved to be hit. After some waffling, she said she didn't know.

We talked about her stepfather. She said she had been terrified of him because she had seen him beat her mother and sisters. Once when he was hitting her mother, Norah jumped on his back to try to get him to stop, but he didn't stop.

I asked her if her mother was mouthy. She said she didn't remember, but then described her mother as sometimes saying bellicose things to her husband and taunting him.

I asked Norah if she didn't see that the relationships she had with her boyfriends were like the relationship her mother had with her husband. She laughed; she said she didn't think so. Anyway, if her boyfriends hit her, she would hit them back. She wouldn't let anyone get away with hitting her, she said.

I thought that if I were married, I'd look into the possibility of adopting her. I wanted to fix her despair. Knowing I couldn't, I still wanted to.

* * *

Norah said she'd had a dream about becoming a counselor for kids and coming back to Ash Meadow and working side by side with me.

* * *

Returning to work after a week off, I found an email from Marty that Jan had forwarded to me. It said the "Administrators"—upper case A; Marty, an administrator, wrote it that way—had approved Norah Joines' transfer out of Wolf Cottage to occur on April 24. The email said also: "Thank you for the good work and of course the willingness of Norah to invest in herself, we were able to accomplish this request."

In the journal I kept during the years I worked at Ash Meadow, I wrote, following the entry of the text of the memo: "Fuck you, Administrators. In the upper case…. And fuck you … for your duplicity."[2]

Norah already knew. Layton had told her. You could see that she was happy, but also that she was afraid to trust them, the Administrators, upper case. I didn't blame her for distrusting them, of course, but I was glad she was happy. In fifteen days she would be in a different cottage, assuming this was not another lie.

* * *

I stayed late to talk with her. She would be leaving tomorrow. She said she wished I worked at Serpent Cottage, where she was going. Apparently Serpent required its residents to write an autobiography and to read it to the cottage. She was afraid of having to tell people she didn't know well about her life. She didn't want to leave herself vulnerable by revealing what had caused her pain. I tried to reassure her.

She moved to Serpent at nine the next morning. I allowed her to wear her regular clothes instead of the orange jumpsuit she had worn for the last six months. I was supposed to transfer her in her jumpsuit, but I didn't. I wasn't sure why I didn't, but I didn't. Unlike last night, she was overjoyed to be leaving, and in her own clothes! She ran all around searching for a place to look at herself—there were no mirrors in Wolf Cottage—and finally settled on the window looking into Jan's office. "I'm cute!" she squealed. "And I know it!" Bernie and I were delighted to see her so happy.

I went to the psych meeting at nine-thirty. I talked about Norah for the last time; it would be up to Serpent to present on her after today. It was as though the psychiatrists had never been told that Norah had been in maximum security for six months. One of them asked why so long and before I could reply, Marty Biggs said it was because she was a high-profile resident. I was immediately angry but let it pass as just another instance of the administration's mendacity.

When I said Norah was estranged from her mother, Marie, the school psychologist, put in that Norah hadn't had contact with her mother in years. I corrected her: Norah hadn't seen her mother in several years, but until four months ago she had talked regularly with her. What happened four months ago, I said, was that the superintendent told Jan, Wolf's cottage director, and me that Norah would be able to transfer to Serpent Cottage at the end of December. I told Norah. December passed and she was not transferred; we were not told why. Eventually Dr. Nader told us that the other administrators had dissuaded him from allowing Norah to transfer out of Wolf. I told Norah and she called her mother to tell her; she had been keeping her mother informed about her progress. Her mother told her that her behavior must have been bad for the administrators to change their minds about her. This was the kind of response her mother had made when Norah told her that her boyfriend had raped her.

"Invalidation," one of the psychiatrists said.

"Yeah. Invalidation. I have nothing else to say." I left the meeting.

*   *   *

Three weeks later, Ash Meadow was in the midst of what we had come to call an "epidemic" of attempted suicide, begun when a girl at Peacock Cottage killed herself. At the psych meeting, Dr. Williams informed us that there had been seven suicide attempts in the last fourteen days. Meg Bellardine, the mental health resource coordinator, came in just as Williams made his announcement. "Make that nine," she said. There had been two more this morning. A few days later a girl in Wolf hanged herself but was cut down by Layton before she expired.

A month after the epidemic abated, Dr. Williams said he was concerned that Ash Meadow was creating mental health problems in its residents by not giving them the opportunity to transfer out of maximum security. He was alluding to Swan Cottage's refusal to accept back a kid they had sent us months before. It had become more the rule than the exception that kids were sent to Wolf and remained there.

I said it was a real morale killer for kids, not to have something to look forward to. I reminded Williams that Wolf was supposed to have kids for thirty to sixty days, but we were getting them for up to six months now. I didn't mention that I had brought up the same issue months ago as it pertained to Norah, but told him I was glad to hear him speak this way because I and other Wolf staff felt as he did. Williams was a man who seemed to believe that any psychological insight that did not originate from within his profession had no validity. And he drew a sharp distinction between the psychiatrists at Ash Meadow and the cottage staff. If he could not deny the validity of something one of the cottage counselors proposed, he repeated it to others as though the insight were his own.

* * *

I'd started visiting Norah at Serpent once a week after I got off shift. One night as I was leaving, Sandra, her case manager, told me, "She really loves you."

* * *

On one of my visits, Norah told me that she sometimes woke up with bruises or scratches on her arm; she thought she might be hurting herself in her sleep. She was afraid to tell the staff at Serpent because she didn't want to be put on suicide watch. She said she had also been having trouble with bulimia. I advised her to tell Sandra, whom she had begun to trust. I told her I didn't think they would place her on suicide watch.

When I visited her next, she said she had confided in Sandra and that Sandra had told her of her own struggles with bulimia when she was Norah's age. Sandra said, too, that she didn't see Norah as being suicidal.

* * *

When Norah was on the outs, she got hit on the head with a beer bottle during a gang fight. The bottle shattered, bits of it becoming embedded in her scalp. In school one day at Ash Meadow, she was scratching her head when a piece of glass fell onto her desk. She was amazed. She showed it to the other kids in her class. They were amazed too.

* * *

She said that when she was at Wolf she was still so angry at Geraldine that she could not separate her responsibility for having assaulted her from her anger at Geraldine for having demeaned her. She said she was past that now. She did accept responsibility for attacking Geraldine even if her anger, although not as intense as it was, was still there. She wished she could write Geraldine to tell her how sorry she was for having hurt her, but she was not allowed to contact her.

*   *   *

Serpent Cottage had been designated a second mental health unit for girls. The superintendent had parlayed the suicide and the attempts at suicide into money to add staff and retrain existing staff. Norah was transferred to Peacock Cottage. A few weeks later I received an email from Peacock's supervisor informing me that Norah's relationship with me was interfering with her new case manager's attempt to build rapport with her; I would not be permitted to visit Norah again. A week after I received this email I saw her case manager at a psychiatry team meeting. He was aware of the email and said that while he did not have a problem with Norah having a relationship with staff outside Peacock, the cottage director did. He was sorry. He knew, he said, how much I meant to Norah.

At Peacock Cottage

At the psych meeting, Tony Dell, Peacock's representative, presented on Norah. Nobody had talked about her in the several months since she moved to Peacock from Serpent, but now her case manager wanted her seen by a psychiatrist because she had become so withdrawn that he was afraid she might try to kill herself. He was the one who discovered Ash Meadow's last suicide and cut her down and tried to bring her back. But Tony didn't talk about suicide concerns. Instead, he said Norah was sneaky and he didn't trust her. She's so sneaky, he said, that she puts her hand in front of her face to conceal it when she gets Ibuprofen from staff. Tony presented on three or four girls; he was angry with all of them. His anger took the form of dismissing the kids he talked about. "I don't know what's wrong with her," he said about one. "She'll intentionally do what she's not supposed to." He left the meeting after he made his last presentation.

Until it was my turn to present, I wrestled with myself over whether or not to say anything about Norah. When my turn came I talked about Birdie Forrest. Afterward, I asked if I might say something about Norah Joines. Nobody spoke, so I began, "I was Norah's case manager for the first six months she was here. Given our experience of her at Wolf, I know that when Norah puts her hand up to conceal her face, it isn't because she's being sneaky—she's feeling shame. And it probably has to do with her relationship with cottage staff. One or more staff is reinforcing her sense of shame. As far as I know, she feels shame about two things. The more recent is her having committed her offense. While she knows she did it, she has trouble accepting that she did. And it was a bad crime. Second, and further back, she gave information to the police that helped send her stepfather to prison. He was a sex offender and the police questioned her, a four- or five-year-old girl, and she answered honestly and he went to prison. She knows he belongs there: his prey were girls the age she is now. But she feels she betrayed him. If Norah tries to kill herself, it won't be a gesture; she will truly intend to do it. She tried once before, when she was in foster care. That's all I've got."

Norah's psychiatrist had been taking notes. "Thank you," she said. She did not look up at me, but continued to write.

Leaving the building, I saw Dick Peck, our chaplain, coming out of Administration. He and Norah had grown close and I relied on him to keep me informed on how she was doing. I told him what I had done. "You may have made a mistake," he said. "Now they can use this to keep you away from her. They can rationalize it by saying you're interfering with their cottage program."

"What program? They don't have a program. They just warehouse girls."

"You know that and I know that, but they don't see themselves that way."

"Well, I considered that I might be giving them ammunition to use against me, or against her, but if Norah killed herself and I hadn't done everything I could to prevent it, I couldn't live with myself."

* * *

Occasionally I would see her at lower court on my way to or from Wolf. The talk was always superficial. I felt each time that there was something more she wanted to say, but there was always someone else around. Once when I stopped to ask how she was doing, one of the Peacock staff who had been monitoring the kids shooting hoops came running over to where Norah and I were talking. Peacock regarded me with suspicion.

* * *

Just before Thanksgiving I ran into her at the cafeteria. She was pouring water for tea. "Tea is good for you. It's better than coffee," she said.

She would be leaving in less than three weeks. A group home. She had been given her choice of three and had chosen this one, even though there was not an opening until December. Dick Peck was angry with her because one of the others was a Christian group home and he wanted her to go there, but she had decided not to because she'd had enough of Christians for a while. Her cottage was going to have a party for her before she left. She was happy, she said, but she was also scared; Ash Meadow had become her home.

I did not see her or hear from her again for almost six months. I left a message for her with one of the group home staff a couple of times but got no response. Then in May I walked into the school library to browse while I waited to pick up the Wolf kids to escort them down to the cottage after class, and there she was. When she saw me, she said, "Oh," and I opened my arms and she came into them and cried while I held her. She kept saying, "I haven't been bad," while I said, "I know … I know…."

At the group home she had gotten angry—about what, she didn't tell me—and tossed her clothes around her room. The staff were afraid that she might be suicidal, so they sent her back to Ash Meadow for a month. Norah laughed: they had never seen anybody throw her clothes around before. Then she said, "They still love me."

"I know they do," I said.

When she had regained herself, she told me she was seeing a boy. Guillermo was still in prison; he had gotten time added to his sentence for fighting. Norah said she didn't think they had anything in common now. She didn't want somebody who was involved in criminal life; she didn't want someone who would leave her to raise their children, when they had them, alone.

She returned to the group home at the end of the month. I visited her at Peacock the night before she left. Peacock had a new cottage director and she had okayed my visit. Norah had put aside some dessert from supper for us and we sat in the dining room and ate lemon cake and drank tea as we talked. She said she would be better about staying in touch with me, but said, too, that she had left messages for me with Charlie Patterson, one of the day staff at Wolf. He hadn't passed them on to me. "You could always write," I said. I wasn't allowed to write her as long as I worked in the system, but she could write me. "Regulations are strange animals," I said. I hoped she would laugh, but she only nodded her head.

*   *   *

It was a year and a half before I talked with her again. If she had tried to reach me by phone, no one had told me. I had tried calling her, but had not been able to connect with her. Finally another Ash Meadow staff who had been able to get hold of her called me and gave me her cell phone number. She seemed happy, he said, and had asked him to pass her number on to me.

She said she would be paroled in three months. She knew she had a lot to do to get ready for parole, to get ready to be on her own, but she was looking forward to it. She had gotten a food handler's certificate and had worked in the kitchen at the school she attended, so she could work in food service if she couldn't find anything else. She sounded unsure, but hopeful.

* * *

In April, the staff at her group home invited me to a surprise going-away party for her. One of the staff got her out of the house before the guests arrived and when they came back she did not realize at first that the party was for her. Her uncle Patrick was there—I recognized him from when he used to visit her at Wolf—and she appeared to be trying to figure out why, and also why I was there. It had been almost two years since I had seen her.

Perhaps it was her confusion at the beginning of the party, perhaps it was something else, but she withdrew to a sofa at the edge of the room and spent most of the afternoon there. From the way she stared at me, I wasn't sure she even recognized me. After a while I went over and sat down next to her. She would be moving in with Patrick next week, she said. He had an apartment in Seattle just down from Capitol Hill. She hadn't been able to find a place of her own; people didn't want to rent to her because she had been in prison. I didn't doubt her. Years earlier, I released a young woman who likewise was unable to find a place to live in Seattle, or a job. It was a terrible situation to be in, especially if you had almost no experience of the world outside of prison. And Seattle is not a city that troubles itself over a stranger's problems.

Norah had failed the written test for her driver's license. Some of the questions on it were not in the Washington Driver Guide. She knew what was in that book and these questions asked about things that weren't in it. I remembered this from my own test, but my experience as a driver had carried me through. She was trying to understand the rules of society, but the rules that appeared to govern it were not the real ones, or not the only ones, and the others were not written down anywhere.

I told her I had gotten married. I wondered if she would be jealous, but all she said was "Oh, really?"

I mingled with the group home staff and spoke a little with Patrick who did not remember me, although he said he did. Finally I told Norah I had to go. A small "Oh" came from her, as if she was disappointed that I was not staying longer, but her expression did not change. She still looked dazed. She gave me Patrick's phone number. The next day I sent her a copy of my book, *How I Learned That I Could Push the Button*; she was in one of the essays, though as an unnamed resident of Ash Meadow.

* * *

No, Norah's not here, Patrick said. Why would I think she was here? No, she has her own place. He gave me her phone number.

Guillermo had been released from prison and he and Norah were living together in an apartment in a suburb south of Seattle.

I asked how she could be living with Guillermo. She said her parole officer had told her that they're not enforcing the element of the parole contract that requires parolees not to associate with felons, because so many parolees are related to felons or live near them that it was impossible for them to honor it. Guillermo was working as a car detailer, she said, and she was thinking about going to cosmetology school. She had some money that her father had put away for her, so she wasn't worried yet. She had read my book, at least the part of it that she was in, and was delighted with my portrait of her, but wished I had used her name.

We talked on the phone a few times over the next few months and Jeanne, my wife, and I took her to lunch once.

During our last phone call that summer, she said she and Guillermo were no longer together. He had another woman. He had said he would give her up, but he hadn't, so Norah kicked him out. She was especially angry because he had used her father's money to pay the rent on his girlfriend's apartment. Norah was seeing somebody else now.

A New Relationsip

She was living in Tucson, she said, but she and her boyfriend were in Seattle to see friends. We had just started to talk when I heard a man's voice in the background. Then she said they were going somewhere and she would call me tomorrow.

She called half a year later. She was still in Tucson. She was bored, and missed Seattle. It was hotter in Tucson than she had expected it to be. She and K., her boyfriend, had been to Las Vegas four times in the eight months they'd been living in Arizona. They went for the excitement. Also, she liked the buffets. She ate an enormous amount now. She was still the same size she had always been, but her body needed some toning up, she said.

K. was in business with a partner. They had an interest in a hotel and a diamond mine and were importing gems from Africa. Norah still wanted to get a cosmetology certificate, but she went to a community college near where she lived and they wanted to enroll her in their regular program. She didn't want that. She didn't want to take courses in reading—she didn't enjoy reading anymore—or writing or math. She had had all that in high school and didn't want to do it again. She had checked into commercial schools offering cosmetology certificates, but they wanted eight thousand dollars for the course.

I suggested she check with other community colleges to see what they offered, and also to ask if financial aid was available for commercial cosmetology schools, but she was discouraged. All the community colleges in her area were the same, she said. Plus, if she went to a different one she would have to drive there, and she still didn't have a driver's license. She said she might be coming up to Seattle soon.

* * *

She left a message, just that she wanted to keep in touch. I called her back.

She was pregnant. Five months. It was all right. She was glad she was pregnant. She just found out a month ago. That explained why she was so hungry all the time. She had had hardly any morning sickness, only a little nausea. She and K. were still in Arizona.

* * *

I had not heard from her in almost a year. She was living with a cousin in upstate New York now and would start business school next week. Tuition was thirty thousand a year, but she had a number of grants to cover most of it, and loans and a job to cover the rest. Eventually she wanted to own her own beauty salon. She had a little girl now, Lily. Her cousin would watch her when Norah was in school.

She said that in August, a few days after we last talked, federal agents burst into her and K.'s apartment when they were asleep and arrested them. It was terrifying. At first she couldn't figure out what was going on and thought they were going to kill K. and her. K. had been charged with various things, including transporting weapons and money laundering. The feds had been watching him for years. The money-laundering account had been set up in her name and they held her for four months until they were certain she really didn't know anything about what K. was doing. When they released her, they told her they might require her to testify against K. He was still locked up.

His family believed she had snitched on him. That was why, they thought, she had been released. She was afraid that he, or they, would send someone to hurt or kill her. He was very scary when he was angry. He didn't know where she was now. She had called me because I was the only person she trusted.

As worried as she was that her life might be at risk, she seemed to be equally upset that she was unable to maintain a relationship with "a caring, stable man." She said she ruined those relationships when she had them.

The counselor in me asserted itself and I said that was understandable: she'd been abandoned early in her life by the men who had mattered to her and she was afraid now to trust a man, but drew back when she caught herself getting too close. But, I said, there was another aspect to this: she chose men— Guillermo, K.—who, she knew at some level, would hurt her. She used them to hurt herself.

She was very quiet. I thought she may have closed her phone and I asked, "Are you still there?"

She was. She wanted to keep talking, but her cell phone was losing power, and in a moment I couldn't make sense of what she was saying.

Intimations of Trouble

Three or four months passed without my hearing from her. This was not unusual and I did not think much about it. Then, at the end of the summer, she was in my thoughts a lot. An image of her as I had once seen her on the walkway at lower court at Ash Meadow, thin, too thin, and uncertain as she came over to talk with me; my memory of her crying after I told her she would have to remain in maximum security ("I've worked so hard. I've done everything they wanted me to do. Why won't they let me go?"); other images, other memories would suddenly appear in my mind, regardless of what else I was thinking about, and they were always accompanied by a feeling of unease, a kind of apprehension. I tried calling her but her phone was out of service. We had exchanged emails when she started business school, and at the end of September I wrote to her at the address from which her last note had come, a single sentence: "How are you doing, Norah?"

She wrote back the same day:

… life is not good for me I'm struggling don't have a job anymore no money family ain't tryin to help me friends can't help don't know what to do to be honest I need a miracle that's all that can bring me out of this my life is hell

I asked what happened. What could I do?

I don't know how u can help I don't got ideas I don't know what 2 do myself what happened is my family drug me out here where I have nothing and know nothing and turned their backs on me they have not done any of the things they said they would do for me

She had had to drop out of school because her cousin's girlfriend "had a thing for me [and my cousin] got mad and kicked me out cause she was jelious [sic]." Norah had relied on her cousin's promise to babysit Lily while she was in class. Now there was no one to leave her with.

I was shocked at the way she wrote: "I don't got..." "my family drug me...." Did she talk like this now too? She sounded like a four-year-old.

Unable to think of anything else to do, I offered to send her money, and after talking with Jeanne, I wrote that if she wanted to leave New York, she could stay with us until she got on her feet.

> Thank you so much and I might have to take you up on the offer thanks for the option I don't know what I would do without you both I will stay in contact with you.

But she did not seem in a hurry to move and she did not answer most of my questions about her situation. I didn't have a street address for her, or a phone number, if she had a phone. I assumed she and Lily were living in a shelter, but I didn't know. And I could only speculate about her state of mind. From the tone of her emails, I thought she was depressed. She'd had a propensity for depression when she was younger, and from the sense I got that she was feeling overwhelmed, from the lethargy I believed I detected in her emails, I thought she had fallen victim to it again. I renewed the invitation to stay with us and offered to send her more money to get her by until she could leave.

To try to get her through what I took to be her inability to make a decision, I listed what she had to do, step by step, if she was going to leave: Pick the day and time you want to leave; find an airline with a decent price for that day; be sure to find out if you have to pay for a seat for Lily; let me know the airline and flight number and when to expect you. I would pay by credit card.

I assured her that Jeanne and I were looking forward to seeing her again. I had taken an early retirement from Ash Meadow almost two years earlier, and while my time had quickly filled, it was my own time and I could adjust it as I needed.

> any help with money right now would be a blessing I can use it so if u can that would be very kind it's hard out here I can't believe I'm struggling like this It makes me crazy, breaks my spirit I never in my life have delt with this before I know after I come out of this and get my life right I will be able to take on anything that might come my way this whole year has been nothing but stress and pain I just want it to end I thank god for u and Jeanne because without the both of u I don't know what I would do I will always have love 4 you and consider u both family I will look up ticket prices I'm on it in the morning and I'll let you know by the end of the day.

The tone of this email was different: she seemed to be able to see the end of something bad and, perhaps, she felt that her life had direction again. I hoped the feeling in this note was not an anomaly, that it really was a sign that something was getting better. I was worried about her misspellings and the lack of punctuation, although, for the first time in her emails to me, she ended her paragraph, if not her individual sentences, with a period. When she was fourteen and fifteen she wrote poetry and read Henry James.

Over the next week I pushed her to get her tickets, but she was unable to decide what the best time to leave would be. She sent me photos of Lily taken at a park. Lily was ten months old. She wasn't walking yet, but could stand up without help. She already had four teeth and a fifth tooth was peeking out. She and Norah slept together. Norah had tried having Lily sleep in a crib, but Lily had cried all night. "I guess she feels safe if she can feel me through the night I like it too[.]" Jeanne and I decided not to buy Lily a crib and started thinking about how we would childproof the house.

Norah finally gave up trying to pick a time to leave and settled on a date.

> the time does not matter what ever flight is the easiest so there is not a crazy lay over if any at all I have to check with the people in Arizona and let them know I'm planning on leaving but I'm sure it should be fine I'll try and let you know 2marrow.

Who were the people in Arizona she had to check with?

> the people I was talking about in Arizona are the pre-trial people due to the fact that mine and K.'s case is not over I may need to go to trial some time … so any time I have a change of address I have to let them know and they say if it's ok or not cause they have to keep tabs on me till everything is over.

We spent the next couple of weeks making and confirming flight arrangements. Jeanne bought a car seat for Lily; Norah's cousin had not allowed her to take the one she had ("all I have is a stroller"). Her cousin had also kept most of their clothes; Jeanne and I decided to buy clothes for them in Washington so they wouldn't have to travel with additional baggage. We asked what their sizes were and what foods they liked.

> her size in clothes I get are 18 months so she can get some wear and still have room to grow as far as food goes lily eats baby food the different fruits any type she is at the point now that she eats our foods she has 6 teeth now so she is learning to chew I feed her whatever I'm eating to learn what she likes, she does not drink our milk she drinks Enfamil Next Step for babies 9–24 months I on the other hand drink milk my food varies I like pretty much everything pasta is my favorite and I like eating salads. my clothes size pants are size 7 shirt size goes from med-large it depends on the style of the shirt I need to get more under garments I'm working with a limited amount, as far as toiletries go I don't have much of anything my plan was to get all of that when I arrive there I'm in to fruity smells when it comes to body wash, lotions, and shampoo. Thank U so much for getting lily a car seat U both are really going out of your way for

us and I can't thank U enough. I have just one question for U off the subject I'm dealing with a real difficult situation and I have not been able to tell any one because I did not want to be judged or thought of in a bad way I'm afraid to talk about it because it is painful and I'm scared I have to tell you but I don't know where to begin to explain what are your thoughts?

"She's pregnant," Jeanne said.

I don't have copies of the emails I sent her during this time, and my memory in this instance is blank, but apparently I responded. Norah wrote back:

thank you it has been so hard for me I have never went through this type of thing before the stress is taking a toll on me along with the other day to day things I face here I will talk with U in person because it's not something one would like to discuss through an e-mail I just needed to be reassured that you are here for me to support me and help me through difficult times considering how there is no one else who knows my past and me as a person … your my confidant I have always held the up most respect for you because you were the only one who helped break down my many walls and see that not everyone in this world is out to get me.

"Something's wrong"

Suddenly she was here, coming up off the escalator after the main rush of passengers had gone. She was wearing a white jacket not much heavier than a windbreaker—it must not have been much protection from the New York winter—and her hair was pulled back as I remembered she used to wear it. She was taller than I remembered, but then I saw that she was wearing stiletto heels. She held a very small child clothed in a miniature pink running suit on her hip. She didn't appear to be pregnant. I tried to see what she was feeling but she moved her eyes away from mine. She looked tired, but it was something other than tiredness that she didn't want me to see. Then her back was to me; Jeanne was reaching for Lily and cooing and then they were walking ahead of me to the baggage carousel.

Jeanne offered to sit in back so Norah and I could talk on the drive home, but Norah insisted on sitting in the rear with Lily. We hardly talked. For a while I thought Norah had fallen asleep, but when I looked in the mirror I saw her staring at me as she had at the surprise party at the group home. There was no expression on her face. We stopped at a Safeway to get Enfamil for Lily and then drove the rest of the way home. At the house we showed Norah where her bedroom and bathroom were, where to find extra towels and blankets, shampoo and soap. She just wanted to sleep, she said, she hadn't been able to sleep on the plane, and she disappeared into her bedroom with Lily.

"I don't think she's pregnant," Jeanne said when we were in bed. "If she is, she's not showing."

"Something's wrong," I said, "but I don't know what it is. Something bad has happened to her that she hasn't told us about."

"Told you about. She wasn't writing to me."

"She doesn't know you. She only met you once."

"That's true. I had forgotten how pretty she is."

"We could ask her to wear dirty clothes and not to wash her face or brush her hair."

"You ask her."

"Okay, I will."

*   *   *

In the morning Norah said she hadn't slept well. Lily had the habit of pinching the skin on Norah's neck and she did that all night in her sleep. "It's always like this," Norah said. "I never get any sleep. I lie down with her to get her to sleep and she sleeps through the night, but I can't sleep at night. So when she's awake during the day, I'm still tired. When I was living with my uncle"—she had gone from her cousin's house to Patrick's brother's when her cousin kicked her out—"he would be awake during the day, so I could sleep then. He worked graveyard shift and didn't go to sleep until late afternoon. I'm going to have to adapt here. It'll be like weekends at my uncle's."

She had a problem sleeping at night when she was fourteen, I remembered. She was depressed then, too.

She had been with us for a couple of days when I took her to the market to buy food for herself and Lily while Jeanne babysat. Norah and Lily weren't eating with us. Norah cooked for herself and her daughter after Jeanne and I had finished our supper. Norah preferred this; she didn't tell us why. In the car, I said I knew that something was wrong, that something had happened to her. At first I, and Jeanne, suspected that she was pregnant, but now we didn't think so.

When I began to speak she turned to face me, but then she turned away. She was looking at the floor.

"I'm pregnant."

When her cousin kicked her out, she found herself on the street with Lily, with no money and no place to go. Her uncle lived in another town. She called the only other person she knew, a man she had met at a party her cousin had had, and he took her and Lily in. She stayed with him for a week until, finally, she got hold of her uncle and he came and got her and Lily. During that time the man she was staying with raped her. She had told no one except one of her sisters and, now, me. She had been reluctant to tell me because she was afraid I would think she was bad for staying with this man after he raped her.

I assured her that I didn't think she was bad. I understood the bind she had been in, I said, having Lily to look out for and not having another place to go.

Norah nodded. She still wasn't looking at me.

Had he hurt Lily?

No. She hadn't let Lily out of her sight when they were at his house.

Had she seen a doctor? A counselor?

No.

She didn't know how far along she was. Five or six months, she thought.

I told her she needed to see a doctor. She could do it while she was staying with us.

She said she intended to give the baby up for adoption. She couldn't bear even the thought of abortion. Her sister was religious and wanted her to keep it and raise it, but Norah didn't think she could love it because it existed as the result of her being raped.

We had been talking in the market's parking lot. We got out of the car and went inside to do our shopping.

When we returned home, Norah went into her bedroom with Lily and didn't come out again that night.

* * *

I did not bring up the possibility of her looking for a job. In the condition she was in, I did not see her winning anyone over in an interview. I did mention school, but she said she was not ready for school.

I called a friend who had helped troubled young women before and she gave me the number of a clinic in Seattle. At the clinic, a nurse interviewed her. The nurse was very nice but said there was nothing they could do for her there. However, she thought Norah was eligible for medical coupons and she gave us the number of an agency that would assist her in applying for them.

Norah did not want to call. I badgered her, telling her that she was not being fair to either Lily or herself by refusing to take care of herself. At one point she told me that I should call if it was so important to me. "It isn't my life," I said. "I know how to take care of myself." Finally, she called.

The agency representative wanted to meet Norah alone. A few days later, I drove her and Lily to a Denny's restaurant and sat in the car while she and Nancy talked and filled out forms. When we got home, Norah told me that Nancy had asked her if she felt safe living with Jeanne and me.

"Do you?"
"Yes."
"Good. I'm glad she asked."

*   *   *

I was under some strain. I was working on a book and I wanted to get it done without distraction. Though we enjoyed her, Lily required a lot of attention and Norah was often too tired to give it. While I had retired from my job, Jeanne had not retired from hers, which meant that during the day it was Norah, Lily, and me. Fortunately Norah usually slept in the morning and Lily seemed content to lie quietly beside her. I used these hours to write and read. Since I had retired from Ash Meadow, I had grown used to spending my days alone. But once Norah had connected with a doctor and a therapist at another clinic, two or three afternoons a week were given over to driving her to and from her appointments and playing with Lily or holding her if she fell asleep, while her mom met with the caregivers.

*   *   *

Norah kept Lily beside her almost constantly. Even when Lily napped, Norah lay next to her. Lily was her anchor, her constant companion. With all that had happened, Norah said, she didn't know why she hadn't gone crazy. It was Lily who gave her balance.

Sometimes she spent the entire day in her room with her daughter. I remembered that she used to isolate herself at Ash Meadow too. (Years later, she told me that she had felt so ashamed by her need and her inability to provide for herself and Lily that she had avoided me when she was living with us so that I could not see her shame on her face.) Then, as now, she only picked at her food when she ate. She had told me once when she was at Ash Meadow that she was afraid of gaining weight, as so many of the girls had. Jeanne and I wondered about Lily, whether Norah was passing on her eating problem to her, but Lily looked healthy. She was wiry, but she wasn't thin. However neglectful Norah's mother had been, Norah doted on her daughter.

At Ash Meadow I had considered Norah antiauthoritarian. I still did. After all, those who had abandoned or betrayed her or had otherwise contributed to the traumas in her life had been people with power over her: her mother, her mother's boyfriend, her stepfather, Guillermo, K., most recently the man who had raped and impregnated her. But now I thought too that some of what I interpreted as anger toward authority was related to her fear of loss. A lot of kids placed in foster care despise authority because they blame it for having removed them from their parents, regardless of how neglectful or abusive their parents may have been.

I brought up again the idea of her going to a community college. Some community colleges had daycares on campus; she would have more time with Lily than if she worked a forty-hour week. She could get inexpensive health insurance through the school. She could get grants and loans. By the time she graduated, Lily would be ready for preschool and she would be in a better position to work full time.

But she insisted on delaying school—she knew she would go eventually, she said—and going to work instead, although she was not looking for a job. She didn't say what she would do about Lily. I wondered if I represented authority to her now. Certainly she was less open with me than she was when she was fourteen, or, for that matter, when we were emailing.

*   *   *

The deterioration of her spelling continued to bother me. And she did not think as clearly as she had when she was younger. She used words like "stuff" instead of saying what she meant. Many people do, of course, but she had been precise in her word choices at one time, and she had possessed the vocabulary to enable her to make those choices. Perhaps now she did not know what she wanted to say, so tried to slide through her sentences by using terms of a kind of fuzzy generality because those that were more exact did not represent the cloudiness of her thinking. Or perhaps she did know what she thought, but didn't want to provide—me, at least—any passage to what it was.

When I mentioned her misspellings to her, she said she knew how to spell but preferred to spell incorrectly. She said she had always had a problem with punctuation, but that wasn't true. She had one now, but six or seven years ago, she had written well. She had also given up reading, except for what she had to read. She passed her time watching movies on TV and attending Lily.

*   *   *

First there was Christmas and then, a few days later, it was Norah's birthday, and then, a few days after that, it was Lily's. For Christmas, Jeanne and I bought Norah a cell phone and a month's worth of minutes. For her birthday, her twenty-first, we took her and Lily to dinner at a local steak house. A year ago she had fantasized about going clubbing with her friends on her twenty-first birthday. But her pregnancy prevented her from drinking, and she didn't have any friends here, at least nobody she trusted enough to allow them to see how she had changed.

At first she ate as though she hadn't seen food in a long time. Then, as if she had suddenly remembered something, she stopped and picked at her food as she usually did. We all got a kick out of Lily's fascination with a man at a booth across the aisle who was eating ice cream.

Lily was a kick at home too. She still hadn't taken her first step. She would stand with her fists clenched in front of her and her toes curled and dug into the carpet as though they were prehensile and she would make small grunting sounds which I took to be her talking to herself, trying to get herself to move, to take that step. At other times, she stood planted in the spot where she had gained her feet and, looking down and wagging her finger at the floor, scolded in a loud, imperious babble whatever it was she saw there. At these times she looked like a tiny but stern first-grade teacher admonishing one of her charges to do better or not to do something at all. We all wondered who she had seen do that; it was not something I had observed Norah doing. For Lily's birthday, Jeanne and I got her a rocking duck—yes, a duck, not a horse.

The Persistence of Trauma and Depression

Norah said she had two choices: she could go to school, but felt she wasn't ready—she said again that she knew she would go eventually—or she could remain on the DSHS rolls, collecting a stipend, getting free health care, food stamps, and rent subsidies for up to five years. She was sure she would be ready for school within five years. She didn't mention looking for a job; working full time would take her away from Lily all day. She didn't want to be away from her until Lily started school.

Envisioning her on the DSHS rolls, I saw her stagnating, depression settling in, perhaps irretrievably, unless she found something besides Lily to provide purpose in her life. I gave her what I decided would be my final pitch to go back to school. I said that by sacrificing now, she would get something better later. Also, she would be establishing a model for Lily to follow in her own life, or at least to refer to. I asked Norah if what I was saying meant anything to her. She said she was listening.

* * *

It had gotten cold. The heating vent in Norah's room was blocked. I advised her to leave her door cracked at night so the heat from the hall would warm the bedroom, but she did not. I understood this. People who have been hurt often feel that they are vulnerable when they sleep. An open door increased that sense of vulnerability. I found a space heater I had used years before, when I lived in a different house, and gave it to her.

* * *

Jeanne and I usually kept the blinds up in the breakfast area where we ate. Norah warned us to lower them. "People will see what you have." The implication was that they would come back and steal what they saw.

* * *

I had a routine. I woke in midmorning, read for an hour before getting out of bed, got up and washed, brushed my teeth and shaved, had breakfast, wrote for an hour and a half or two hours, then did errands or drove Norah and Lily to the clinic. In the evening I ran, showered, ate supper, read or caught up on email, then watched some of the late-night interview programs with Jeanne. Afterward, I often worked at my computer or read or watched TV if I had nothing that required doing.

Norah was amazed. She had heard about people like me, but had never actually met anybody who was so set in the sequence of their daily activities until she came to live with us. I don't think she was being critical; I think she was truly amazed. I told her I felt I needed to accomplish certain things every day, and in order to do this a routine was necessary. It was like a job, but I didn't go to an office and I didn't have a boss and I set my own hours.

She didn't think she could live like that. It depends on what you think you need to do to give your life meaning, I said. I was fortunate in that I was able to live so that I could try to create a little bit of meaning for myself almost every day. But it meant giving a large part of my life over to routine.

* * *

The baby was overdue. The doctor would induce labor on Friday. Norah would have to be in the hospital overnight, maybe two nights. The adoptive parents, whom Norah had met through Nancy, had been notified. They were a young, athletic, professional couple that liked to hike, and Norah had been impressed by them. They would pick the baby up at the hospital. Nancy offered to pick Lily up on Thursday night and keep her until Sunday. Norah had confidence in her and I jumped at the offer. I was trying to finish the book I was writing and I did not want to delay work for two days in order to care for Lily. (Yes, I can be obsessive.) Also, I wanted to be available should Norah need me at the hospital.

Nancy, Lily and I accompanied Norah to the hospital on Thursday afternoon. After Nancy and Lily left, I sat with Norah until there was no reason to. Finally Norah told me to go home, there was nothing more I could do for her tonight. I tried to think of a reason to stay a while longer, then realized what I was doing and got up and left.

* * *

I arrived at the hospital a few minutes late. The baby had been stillborn, its umbilical cord wrapped around its neck. Both Norah and the adoptive father appeared to be in a daze. The adoptive mother cried, unable to stop. Finally the would-be parents left the hospital. Nancy and I sat with Norah until a nurse injected her with a sedative and she fell asleep.

She returned home at midday on Sunday, seemingly in good spirits. Despite the soreness, she felt her body had been returned to her and she took Lily for a two-mile walk in her stroller. She returned early in the evening, exhausted, and slept the rest of the night.

She spent most of Monday and Tuesday in her room. Her depression had returned.

* * *

It had been a month since Norah's baby died. Nancy thought, and I agreed, that Norah needed to be someplace that provided more distraction and opportunity, where public transportation was easier than where Jeanne and I lived. Nancy suggested Norah return to Seattle; Norah did not object. Her uncle Patrick still had his apartment. She and Lily were welcome to stay with him while she looked for her own place. Nancy would help her.

She left before I was ready to see her go. She and Lily had been with us for almost four months. I didn't know I would miss them as much as I did when they were gone.

I talked with her a few days later. She had a job interview coming up at the YMCA. She thought she had a good chance of getting it.

Love and Other Changes

We hadn't heard from her in a couple of months. Finally Jeanne called her. She was in Kansas, staying with a friend. K. had been convicted and was at home in Tucson, wearing an ankle monitor while he awaited sentencing. He had told some people that he was going to kill her. She had gone to Kansas because she was afraid of him and he knew no one in Kansas and she had a friend there.

Over the next several weeks Jeanne left a message for her twice and I left one for her on Patrick's phone. Finally she called. Her phone hadn't been working but she had finally been able to retrieve one of Jeanne's messages. She was living with Patrick again but was unaware I'd called.

K.'s sentencing was scheduled for later this week. He'd been in jail since he was picked up after threatening to kill her. He told the judge that he hadn't done it, that Norah had made up the story and gotten her friends to say he had threatened her. But the woman who told Norah about the threat said that she had grown up with K. in a particular part of Georgia and that in the letter K. wrote her, he had used certain phrases that no one who had not grown up there would know. The judge believed her.

Lily was going to daycare every day. She was talking a lot more. Norah had taught her to say "people" and Lily would look out the window and point to cars in the street and say it: "People." Patrick had taught her to say "Oh, man" when she dropped something. As we talked, I heard a clatter in the background—maybe a plastic dish hitting the floor—followed by a tiny voice: "Oh, man." I reminded Norah how hard it was for her, only a few months ago, to even think about putting Lily in daycare.

She had a boyfriend she had met through her friend in Kansas. His name was Eugene. He was staying with her and Patrick now. He was going to college in Kansas on an athletic scholarship. In Seattle he worked at a gym, which was perfect for him as his job allowed him to stay in condition during the summer months. A couple of years ago he left school to care for his mother when she went into a depression and became suicidal. (So, I thought, he had an ability to care for a woman in crisis.) But he was back in school now. Living with Norah, he turned his paycheck over to her with instructions on how to use it: first, get what Lily needed, then get what she herself needed, then save what was left. Eugene wanted to marry her and had asked Patrick if he would object to their getting married. Patrick was all for it; Eugene was the only one of her boyfriends Patrick had ever liked.

*   *   *

Norah called. Eugene was back in Kansas for football camp, but they talked a lot by phone. She would be going to Tucson in a couple of months for her sentencing hearing. (What? This was the first I'd heard that she was facing sentencing. But she seemed to think I knew all about it.) Her lawyer told her this morning that he would be sending her a probation packet.

*   *   *

It was nearly two months before we heard from her again. She emailed Jeanne that she was in Kansas again. K. had learned that she was staying with

Patrick, so she took Lily and left. Her hearing had been pushed back until after the first of the year because she couldn't afford to travel to Arizona. She was changing her life, she said, and was avoiding the kinds of people who would obstruct her path toward a better life for herself and Lily. She was blessed to have Eugene in her life. He had brought out in her qualities that she had kept hidden because she had been afraid to reveal them.

> I can be myself open up and know that he's here to love and support me in the things I want to achieve in life I believe I truly have found a companion and I look forward to spending my days with him we do plan on getting married at some point....

A New Life

January 19, 2009.

Hello jean I just wanted to let you and Jerry know that we got back from court in Arizona Saturday night everything went well for the most part I'm on probation for at least 3 years. With that said everything else is going just fine for us Eugene is working and with the money he gets from that and his scholarship along with the money I get each month we are able to take care of everything we need. my phone is off till next week so if you need to get a hold of me just shoot me another e-mail. we miss you guys and will talk to you soon.

February 10.

hey Jean sorry it's bn a while since i wrote you we have bn real busy i never told you i don't think but Eugene and i got married last month on the 6th we have bn members of a real good church and the pastor married us after we did pre marital counseling for a few months before our big day we moved into a real nice place and are doing well I'm very happy my phone will be on Friday we are supposed to be getting our taxes back so I'll be paying my bill talk to you soon hugs.

She called. She sounded happy. Eugene was doing well. He was getting better grades than anyone else in several of his classes. This achievement had earned him a paid internship for the summer in an accounting firm. She sounded like a proud young wife. She intended to take some business classes next summer. K. was serving a thirteen-year sentence on weapons charges and money laundering. Eugene wanted to adopt Lily. Norah had visited her father to tell him about her life, but he had Alzheimer's now and didn't know who she was for much of the time she was with him.

She said she'd call us again. Jeanne and I were on her favorites list, so she didn't have to pay to talk with us.

May 18.

hello Jerry how are things going with you guys? I hope all is well these are a few pictures from our wedding that i thought you might enjoy the wedding was put together by our pastor and the rest of the church they made that day so special for me Eugene and I are truly blessed being married is not always easy we have had our trials even in this short time of being married its almost been 5 months we love each other and want to make it work and believe we have the desire and the tools to make it last i can honestly say i am happy at this point in my life i can't ask for anything else. I finally got my permit and this Wednesday I take my driving test so keep your fingers crossed well that's all the news I have for now i'll write again soon take care Lily and i miss you guys so much.

She failed her driver's test. She had done everything right except for rolling through two stop signs. A week later she wrote:

hey Jerry I wanted to share the good news with you guys today I got my license I'm legally able to drive and am so happy i never thought i would get it the written test was so challenging the driving part was pretty easy once i stopped running the stop signs.

I wrote back: "Well, congratulations! I've been imagining you, with the examiner beside you in your car, running not one but two stops. Every time I think about it, I laugh. What's Lily up to?"

May 28.

Lily is ok she likes to play with everything we found a baby sitter for her to go to twice a week so I can get a break she is getting so smart she knows her colors, numbers, and objects the head start people said they would accept her early because she is so smart I'm happy my little girl is growing up and so smart. Today I had to go to the school campus to do a walk-through I had to also get my I.D. picture and buy books classes start monday and go till july 23rd I'm really happy that I'm doing this things are looking up for me these days.

She was going to take remedial classes in math and English. It had been so long since she had done schoolwork that she couldn't remember how to do everything. She wasn't accepted by the university Eugene attended and was advised by a woman in Admissions to take on-line classes through a community college and then transfer. She had been working out, yoga and Tae Bo, and running three and a quarter miles with Eugene every Saturday.

May 31.

it's working wonders on me. I feel good about myself and love the support he gives me plus it's nice because we take Lily to a baby sitter and get the chance to have an hour to ourselves to talk about whatever I can see why you love to run every night....

In September she wrote that she had failed her classes and was taking them again, but as a regular community college student rather than on-line. She said, too, "we are expecting the latest addition to our family here soon and are very happy about that."

I told her that I admired her persevering with her schooling. "It must be frustrating for you. But when you finish school you will know you earned it. What addition to your family? Are you pregnant?"

She didn't write again until December. She was getting ready for finals. School had been hard

but I really need this for myself and for Lily she deserves to have a mother who is successful and can be a positive role model so she will grow to know the importance of an education. Yes we have another addition to our family It is a boy Eugene Weaver the 6th he was born a little while ago now I prayed that God would bless me with a son and he did. His birthday is March 13th he was born early but was perfectly healthy he weighed 7 lbs. 4 ounces and was 17 inches long I had a natural birth it took 27 minutes can you believe that I went to the hospital when I was dilated at 7 cm I didn't even feel the contractions I was up walking around talking and everything the nurses couldn't believe it they all said I make it look so easy Eugene's brother flew in and stayed home with lily at night I was in the hospital for two days and Eugene was with me the entire time lily spent the days at the hospital at first she was real jealous and didn't like the baby but now she loves him….

Replying to an email from Jeanne, she wrote the next day.

December 13.

OK I will send you guys pictures of the kid. I am going to be transferring to Eugene's school down the road … when I get to his school I'm gonna be working on my AA in Human Resources I'm happy about it. Yes it is hard being a student, wife, and a mother of two kids who require a lot of my time but I would not change anything. the kids are in daycare 5 hrs a day so I manage to get my work done in the two hrs I have after I get home from class and after they are in bed. Sacrifices have to be made for the greater good of our family is what I tell myself we want to give our kids the best possible opportunities if nothing else I want to know as a parent I did right and my kids had all the tools to be successful. We do miss you you both are dear to my heart you're like the family I never had you guys showed me what love and understanding are and made me a better person I will make sure Lily never forgets you.

To me, she wrote:

December 15.

My mother calls me from time to time she understands we will never have a great relationship and may never talk more than twice a month but she says she cares, is so proud of me that I'm able to be a better mother than she was, that was a big step for her. I have made my peace with her some what I had to forgive her for all of those horrible things she put me through for myself I don't want to have hate in my heart anymore I have the strength to be kind to her over the phone and if I don't have expectations like I had in the past I won't be let down or hurt. On a happier note Miss Lily has learned her ABC's and how to count to ten. She can also draw a circle, triangle, and square.

* * *

The next summer Norah and Eugene and their children came out to Washington for the memorial service for her father who had died a couple of months earlier, and they spent an evening with us. While I was sitting on the floor in the living room where we were all talking, Eugene Junior toddled over to me and dropped himself into my arms and proceeded to squirm until he had made a little nest for himself between my chest and my arm. I thought, A kid who can put this much trust in an adult he has just met has got to be a happy kid.

Lily had grown, of course, and spoke fluidly. She spent the evening listening to the adults until she fell asleep. Eugene was a stocky, muscular young man who was intense about everything we talked about, from his family to physical training to his ambitions to proper behavior under different situations. His aims were wealth and status, but he was able to accept the frustration of having to focus on short-term goals, convinced as he was that he would achieve his aims in the longer term. He succeeded in impressing me. Norah had just completed her first year of college. She had gained weight and she looked happy and at ease with herself for the first time in all the years I had known her.

*   *   *

Of course I continue to worry about her. I worry that her depression will come back, that it will wait and it will find an opportunity and it will return. But then I tell myself that maybe she has seen the worst that she will experience in her life, that even if there is further tribulation, she has learned to surmount it and she will find a way to overcome whatever else she must. For now she is happy, and I am happy that she is.

So here is where I'll end this story. Everybody loves a happy ending.

VI

Kyle Payment
Institutional Man

Whenever I mention Kyle Payment to someone who didn't know him at Ash Meadow, I tell the story of how Kyle once defecated in his room and placed a turd of nine or more inches just inside the threshold, and then tore the light fixture out of his ceiling with the idea that a cottage staff member would come into the room in the dark and step on the turd. When Security took him out of his room in handcuffs, he was wearing a smile that connoted both happiness and insolence, even though the security officers had avoided the turd.[1]

Another thing I mention is that Kyle was locked up when he was thirteen and, except for a couple of short breaks, he has been in prison, juvenile and adult, ever since. The last time he was returned to us was for taking a sledgehammer to his grandmother's car. We all thought this was odd because his grandmother was perhaps the one adult he truly loved, but then Kyle was odd and he often did things that were contrary to what we might have expected.

In those days I taught a class called Aggression Replacement Training that Kyle attended. It was a combination of "anger control" (including aspects of anger management), social skills designed to replace outbursts of anger, and moral reasoning. In Washington State, it reduced recidivism by 24 percent among kids who graduated from the class.[2] The class ran ten weeks, one hour a day—I often extended the time to ninety minutes—three days a week, and kids received high school credit for completing it.

On the final day of class, Kyle refused to participate and left the classroom almost as soon as the session began. He had missed several sessions over the course of the class, and if he missed one more, he would not be permitted to graduate. He knew this and I reiterated the rule to him several times before he walked out of the classroom. I can still see the tentative smile on his face, as if he was not sure where this would lead, but he was doing it

148

anyway. His case manager's response when I told him was "Kyle can be a jerk sometimes." Which, of course, was not an explanation at all. I don't generally share this memory, probably because it doesn't in itself reveal enough, except about the case manager. (In fairness to Charlie Patterson, Kyle's case manager, Kyle's psychiatrist said almost exactly the same thing when I mentioned the episode to him.)

Another episode I don't usually talk about was the time Newt Smith, our Chief of Security, brought Kyle back from the health center where a nurse had checked his blood pressure—he was on a new medication. Newt and Kyle were in the foyer. I wasn't paying much attention, but I could hear Kyle yammering insults, as usual. Then I caught a flash of movement and suddenly Kyle was on the floor and Newt was bent over him. Kyle was yelling and Newt was yelling over Kyle's voice, "Don't you put your finger in my face! Don't you *ever* put your finger in my face!"

Newt took him to our quiet room and strip-searched him, probably to demean him rather than because he suspected Kyle of concealing something, all the while Kyle screaming, "Ho!" "Bitch!" "Motherfucker!" After he locked Kyle in, Newt said—to me? to himself?—"No kid is going to put his finger in my face! No! No! I'm not going to let *any* kid do that!"[3]

As soon as he left, Kyle escalated his tantrum, yelling that he had cut himself, though he hadn't, and otherwise screaming incoherently. I had seen this kind of rage once before, when I worked in a different cottage and another staff and I took a boy down, bending him over the back of a chair by way of restraining him, and he began to scream what sounded like nonsense words— babbling, really—the words and curses pouring from his mouth, seemingly unconnected to one another. Some time later I learned that he had been raped by his stepfather after having been forced to watch as he raped the boy's sister. But I did not associate Kyle's performance with the other boy's actions then.

One incident I have shared was my own taking Kyle to the floor, triggered by his jabbing his finger at me as he had done with Newt. I don't know what this act, this finger-thrusting, signified, either to Newt or to me—perhaps in my case, it recalled a vague memory of being humiliated by a teacher—but the reaction it prompted was my grabbing his arm, and then when he pulled away, I grabbed his leg and pulled him off the fireplace platform where he had been sitting and put him on the floor. I knew even as I did it that I didn't have to do it, that he wasn't a threat to me or to anybody else, but I did it anyway. Ordinarily I felt sorry for a kid after taking him down, but this time I felt good.[4]

I don't know why I have told this story over the years. I have regretted my action that evening ever since. Perhaps by talking about it, I have tried to diffuse my sense of shame. Or perhaps I've only wanted to indicate how irritating Kyle could be.

Kyle was paroled in mid–March 2000 when he was still thirteen, and was arrested again at the beginning of April. This time he got two and a half years for Taking a Motor Vehicle Without Permission and fourth-degree assault. He was returned to us in September. He was fourteen now. He was a little taller. His voice hadn't changed yet.[5]

He was more aggressive. On one occasion, he was sent to a quiet room in another cottage for going off in his room and trying to get other kids to go off with him. While he was gone, staff stripped his room of all his belongings, a reminder that we, not he, controlled the cottage. When he returned in the morning, he took his shower and then asked who had stripped his room.

"Staff," I said. He demanded that I tell him which staff. He walked into the office where I was preparing to give out the morning meds.

I told him to get out of the office.

He told me not to shout at him.

I told him again to get out of the office.

He told me again not to shout at him.

We went back and forth like this as I moved toward him, shepherding him out.

He picked up the trashcan and threw it into the living room, then threw his towel at me. He had never assaulted a staff member before, even if it was only symbolically. Bernie, who had been monitoring the floor, came bounding across the living room and grabbed Kyle by the arm and walked him to his room, Kyle yelling that he was going to punch me in the mouth the next time I shouted at him.

Later that morning, I reported the incident to Dr. Williams, Kyle's psychiatrist. He said that Kyle was acting out because he felt unloved. I could not believe that banality had come from Williams. When I told Dick and Bernie what Williams had said, we all had a great laugh.

After lunch, out of his room for a head call, Kyle threatened me again, telling me he was going to break my glasses.

A week later, he tried to hit Gil, our newest staff member, with a flashlight he had snatched from the office when Gil was giving out meds.

Two weeks after that, Kyle picked up a pair of scissors from where the art teacher had left them on the kitchen counter and raised them as though to stab James, another recently hired staff. James and Charlie took him to the floor and James pried the scissors out of his hand.[6]

At the beginning of May 2001, two days after Kyle turned fifteen, Dick and Layton stripped his room of everything that was not attached to the floor, the ceiling, or a wall while he was at school. Then they removed everything from the top of the staff desk at the edge of the living room and the bookcase behind it, as well as the table where the jumpsuits and sweatpants and sweat-shirts were folded and set out for the kids to pick up and take to their rooms. Then Dick called Kyle up from the school.

He came up and Layton told him he was being transferred to Elk Grove, one of the two juvenile institutions that took older boys. Kyle looked around and gave a small laugh. He did not go off. Layton gave him his street clothes and told him to go to his room to change. Kyle laughed again when he saw his bare room.

He asked Layton why he was being transferred when he'd been good lately. Layton said he'd been good for a few days, yes, but only after several weeks of being terrible, and staff knew him well enough to know he would be terrible again.

Three years later, we heard that Kyle had beaten up a staff member at Elk Grove and had been transferred to the adult system. I wondered if the person he had beaten up was a woman. It had seemed to me that as Kyle had gotten older, he had become more aggressive toward girls. One of the reasons we moved him when we did was that we had learned that he was trying to put together a coalition of boys to beat up Norah Joines before she transferred to a girls' cottage.[7]

*   *   *

I had not expected to meet or even to hear anything about Kyle Payment again. He had not been on my caseload when I was at Ash Meadow. Though I had sometimes sympathized with him, we had not been close. He had not confided in me and I had not tried to explain the world to him and how to navigate it—I had not been his mentor or adviser. So the first letter from him, twelve years after I had last seen him, came as something out of the blue.

What should I say about this letter and the dozen and a half that were to follow? Together, they brought back the sadness I had felt all the time I worked at Ash Meadow. It had seemed to radiate from the kids imprisoned there and had been like a constant weight on my chest. It was years before it finally lifted, and now it had returned. In fact, I had not realized it was gone until I felt it again, beginning with Kyle's second or third letter.

Reading his letters, I recognized certain aspects of his personality that I had seen when he was a child: his chronic anger; his tendency to blame authority, or "the system," for his imprisonment; and his habit, like that of a

politician or a political commentator, of distorting information or exaggerating it so that it takes on a different meaning altogether. For example (one
that is fictitious), someone might pinch him and Kyle would claim afterward
that he had been assaulted. To be certain, the criminal justice system has
much to account for, but I caution the reader that all of the information about
Kyle's imprisonment as an adult comes from Kyle. Still, I had never known
him to make something up out of whole cloth.

I felt there was something essential in Kyle's experience of life that he
and I had not talked about, although I didn't know what it was. I sensed
he was holding back, even during our correspondence. He would say he
was going to send me something—his psychological assessment, for
instance—and then he wouldn't. He never told me what he was charged
with while in adult prison, other than his defending himself against an
assault by two guards. But this event, whether it was an assault initiated
by him or by the corrections officers, happened only once; apparently there
were several charges that arose from incidents that occurred in another
prison.[8] I felt sometimes that he was distracting me, intentionally or not,
from things that were important, but I didn't confront him on it. Neither
of us brought up the influence of possible mental illness on his behavior,
although each of us may have implied it. I've thought about it and I'm sure
he has too.

What I did not see in Kyle when he was a child is his ability and willingness, present now, to see and accept that he has contributed to his situation.
This, and his desire to educate himself, allow me to maintain my belief that
people can, and do, change.

*   *   *

Kyle was in Clallam Bay Corrections Center in northwest Washington
when he began writing me; he had not been out of prison since the last time
he came to Ash Meadow in 2001. He had read my book, *Paranoia & Heartbreak: Fifteen Years in a Juvenile Facility*, and had recognized himself in it,
even though I had changed his name and altered certain facts of his life. He
said he had been skeptical when he started the book, but then realized that
I "was not protecting any interests and [was] letting the world know about
some hard pills to swallow. I appreciated your honesty," he wrote, "even about
your own faults … but cannot think of one instance where I can say that you
were out of line."

My portrayal of him in the book was "on point." Now, he said, "I am
doing the best I can." He had eight years to go on his sentence. After reading
Paranoia & Heartbreak, he began to write his own journal that he hoped to

publish someday, as I had mine. He spent most of his days reading and writing. He said he was pretty well versed in the law now, and had even completed a paralegal course.

He had a friend who taught at one of the state universities in northern California. Kyle did a lot of writing for him. "I feel verry good about doing this as it gives me an avenue for my voice to be heard." He was also writing his life story with the help of another friend who taught at a university in Washington State. He hoped to publish this, too, after he completed it, even if he had to self-publish it.

He ended his first letter by inviting me to write back, and added a postscript: "I am old now, Jerry (27) with gray hairs (just a couple). What is the world coming to?"[9]

He had written the letter with a blue ballpoint. He did not use cursive, but printed each word in capital letters. I wondered if he knew how to write script. Some kids I had known at Ash Meadow had not been taught to write it, or even read it.

I wrote back, telling him that I was glad he liked my book. One reason I wrote it was to remind readers on the outside that prisoners are also human. And I wanted there to be a record of the people I had known at Ash Meadow, even if I used false names. I had received a number of phone calls from staff at other juvenile institutions congratulating me on the book, but I had heard also that a couple of the staff at Ash Meadow were hurt or angry, believing they had recognized themselves behind the fake names. I had written the book as honestly as I could, but I had changed the names so that someone I had depicted would be able to say, "Oh no, that isn't me. I would never have done that." I had thought more about some of the staff in this context than about the kids, although I thought that a kid getting out of prison should not be burdened by his or her past either.

I wrote all this to Kyle, and I wrote,

> I appreciate your saying that you can't think of an instance where I was out of line. But I can think of one. I took you down once when I didn't have to. I did it because I was pissed off at you. So I want to apologize now for doing that. I probably had a good reason to be pissed off, but I shouldn't have acted on it.
>
> You say you are constantly at war with yourself. That is how I remember you too—a kid who wanted to do well, but wouldn't allow himself to accomplish anything. You'd get to the edge of success in whatever you were trying to accomplish, and then you'd do something to thwart your own effort....
>
> Recently I ran into a middle-aged man I had known when he was ten or eleven years old. He recognized me ... from my name. He had been a friend of my sons, and after I was divorced he would come with them to spend Saturday and Sunday at my house. I knew he had gone to prison as an adult, but I hadn't known he had come under the "three-strikes rule," so was doing life. But eventually he applied for and received

clemency and now he's a paralegal working in a law firm in Seattle. He specializes in clemency appeals for people who are still locked up.

I wrote this to offer him a model that would encourage him to persevere. I didn't know how he would interpret this story—he might have thought I was trying to make less of his own experience—and considered deleting it from the letter, but decided finally to leave it in. I asked what was the purpose of the life story he was writing—"To help you think things through?"—and said I liked his last paragraph, "telling me you're old at 27. Kyle, on my next birthday, I'll be 70. I can hardly believe it. Seventy! I had expected to die before I was 30."[10]

* * *

"Wow! What a surprise! I am still … jazzed about receiving your response," Kyle began his second letter. No one—not other inmates or guards or his family—had believed that I had written about him in my book. After all, "Lyle Munson" was a name I had made up and how could he know I was talking about him? But my letter was proof.

He said he was glad I had responded and that I was doing well "at 70!" It was hard for him to believe I had gotten so old, or that he himself was getting there. Every time he found a gray hair in his comb, he "freaked out, like … this is not supposed to be happening."

He wanted to emphasize that I had nothing to apologize for. He remembered the incident where I took him down, but said it happened as he had intended, that he had wanted me to take him down.[11]

He said the life story he was writing was focused on his experience of incarceration more than the history of his childhood, though of course the two were related. He did not want to convey a "poor me" message, but rather to show how the prison system is broken so that it may be fixed.

Still…. He knew he was "far from innocent," but he had documents that proved the state of Washington knew his uncle was abusing him, so that when he was eleven he was afraid to go home after his release from juvenile detention because he knew his uncle was waiting for him. He was, in fact, so scared that the security officers had to carry him out of the building, and he punched one of them and was promptly re-arrested and brought back to detention, "to my own relief."

He said he had documents saying he was not to be given over to his mother when released from Ash Meadow, yet he was returned to her. He said he had suffered from mental illness since he was very young and that it was responsible, in part, for his behavior. "[Y]et nobody took any initiative to treat it and merely responded by locking me up and throwing away the key… [S]hit like this should never happen to another child."

He admitted to being bitter. He wrote that when he was thirteen he was locked up

for 21 years for stealing a car and spitting on a guard.... There [are rapists, murderers,] etc., all doing less time than me. Does that make any sense?[12] My point is, I may not be able to do anything about my sentence, but by golly, I will put this voice of mine to great use, and scream at the top of my lungs, through this pen and paper, to hopefully prevent another tragedy of this nature [from taking] place.

When you lock up a child, you break his spirit, Kyle wrote, and the child is transformed into "an immoral creature" who comes

to love no one more than himself and adopts the "me against the world" mentality, to [his] own detriment. Braking [sic] out of this prison of the mind takes time, some serious self-evaluation and the dedication to follow through [with] restructuring [his] cognitive distortions.
 I better stop there before I make you think I am crazy. I am so serious about all of this I could go on for days.

He reminded me that I had mentioned a friend whose life sentence was commuted and who worked now as a paralegal for a law firm that specialized in clemency appeals. Kyle asked me to send him contact information for the paralegal. He closed by saying he would spare me "further ramblings" and anyway, "my hand is killing me from writing."

He asked me to send him my phone number and said he would call me, pre-paid, but said too that he wouldn't have any heartburn if I didn't feel comfortable giving him my number.[13] (I didn't give him my number.)

I had known other kids—of course, Kyle was not a kid now—who wanted their lives to mean something more than only the experience of living it, and who chose writing as the way to communicate to others what they thought, or hoped, it all meant. There was the fourteen-year-old who wanted me to help him with his autobiography. He believed he would die before he was eighteen and wanted his life to count for something, even if he couldn't define what that something was. When I suggested he might find comfort in religion—he had been baptized a Catholic when he was an infant—he dismissed my suggestion, saying life was too cruel for there to be a God.

There was another boy who kept writing the first two pages of a short story over and over until he finally gave it up. And another boy who wrote memoirs rather than fiction, writing one lengthy piece and then a shorter one that he didn't finish. I was astonished by his ability to put sentences together so as to arouse an emotional response in his reader, at least in me. But while writing his second piece, he came to feel that he had no more to say, and he stopped writing before he completed it. He was also fourteen. The short-story writer was fifteen.

So Kyle's wanting to make his voice heard did not surprise me. In fact, I had often wondered how anybody, in or out of prison, could find or manufacture meaning in his life if he was not called to one of the arts and was unable to accept religious belief. (I recognize that this represents a limitation of my imagination.)

*   *   *

Kyle's confiding that his uncle had abused him helped me make sense of much of his behavior when I knew him: his preferring the company of women and girls to that of men or boys; his unprovoked cruelty toward girls, at least some girls; his chronic anger; his quickness to re-offend after each release from prison; his defying staff even when it meant harming himself.

Why did Charlie Patterson, Kyle's case manager, not pick up on the abuse, instead attributing Kyle's behavior to his being "a jerk," and Jan, our cottage director, go along with that characterization? "Sometimes he's just a jerk," and "Kyle can be a real jerk," I can recall her saying, parroting Charlie.

Both Jan and Charlie had health problems, Jan struggling with the cancer that would eventually kill her, Charlie with diabetes. Perhaps on days when they were feeling overwhelmed by their lack of energy and demands on them that could not be deferred, the temptation to take the easy path—call the kid a jerk and move on to a kid who was less complicated—became irresistible.

I wrote Kyle,

> I had no idea that your uncle abused you. Did you tell anyone in Wolf? In our staff meetings, we spent I don't know how many hours discussing you, and your having been abused never came out. Charlie thought you might be bipolar, and the chief psychiatrist—I don't remember his name—didn't know what to think. Everybody knew you had mental health problems, but no one except Charlie felt confident enough to put a label on them, and he was probably wrong.
>
> One of the difficulties in trying to figure out what mental problem affects a child is that the problem often doesn't become clear until adulthood. But your telling me now that you were abused does put a lot of your behavior in perspective. Now that I know, I don't know how I could have missed it. Or Jan—had she known, we would have adopted an entirely different treatment plan for you. If you ever get a chance to have therapy, either in prison or after you get out, I'd advise you to concentrate on the abuse. If you can come to terms with that, and your anger about that and about the system failing you, I think you'll find that the quality of your life will be greatly improved.
>
> Your library probably has some books dealing with child abuse. I think reading a couple of first-person accounts of abuse, whether sexual or physical, would be a big help to you. I used to recommend certain books to kids on my caseload who had been abused. Most of these books are written by women recalling their abuse when they were girls, but I found that boys got a lot from these books too. What is most important is discovering that other people's experience resembles yours.
>
> Jan really liked you, by the way. And the chief psychiatrist did, too. But we didn't

know what to do for you in terms of mental health, and you were getting more aggressive. Your aggressiveness was the reason for transferring you to Elk Grove.

I reminded him that in his last letter he said he had spit on a guard, and asked him if this was the assault he was charged with at Elk Grove. At Ash Meadow we were told that he had beaten up a member of the Elk Grove staff badly enough to hospitalize him or her.

I agreed with him, I wrote, that there is a lot about the criminal justice system that is unjust. For several years I had corresponded with a young woman who, as a juvenile, had been on my caseload at Wolf Cottage. She had come to Wolf about a year and a half after Kyle left. She was fourteen when she came to us and eighteen and a half when she was transferred to Purdy, the adult women's prison. She had gotten a twenty-two-year sentence, even though she had never been in trouble with the law before.

> When I tell people, including lawyers, what her sentence was, and that she was only 13 when she did her offense, everybody is shocked that she got such a long sentence. Had she committed her crime in Seattle or Tacoma, she would have been sentenced as a juvenile instead of an adult. But she was from a hick county with a hick judge and he agreed with the prosecutor to sentence her as an adult. I get pissed off even now, thinking about it again.

I told Kyle I'd emailed the paralegal I'd mentioned, but hadn't received a response yet. I said I felt I had to get his permission to give out his mailing address.[14] I included with my letter several photos my wife had taken on our recent trip to southwest France.

Kyle thanked me for the photos. He always enjoyed seeing "the wonders of the world," he said. But what most surprised him was that I looked the same as I did the last time he saw me. I even wore the same brand of jeans and the same kind of denim jacket. "That's the Jerry I remember."

He had been reading *Trauma and Recovery* by Judith Herman. He found it "very intriguing, to say the least. It has allowed me to learn about the psychology behind a lot of how prisons treat their captives. It's the littlest things that have a major psychological bearing on the prisoners, but to the untrained eye, it seems so innocent."

He recommended my reading *The Lucifer Effect: Understanding How Good People Turn Evil* by Philip Zimbardo, about the Stanford Prison Experiment where university students in the role of prison guards arbitrarily victimized other university students playing the role of prisoners.

Kyle asked me to recommend some nonfiction books. "I am open to anything and love to learn." He asked if I had read Nelson Mandela's *A Long Walk to Freedom*.

He had enclosed a two-page essay he had written, "The Essential Nonexistence of Loyalty in the Prison Context," and he asked for my thoughts on it. In it, he characterizes prison as "a place … of hopelessness and despair … a place where every man must come to grips with its stark realities and … must come to know a few dark truths."

One of these truths is that one's fellow prisoners will be disloyal, their nature—human nature—compromised by "immorality." Disloyalty arises from the hopelessness engendered by prison life. Hopelessness leads to "dehumanization" and a sense of inadequacy, of being incapable of accomplishing "anything of significance in one's life."

Prison alienates the prisoner from "worldly perspectives"—i.e., the opinions, norms, and mores of people on the outside—and leads to an "immoral" lifestyle on the inside. "Loving and sincere relationships" are resisted in the prison (presumably because of the lack of trust between prisoners).

In lieu of a sense of community, "it becomes all about the individual…. [C]onsciously or unconsciously, one sabotages any and all meaningful relationships in exchange for a well-fed immoral ego…. The prisoner must rely on his ego for a sense of worth."

The only way to do this is by making himself into what other prisoners want him to be. He must make himself into the image of himself he presents to others.

> He refuses to give, yet he takes. He longs for fame and acceptance at any cost. His celebrity is worth more than his very soul, and his ego is paramount [above] all else…. This is the immoral nature of man in the prison context. [Prison destroys] … our ability to progress into better beings, [and destroys] all hope of a better tomorrow, and finally [destroys] any and all sense of solidarity….[15]

He wrote again before I could respond, this letter coming from Stafford Creek, where he had been transferred; he didn't say why. My last letter, which I had sent to him at Clallam Bay, had been forwarded.

In this letter, he answered the questions I had asked. He said he had been transferred to the adult system because of the spitting incident. (In the age of AIDS, spitting on someone is considered assault; it may even be considered assault with a deadly weapon.) However, he had, in fact, hospitalized a member of the Elk Grove staff. He didn't identify the staff as male or female.

He had been placed in waist restraints and left in his room. He didn't say why he had been placed in restraints, but said it was a form of punishment used at Elk Grove. He was able to slip out of the restraints and when the staff came into the room Kyle attacked him or her with the chain, at the end of which was a heavy padlock.[16] The staff was struck several times in the face, fell and hit his or her head on the concrete floor and went unconscious. Kyle said he was "in awe" of what he had done, and thought, "Damn, that was a little too much."

But, he wrote,

in all honesty, I've got so much anger built up towards the "system," I cannot say I regret it, and I don't, and am actually glad that I did it. However, I can say I feel, and felt, bad for the staff because they did not deserve it, as they were one of the better ones. I know that is somewhat of a contradiction, but it is what it is. The processes of … the human mind are never simple.

He said he was not charged with this assault, but did not say why not; it is possible that he did not know. It occurred two months before he turned eighteen. Nine days after his birthday, he was transferred into the adult prison system.

Regarding his uncle's abusing him, Kyle said he didn't tell anyone "until maybe 5 years ago, when I realized that DOC was not going to give me any treatment unless I admitted to it." But DOC was not interested, or if they were, they were not interested enough to offer counseling or therapy.

He asked if I had read *Oliver Twist*. He felt "like little Oliver's struggle is my struggle, just different circumstances…."[17]

In my response, I said that while I was not condoning his attacking the Elk Grove staff, I thought he deserved credit for being honest with himself about his emotions at the time and since. I asked if this self-examination was a consequence of his reading and writing as much as he had, or did he think he would have become this thoughtful so early in his life anyway?

And I asked him if he thought his anger dominated him. "Does it affect your decisions on a daily basis, or only occasionally, or at all? I realize this sounds like a counselor's question, and maybe it is, but I am interested."[18]

Kyle's next letter came a few days after I posted mine; they had crossed in the mail. He said he had heard on the radio that Sonia May had been recommended for clemency. While I hadn't mentioned her name—in fact, I had not written him about Sonia, but about Caitlin Weber,[19] also without mentioning her name—he recognized the case as it was recounted on the news and assumed Sonia was the young woman I had been talking about. He asked me to congratulate her on his behalf and to tell her that he hoped she got her clemency.

He brought up Black Heron Press, one of my publishers and of which I was one of the founders (though he probably did not know this), and asked if it was one of "those … self-publishing situations." He had a lot of raps and poems that were "reminiscences of my upbringing and portrayals of the present [and] the emotional aspect of it all. I also plan [on] outlining my life story from the prison standpoint. This is something that [a friend on the outside] has been trying to help me organize."[20]

I told him that Black Heron Press was "a traditional publisher" in that it financed the production of the books it published and then marketed them as best it could. "This is a very different model from the self-publishing model. It is the way most publishing used to be done."

I encouraged him to write his memoir, even if it was difficult and he grew frustrated. "Writing means searching inside yourself, and this can be painful. But over the long haul, the insight you gain is worth the pain. Writing can give meaning to your life, Kyle. I would be interested in reading your life story when you have finished it. I can see from your letters that you write well and, as I have said, you are thoughtful."

I brought him up to date on the staff he had known at Ash Meadow. I talked with Dick Teale now and then. Layton had retired. Bernie was working security for Bill Gates now. Charlie Patterson had transferred to the juvenile parole system.

> I don't know if you heard, but Jan died from cancer a few years ago. It was quite a surprise for me. I actually learned about it from Sonia who heard it from [one of the Ash Meadow school staff who visited her occasionally]. I would have expected Dick to tell me, but he didn't think to. I thought the world of Jan, and had talked with her only a month before she died. She really liked you, by the way. I think I told you that.[21]

Writing back, Kyle said he'd had some bad news, "probably better labeled news I don't like." The prison had just placed him on an "indefinite program," meaning he would be housed in Segregation, "the hole," indefinitely. Normally, he wrote, they give specific sentences—six months, say, or a year—but recently they had been confining some inmates, "mostly gang leaders," to the hole indefinitely. Before, when he went to the hole, he knew how long he would be there if he behaved well, but now there was no specified time he had to serve. "[T]hey will let me out whenever they desire, if ever. Sounds like the story of my life!"

Replying to the questions I had asked two letters back, he said,

> I do not believe I would have been so thoughtful, had I not had many years of no choice but to reflect and get to know my inner self, as tormenting as it is at times. It's safe to say, and very sad, but had I been on the streets I would probably be highly addicted to meth[,] living a criminal lifestyle. My whole family, minus a ... few, suffer from this addiction. I say this because practically my whole life I have idolized my father and wanted nothing more than to be just like him. This is how I got into stealing cars. I stole cars because that's what my dad was notorious for, and I felt like I needed the same reputation. I had no other reason to steal cars. So, in a way this imprisonment was/is a blessing in the sense that it gave me a realistic perspective on life.... You asked if my anger dominates me.... [I]nstinctively I want to say yes, but as I pondered the question, I would say no ... because I don't even have to be mad ... to do something. What I think dominates me is my ego.... I've found my ego to be quite disturbing in

the sense [that] it is extremely hard to suppress, especially when it has controlled me for so long.[22]

A week later, he wrote that he was saddened to hear about Jan's death.

As I think about it now, I seem to remember her going through chemotherapy.... I remember her losing her hair and coming in with a hat on for some time. She was a nice and compassionate woman, even though she could be stern and I didn't like it [when she was stern]....

I am not sure if I have actually told you this, but I hated (as strong as the word is) all of you back then. But as I have matured and have had time to reflect on my own actions, I have realized a lot of people were actually trying to help me. It is probably safe to assume that the reason I wasn't able to be helped then [was] because of my distrust [of] authority figures.... [N]obody was able to brake [sic] my shell.

Growing up, Kyle had seen his father arrested and "taken away from me" many times, and he thought that the reason he had developed a hatred for authority, especially law enforcement, was because of this. He also remembered "talking shit" about the military and saying, when he heard about a soldier dying in one of our wars, "That's what they get," as though, because he wore a uniform, the soldier deserved to die. But now one of his favorite songs was "American Soldier," and every time he heard Toby Keith sing it, "a cloud of depression, sorrow and uneasiness sweeps over me." He admired soldiers' bravery and strength, he said, and thought his change of heart about them indicated his own growth and maturation.

He mentioned Bernie, the Wolf Cottage staff, who had become a friend of his grandmother after they ran into each other at a Costco. Kyle remembered that the night before he was transferred to Elk Grove Bernie brought him a slice of strawberry cheesecake. Bernie's birthday had been a day or two earlier, as had Kyle's, and he had saved a piece from his cake to give to Kyle. "That cake was delicious!" he wrote. He couldn't imagine Bernie as a bodyguard now.

Kyle said he would be getting a TV soon. In the hole, prisoners had to earn the privilege of having a TV. He figured that in about three weeks he would have earned enough points from good behavior to get one.[23]

It was a month before I responded. I had been traveling, and with the travel and the jet lag and my beginning to think that beyond reminiscing, Kyle and I did not have a lot to talk about, I delayed writing.

Kyle, however, wrote again only a couple of days after posting his previous letter. He said he had a court hearing scheduled for September 30th that was stressing him out. He said, too, that he was going to send me a copy of "a full psychological evaluation" that was done on him a couple of years ago. He wanted me to read it.[24] (I never received it.)

I finally wrote at the end of October. I said I had talked with the paralegal I had told him about, and he said he wanted Kyle to call him. I gave Kyle his work-phone number.

I asked how his hearing had gone, and asked, too, what it was about.[25] (Kyle never told me.)

In his return letter, Kyle wrote that he was agitated because he had just received a proposed plea agreement from the prosecutor. Again, he did not say what he had been charged with. The prosecutor was offering a ten-year sentence added to the sentence he was serving now. Kyle said he would never agree to that.

> That would leave me with a release date when I am 45 years old. I have already been [in prison] since I was 13 years old. I don't even see how they … find some rationale in their heads that … even [seems] fair. Truthfully, I have prepared myself mentally for never getting out of prison. I am so used to this place, I can't even say I would be successful [in adapting to life outside of prison] when I got out, even though I would want to be.
>
> A lot of people do not realize that modern day oppression goes on right here, right now. It is just … masked.
>
> He said his older brother had just been returned to prison for the third time. He was in Walla Walla. Kyle had gotten permission to write him and had already received a letter from him, so was pretty jazzed about that. He had been really moved, too, to see so many from JRA involved in Sonya's case.[26] Never would have thought that people [who were] a part of the "system" cared enough to take time out of their personal lives to advocate for justice. I guess there is humanity of sorts in those in the system. If you get the chance read this book called *The Lucifer Effect: How Good People Turn Evil*, by Philip Zimbardo. Great book!![27]

He asked me how my trip to Germany went. "What did you do, see, etc.?" And he thanked me for giving him the paralegal's phone number. He said he would ask for approval to call him.[28]

* * *

"I'm glad you were moved [by the turnout for Sonia's clemency hearing]," I wrote, "but I was also a little surprised. Weren't you aware of how fond Jan was of you?" I remembered that I had mentioned Jan's affection for him in earlier letters, but repeated myself here because Kyle seemed to be slipping into the mode, once again, of denigrating authority even when it was not justified.

> And your psychiatrist—I don't remember his name—could always find a way to downplay your acting out….
>
> Staff, some of us, grew very fond of some of the kids we worked with. Jan and her husband adopted a boy they had worked with at The Rivers; they worked at The Rivers before coming to Ash Meadow. I would have adopted a kid I worked with, but I was

single then and didn't think I could give a troubled kid the attention he would need.... Bernie and I used to talk about how just plain lucky we were—with less luck, we could have been born into poverty, which would have increased the likelihood that prison lay waiting for us....

I'm probably pissing you off by harping on how life is unfair. You know it is. I once had to talk with a well-known man whom I disliked owing to his reputation—I had not met him. He was very wealthy, lived in a great, brick house, etc. I was going to ask him to donate money to something. (I had some unusual jobs when I was in college.) His wife answered the door. He was sitting behind a table in the room he used as an office. We had been talking for quite a while before I realized he was in a wheelchair— he had a blanket over his legs and the wheels, so I had thought it was an ordinary desk chair. Then he told me that his son had recently committed suicide. This man was in agony. By the time I left him—he did make a donation—I was grateful that even with the difficulty I had in my life, I did not have his.

One of the things I've learned is that nobody gets through life unscathed. Some have it worse than others, and those who have it better should (I think) do what they can to ease others' pain, but everybody experiences pain of some kind.

Okay—enough preaching.[29]

Kyle said he had talked briefly with the paralegal, but the paralegal asked him to call back in five minutes—something had come up—and when Kyle called back, no one answered. He hadn't had the opportunity to try again, but intended to.

He said he knew that a lot of staff at Ash Meadow cared about the kids there, "but like I told you before, I don't think I actually knew it then. Layton was always good to all of us, although when he got mad he could be stern. It's funny because when I run into people until this day, who were at Ash Meadow, we always start making Layton impressions."

Kyle hadn't known that Jan had adopted a boy from The Rivers.

That gives me a whole new outlook. These are the types of things I believe that staff need to be telling kids, because I honestly believe that it will humanize the relationship between the staff and kids. Really[,] all of you were like strict parents who provided structure that a lot of us never had.

Here's something else I have always had a problem with, putting us in quiet rooms.... [F]or myself, all it did was reinforce my anger and hatred at the time, and ultimately it hardened me in a sense beyond repair. A lot of times if someone would have come to talk with me, I would have calmed down.... Listen to me, Jerry, that stuff was not cool at all. Imagine yourself at that age, locked in a small box, with nothing to do except listen to everybody else laughing and watching TV....

Alright, Jerry, I'll stop chomping on your ear for now. Take care and I hope to hear from you soon.[30]

I encouraged Kyle to try again to contact the paralegal. "I think he's a straight arrow," I wrote, "and would do for you what he could...."

You said you thought staff at Ash Meadow should have told kids that some of us adopted children we had gotten to know in prison. I agree that it would have humanized the relationship between staff and kids, but only a few staff did this. How would a kid feel who wanted to be adopted, and knew of it happening, but who was not himself adopted? Wouldn't he feel rejected? And, if he had parents or grandparents, how would they feel about a staff wanting to adopt their kid or grandchild? They have the legal right to refuse.

Also, it was against the rules for a staff to have a relationship with a kid after he/she left prison. The idea was to protect the kid against being exploited by a staff—in fact, I can think of one case where a staff tried to pimp a girl who was released to parole. (He was fired.) And I know of another case, at a different institution, where a female staff got involved with a boy after he got out—his parole officer found out and she was suspended from her job for a year.

But you're right—kids want to personalize the relationship, and I guess staff do too, some of them. Officially, staff weren't supposed to buy Christmas gifts for the kids, but so many staff ignored this rule by buying presents for the kids on their caseloads that the administration overlooked it. Kids, after they were released, would sometimes try to maintain, or reestablish, a relationship they had had with a staff they liked. Staff could have such a non-intimate relationship with a former resident as long as the staff got permission from his cottage director. So I, for instance, kept up with a couple of kids I had known who had gone to group homes. But I had Jan's permission, and the group homes agreed to it, too. Kids I had known years before, when I worked at Swan Cottage, used to call me at Wolf just to make sure I was still around, or because they needed someone to talk to.

Your point about our putting kids in quiet rooms when what they needed was to talk to someone is well taken. The purpose of the quiet room was to defuse a situation— for example, if two kids had been in a fight—or to protect a kid from himself—for example, when a kid was suicidal—or someone else, or to keep a kid from harming another kid. But certainly some staff used the quiet room as punishment. Which was not what the quiet room was meant for. Also, if you have a staff taking time away from the cottage routine to talk with kids, the other staff will resent it, because it means they have to cover for him on the floor, or delay doing other work until he is finished. It was a constant complaint that I, for instance, took too much time talking with kids in the office. But it was important to me to get to know a kid, and talking with him as long as he needed to talk seemed the best way to do this. At Swan I used to take kids on my caseload out for a walk and a talk during quiet time, but you couldn't do this at Wolf.

That was funny, what you said about people who knew Layton at Ash Meadow imitating him. Did I tell you he retired? He did, a couple of years ago.

Well, Kyle, enough for now. Tell me how your life is going now. If we talk only about Ash Meadow, we're going to run out of things to talk about.[31]

A week later, he wrote:

You asked me about my "life" as I know it now. I propose the questions, what is "life"? Is this … "life"? Can a person have a legitimate "life" … when they are … trapped inside a concrete tomb of hopelessness and despair?

I don't even know where to begin. The simple answer is, my "life" now is fucked up…. I am still going to court in Mason County and Grays Harbor County, where these crooks are persistent in their efforts to make sure I never get out of prison. They want to give me 40 years! You are not that old, Jerry, your eyes are not playing tricks on you, you read that correctly.

About a month or so ago, the prosecutor offered me a consolidated "plea bargain" with the Mason County cases and Grays Harbor County, in which I would plead guilty [in exchange] for a 10-year sentence. I laughed and ripped up the paperwork…. There's no way I am taking that. That would put my release date at 2031, when I am 46 years old [sic]. Bear in mind I have been in [prison] since March 11, 2000, when I was 13 years old. The reality is after a 13-year-old child gets locked up for 31 years straight, he is not going to want to go home, for the simple [reason] that he will be too damned institutionalized. This is all he knows. Cars will be flying by then!

Now on top of this, I've got these corrupt judges (no exaggeration) that are clearly in cahoots with the prosecutor, and are looking to hang me. I promise you there is no justice, and this court shit is all a sham. My only hope is 12 reasonable jurors who have enough morale [sic] to see through DOC's lies, propaganda, and cover-ups.

Don't get me wrong, I am not saying that I did not do [anything], because I did—that something was [to] defend myself from an attack perpetrated by two guards. It's called self-defense, so what I did was not a violation of law. Of course, they *destroyed* the camera footage of what really happened, and made it my word versus theirs, and we both know how that battle turns out.

That's one piece of my puzzle of existence. On top of all of this, my whole family are all dope fiends and have officially turned their backs on me. This includes my sister, mom, brothers, everyone! Earlier this year, my own mom stole $200 of mine that was given to her by my friend to put on my phone account, just so she could buy meth. Then after she stole it, [she] had the nerve to tell me "Fuck you, boy, don't call me." I [would] kill her if I had the chance. I know that is extreme, but it's a reality in my mind.

That's what is going on in my life right now amongst the other miscellaneous b.s. going on as a part of daily prison life.

Hopefully I did not overload you with too much. But the truth is, some things in life are what they are, and we can't do anything about them.

Happy holidays, and I hope to hear from you soon. What's going on with Sonya? Take care.

PS. No, I have not been able to get ahold of [the paralegal] again. I don't know what the deal is. It's kind of disappointing though.[32]

Neither of us wrote over the next six months. On my part, I could think of nothing to say that I hadn't already said. I suspected Kyle felt the same. Then, in June, I received a letter from him. He had seen a documentary on TVW about a girl who had done time in Ash Meadow. After her release, she earned a BA in criminal justice from Washington State University. Governor Gregoire, the governor then, pardoned her and she now worked in the Juvenile Rehabilitation Administration.

Kyle wrote: "It's a great story that gives me hope, or shall I say, renews and reinforces my hope. It really is how I envision myself—an effective champion of youth." He said he couldn't sleep that night after he watched the program. "[M]y head was spinning, and I ended up having my dreams dominated by her. Crazy, I know!"

He said his friend who had been teaching in northern California was going to move to San Marcos and would teach at the state university there. So, beginning in the fall, Kyle would be taking his classes "unofficially"—that is, not for credit. "But it's going to allow me to learn, as well as lend my voice and perspective in the classroom. I am looking forward to this."[33]

I wrote back that I hadn't known the girl in the documentary. At least, I didn't remember her.

I told him my wife and I had been to Europe again, and asked if he wanted me to send him some photos. And I asked what he was reading now.[34]

I really had nothing to say. I was only trying to maintain contact.

In another letter, written two weeks later, I described some of the pictures my wife had taken on our trip: one of me on a bicycle in Bruges; the Eiffel Tower; Les Invalides; the façade of the Anne Frank House.

I told him that the governor had refused to grant Sonia clemency, but had suggested she try again in three years. "So she's doing what she needs to do to try again." Meaning she was continuing to take college courses, working at her job in the prison, and doing volunteer work.

Again, I had nothing to say, but was only making small talk.[35]

Two weeks later, I wrote Kyle that I had sent him a letter with photos, but the prison had notified me that the letter was rejected because I had enclosed too many pictures. Apparently an inmate was permitted to receive ten or fewer. The photos were not returned.[36]

*   *   *

Kyle had not been writing me, though I had sent him three letters since his last one. I didn't know why he had stopped writing, but I was reluctant to drop my correspondence with him. I searched through his letters for something to respond to.

He had asked a couple of times if I had heard of the Stanford Prison Experiment, from which much of *The Lucifer Effect*, the book by Philip Zimbardo, is drawn. I had. "It created quite a stir," I wrote now.

> People didn't want to believe that we (human beings) are as susceptible to authoritarian rule as we are. But another point that I have not heard addressed is that this experiment indicates also that the human conscience, at least in young people, is easily manipulated. It wasn't known at the time the experiment was done, but we have learned since that the conscience is not fully developed until people are in their mid–20s. The experiment was done mostly with undergraduates, people in their late teens or early 20s. It would be interesting to do the same experiment with older people, say people 30 years old or older, in the role of the guards. Although, I have to say, I would not want to be the person to design that experiment, and I would not want to participate in it.

I wrote that Sonia was doing well. "[S]he gets a lot of support from other people, her family especially, and she has kept her spirits up by [helping] other people. She is known for this and, in fact, the prison authorities have encouraged her."

Kyle had asked me in one of his letters to recommend some nonfiction books to him.

It's been a while since I read it, but Barbara Tuchman's *The Guns of August* sticks in my mind. It's about the run-up to World War I, and how none of the European powers, except Germany, wanted to go to war, but all of them fell into it because they didn't anticipate how other countries would respond to their actions. This goes for Germany also, who thought it would be a short war and that they would win it. The British also thought it would be over by Christmas. It lasted four years and millions of people were killed.

President Kennedy had read the book and it influenced the way he handled the Cuban Missile Crisis. Curtis LeMay, the Air Force Chief of Staff, wanted to bomb both Cuba and Russia with nuclear weapons, but Kennedy refused, insisting on a diplomatic solution, which is why we are all still here.

Recently I read Norman Maclean's *Young Men and Fire*. In 1947 or '48 (I've forgotten which) a smokejumper crew parachuted into a small fire in Montana.[37] They thought they would be able to put it out in a day. But the wind caught it and it crowned (rushed through the tree tops). At one point, the flames were over 30 feet high. All but three of the crew were killed—burned or suffocated. It is the worst tragedy in smokejumper history. The author spent decades investigating it. The most fascinating finding, for me, at least, is that all three of the survivors saved their own lives by doing something they had not been trained to do, or that was counter to the training they had had. Their thinking was sound, if unorthodox, but the thinking of those killed was also sound. But none of them had ever been in a situation like this, and the training they had had simply did not apply.

Another book I read recently was *Former People* by Douglas Smith. It's about the destruction—meaning the killing—of the Russian aristocracy during the Russian Revolution in the early 20th century. The title, *Former People*, indicates they weren't regarded as people by the revolutionaries. So when they were sent to labor camps in Siberia, they weren't entitled to write or receive mail, and when they were executed, their relatives might not be told, but would go on believing that their husbands or their sons were still alive.

I can't say this was a fun book to read, but I think it's important that people (we) are informed about other people's suffering. For one thing, it gives you a perspective on your own place in the world. You remember Bernie at Ash Meadow? He and I used to say, when we looked at some of the kids we had in Wolf, "There but for the grace of God go I." We didn't mean that God loved us more, but that we just lucked out by not being prisoners ourselves. In especially bad times in my life, I've reminded myself that there is someone who has it worse. And there is always someone who has it worse.[38]

Kyle wrote back, saying he had received ten of the photos I had sent, but the prison had rejected eleven others. He had appealed this decision, but the prison authorities had upheld it. Limiting the number of pictures a prisoner could receive was a new policy, he said. It went into effect only two weeks before he received them. He thanked me for sending them, and said he was going to mail the rejected photos back to me so I could send them again. "I enjoy seeing the wonders of the world." He had used these exact words once before, referring to the photos I'd sent in an earlier mailing.

He was trying to remember the title of a particular book, something like *The Life of a Boy Soldier*. He could see in his mind the cover of the book—a young African boy with an assault rifle, standing alone. The author, who Kyle thought might be from Somalia, was eventually rescued and rehabilitated and came to America, "where he is thriving…. This book came to mind when you mentioned the book, *Former People*."

He referred to my mention of the Stanford Prison Experiment in my last letter. "Yeah, the Stanford Prison Experiment was pretty revealing[,] to say the least. I've got the book called *The Lucifer Effect*…. I [saw] a lot of parallels to the modern day prison that I now endure. A lot of people may not see it, without actually living in the middle of it."

He asked if I read fantasy novels, and recommended Terry Goodkind's Sword of Truth series.[39]

In a postscript, he alluded to Sonia May's loss of her appeal to the governor for clemency. "That's straight B.S. how they did Sonia.[40] That don't make no sense. What more could they ask for? Stuff like that extremely irritates … me."

In my response, I wrote,

You said in your last letter that you were trying to remember the title of a book. It's *A Long Way Gone: Memoirs of a Boy Soldier*, by Ishmael Beah… [H]e has another book out, *Radiance of Tomorrow*. The first one is nonfiction and the second one is a novel. I read the first one, and thought it was wonderful. I bought *Radiance*, but haven't read it yet.

Beah has been to Seattle a couple of times, promoting his books. I saw him at a small bookstore in north Seattle when he was talking about *Radiance of Tomorrow*. He's a small, fit-looking man and a very polished speaker. If I remember correctly, he's from Sierra Leone in West Africa. He's a gifted writer, as you know, and seems to have come to terms with the killing he did. I asked him what became of the kids who hadn't been able to make the transition to civil life after a childhood at war. He said they remain in the rehabilitation camp. I gather these are people whose paranoia or PTSD is so severe that either they don't want to be released or the government doesn't trust them enough to release them.

Beah doesn't use quite the same vocabulary you and I do. I doubt that he's familiar with the concept of PTSD in anything but superficial terms. I was there with a journalist I know who also suffers from PTSD, owing to the several wars he's covered. When Beah shrugged off [my question about] the kids … who remain in the camp, my friend said that those were the people he was interested in. They are the ones I am interested in too….

I recently finished reading *The 900 Days* by Harrison Salisbury. It's a history of the siege of Leningrad (now called St. Petersburg), the cultural center of Russia, by the

Germans throughout most of World War II. It was so moving that I keep thinking about scenes in it even though it's been two or three months since I finished it. The biggest problem was starvation. Over a million people starved to death. They ate everything they could: shoe leather, their pets, some people ate other people, but, except for those who turned to cannibalism, they continued to die of the effects of starvation.

Well, with that cheery note, I'll sign off for now. Let me know what you're reading now.[41]

Kyle did not write back. It was almost four years before I wrote him again, informing him that I was including him in a book I was working on. He wrote me, full of enthusiasm and insisting that I use his real name. I tried to dissuade him—neither of us knows what the future will bring, I said, and he might someday regret allowing readers to know his identity—but he was adamant and I acquiesced.

We corresponded for several months and then stopped again. I anticipate writing him again eventually.

VII

Jan Boats (1942–2009)

I do not remember when I met Jan. She probably came over to Swan Cottage when I worked there and Herman, her husband, was the cottage director and she was the director of Ram Cottage next door. I do not remember speaking much with her in those days, although I did have lunch with her and Herman once when all three of us were attending a conference in Tacoma.

Around the time she transferred from Ram to Wolf Cottage she was diagnosed with breast cancer. When I moved to Wolf a year later, she was ill from chemotherapy. She used to lie down on a mat in the cottage craft room, away from the phones and the fax and the kids and her staff, and take a twenty- or thirty-minute nap every day. One of the staff, her longtime friend Margareta, would stand guard at the door to prevent anyone from disturbing her. She had been fighting her cancer for almost a year then, and she fought it for another ten years before it took her. First her breast, then her spine, then her liver. Each time she pushed it back with new chemicals, different therapies. Then it was her liver again and her kidneys, and this time she couldn't fight it off. Even at the last, though, she thought she still had a chance; she applied for Social Security three days before she died.

We were devoted to her, most of us, her staff. We were a solid team at first, and Dick, Bernie, Layton and I were its stalwarts. In Wolf, we talked at staff meetings in a way that would have been discouraged or even squelched elsewhere. That was my experience in Whale and Bull when I worked in those cottages. A number of us at Wolf had graduate degrees or were working toward a graduate degree, and four of us had retired from military service. Three of us had been to war. This combination of personal histories was not to be found in any other cottage. The resourcefulness and tolerance you learn if you have spent years in the military, especially if you have been to war in a country not your own, and the habit, perhaps even the love of refining your ideas through discussion and argument all came into play in our staff meetings, in defining problems and searching for solutions, or for ways to avoid implementing administration dicta.

Jan told me once that all of us who worked for her would be considered misfits in any other cottage. Certainly a number of us had had problems elsewhere. I had been forced to leave Whale when a staff member with more influence than I had complained about me to the director.[1] Charlie Patterson had also had to leave another cottage. Layton, for his own reasons, had followed Jan to Wolf when she transferred from Ram. As far as I know, Layton's and Dick's and Bernie's records were relatively clean.

If we were an uncommon collection, Jan was an uncommon cottage director. Had we had a director with less breadth of experience—she had been a teacher, a college administrator, a state legislator, a city councilwoman, and the mayor of the city she lived in—the work would have been less stimulating than it was and we could not have accomplished what we did. For five years, we had the only sustained Aggression Replacement Training program on campus.[2] We had the only anti-violence therapy group on campus. We were one of only two cottages that had a treatment group for boys who had been sexually abused. And, when we began getting girls who had been sentenced as adults and had many years to serve, we transformed the cottage from a place where we limited kids' activities to school, work details, minimal recreation time, and residing in bare rooms devoid of color to one of livability where kids, depending on their behavior, were allowed radios in their rooms, books, playing cards, jigsaw puzzles and posters, and where they had as much time out of their rooms as staff could manage.

For a number of years, there was almost no turnover, and then there was—not among the four of us, Jan's stalwarts, but with some of the staff that decided to go to work in one of the parole systems, adult or juvenile, or opted for office work in the upper echelons of the Juvenile Rehabilitation Administration. One went into the army. Another transferred to a sex-offender cottage. I believe the beginning of the departures from Wolf coincided with the first recurrence of Jan's illness and the diminishment of energy she could commit to the cottage. She missed work and Layton, who was the staff supervisor now, was not an adequate substitute.

It was during this period that Jan hired several staff who, in the opinion of many of us both inside and outside the cottage, should not have worked with kids. She hired a man who had been laid off from a career job in the private sector and was unable to find another until Jan offered him a slot, but who so feared being on the floor with the kids that he spent every minute he could at the computer, even stealing computer time from other staff; a (white) woman who complained that she had been treated unfairly by her supervisor at the boys' cottage she had worked in previously, implying that the unfairness was gender-based, and who treated with contempt black males and males she suspected of being gay; and a (black) man disliked throughout the campus for his rudeness and his tendency to ignore or deprecate what other staff said. This man fought verbally with all white male staff and often pretended not to hear black women when they spoke to him. Eventually he was suspended for beating up a resident and did not return to Ash Meadow.[3]

Race was important to Jan. Like Herman, she believed that one way of compensating for the effects of discrimination against African Americans was to hire them when you could. But her sympathies were not limited to African Americans. Like Herman in this way, too, she felt for anyone who she thought had not been given a fair shake. And this sympathy, I think, combined with the loss of energy caused by her cancer and the punishment she took from Ash Meadow's administration, sometimes impaired her judgment.

As we line staff tended to regard the residents, so Jan looked at us through the lens of our personal histories. Frank, the man who was afraid of working the floor, had been damaged by a difficult divorce, she said. Likewise the woman who disliked gays and black men and boys. (Jan eventually concluded that this woman simply hated men of whatever stripe.) Jan never confided to me what in the background of Julius, the man who beat up the resident, invoked her sympathy, but it was clear to all of us other staff that there was something.

She told me once that when I transferred to Wolf from Whale Cottage, I looked broken, like someone had beaten the hell out of me. But my own history was not always important to her. I remember her saying on another occasion, "If you weren't so good [a counselor], I'd fire you." I had no idea what she was alluding to, but she was serious, though apparently not angry. I was at the computer in the staff office and she was standing at the counter near the med box, looking at the announcements and memory joggers on the corkboard above it. I laughed, but she did not. This was during a period when Frank was badmouthing me; Jan was quite fond of Frank. I loved her anyway.

She did what she could to protect her staff and the kids in the cottage from an administration seemingly bent on doing us harm. Herman had sued the institution, JRA, the superintendent, and one of the associate superintendents for having demoted him without cause, and he had won. Given another position as cottage director, he was then fired owing to allegations about him, the nature of which were unclear and which I cannot recall now.[4] He sued again, but this time accepted a cash settlement accompanied by an apology, and then retired.

For years afterward, several of the administrators retaliated against him by punishing Jan and after Clara Beam, one of the associate superintendents, came to work at Ash Meadow, Jan's staff. Jan was not always successful at deflecting the administrators' wrath, but we appreciated her trying.

She bent when she had to, when nothing else was left to her. When every attempt to evade a dictum she knew would be damaging to her cottage or to her staff failed, she gave in. She would eventually rationalize her defeat by saying that the administrator who was the perpetrator was misunderstood, that actually he or she had good intentions. This was a way of salving her self-esteem, of course, lying to herself in order to convince herself that her loss was less damaging than it was. But it was also an attempt to accommodate herself to an adversary more powerful than she was.

A couple of years after I left Ash Meadow, she tried to persuade me, as she had before, that Clara Beam had changed and was trying to be helpful now. I didn't buy it, as I had not bought it before. Clara, I thought, was someone who needed to inflict harm; one after another, she targeted cottage staff, in Wolf and in other cottages, until they left Ash Meadow.[5] If Jan was apologizing for her now, it meant that Clara had found another way to screw her.

In appearance, Jan reminded me of Hillary Clinton, although I may have been the only person who saw a resemblance. She was short, with blond-brown hair until she lost it from chemotherapy. When it grew in, it came in gray and she did not change it. She may have tended toward weight gain anyway, but this was made worse by her body's response to the chemo. It must have been hard for her; she told me that when she was younger, she used to run seven miles a day. She reminded me of Hillary Clinton, too, in her perseverance, her singular determination to see something through. Yet she was capable of putting something aside, perhaps forever, if she became convinced that she could not get others to espouse it.

She knew bureaucracy and she knew politics. We shared the view that bureaucracy is made up of human beings who, in large part, are out to serve themselves, to advance their own influence and careers. In this, they are like corporate executives, but you would have to add the accumulation of personal wealth as a driving force in order to draw an accurate picture of the latter. The description of high-level bureaucrats applied also to most politicians, but because politicians' careers are often more volatile than those of bureaucrats and businessmen, they are more open to horse-trading. But Jan believed that there are idealists in all of these arenas, even if at times they have to disguise or conceal themselves.

She idolized Al Gore (and correspondingly regarded George W. Bush as akin to the anti–Christ) and also Bill Clinton. She did not see a correlation between Clinton's sexual escapades and his ability to govern, except as the Republicans were able to cripple his administration by ballooning the significance of his infidelities. She respected Hillary Clinton, regarding her as a political extension of her husband, but abandoned her for Barack Obama early on. Obama, she thought, had vision. He was refreshing.

"For a Democrat?" I asked. We were on the phone. This was in 2008 and she and Herman had just got back from attending the Democratic convention in Denver. Cancer had been detected again, marking the end of her most recent remission. She seemed confident that she would beat it this time too.

"After all," I said, "Bush had a vision too. Or maybe it was an hallucination."

This made her laugh.

*   *   *

I retired early in 2006. After I retired, I was free to re-establish contact with kids—now adults—I had gotten to know in Ash Meadow. By "free," I mean I did not require the permission of anyone at Ash Meadow to do anything. Had I still been employed there, my wife and I probably would not have been permitted to invite Norah Joines into our home after she was raped and made pregnant.

Caitlin Weber had also been on my caseload, and our relationship has carried through all the years since she transferred to Purdy, the women's corrections facility in western Washington, when she was eighteen.[6] Since her transfer, my wife and I have visited her regularly and talk on the phone with her several times a month.

It was during one of these calls that I learned Jan had died. Sonia May, who was also in Purdy, told Caitlin. Ms. Johns, from the school in Ash Meadow, had told Sonia. Ms. Johns visits Sonia as my wife and I visit Caitlin, though not as often. When she told me, Caitlin said she knew I would be upset, but she thought I would want to know. I thanked her for telling me.

I was upset. Jan had been my boss, true, but we had also worked together as colleagues and I had regarded her as my friend. I had worked in Wolf Cottage for seven years and, with her and Dick and Layton and Bernie, had gone through a number of hard times there.

I waited a couple of days to call Dick because I wanted to give the distress I felt time to diminish. Dick, who still worked at Wolf Cottage, said the memorial service had been the best he'd ever been to. Herman had really done it right; everybody had complimented him on it. Dick apologized for not calling me. Although I had spoken with him and Jan occasionally since I left Ash Meadow, I had retired three and a half years before and I was certain he simply had not thought to call.

He said there had been no announcement in the *Daily Bulletin*, the internal information sheet distributed at Ash Meadow, that Jan had died. Four days after her death, the superintendent came down to the cottage to talk to the staff. No one spoke to him.

When I picture her now, she is most often at the coffee pot in the staff office in Wolf Cottage, or at the microwave oven beside it, or she is at the computer on her desk, talking to me or another staff member about something entirely unrelated to what is on the monitor. Once I found her playing a game on the computer. I hadn't known she did that. I knew Herman read fantasy novels in his office, but I hadn't known Jan played computer games. When I teased her about it—it was an institutional no-no; computers were to be used only for Ash Meadow business—she laughed and said, "Caught me," and went back to her game.

VIII

Further Observations and Thoughts on the Residents of Ash Meadow

"[Y]outh who ... receive the harshest penalties in the criminal justice system (1) are disproportionately youth of color and (2) may be those in most need of assistance from the state and the very systems that punish them. Several studies show that these individuals tended to be raised in poor neighborhoods, had limited education, had mental disability, and were themselves subject to physical and sexual violence. Some individuals ... report that they, or else a parent or sibling, had been victims of violent crime prior to their offense; many others spoke of being abandoned and surviving without a stable home prior to their offense."[1]

Children in Prison is my third, and final, book concerned with the experience of children incarcerated in "Ash Meadow," a facility in Washington State. The first two books, *Paranoia & Heartbreak* and *In the Spider's Web*, were set almost entirely in the prison. *Children in Prison*, focusing as much or more on the lives of children before and after incarceration as on their lives during, allows us to view them in a larger social context, letting us also gain insight into the relationship between the lives of these children before prison and what happens to them later.

This approach may be troublesome for some readers, because it can confuse ideas of guilt and responsibility. What may be easy to see as an issue of individual guilt when listening to a resident's recollections of his life before prison may become cloudy when exposed to the experiences behind those recollections as they were originally lived, or as close to being lived as words and memory allow.

In this book, I have concentrated on the lives of six juvenile offenders.

For the most part I have eschewed statistical studies of juvenile crime, its precedents and its aftermath, except to educate myself. I have found little in these studies to disagree with. In fact, I have found that my own experience and research on youth offenders reinforces the statistical data. But statistics do not reveal much about the lived lives of those they try to describe. I have tried, rather, to portray the lives of young people I've known, including the emotional aspects of their lives, in such a way as to allow the reader to see the bonds of humanity that link people outside prison with those inside, to perceive that much of what separates those inside from those outside is the result of things beyond the control of either: the family, neighborhood, country they were born into; their race or ethnicity; their place in the social and economic hierarchies; the quality of education available to them; their mental stability and health; the availability of health care and counseling; and the variety or limitations of choices available to them.

I have presented the lives, or at least aspects of the lives, of these six young people in such a way as to show how they represent the lives of others in similar circumstances. Norah Joines, for example, embodies the impact of rape and neglect on a child. Her life and Reggie Greene's show the estrangement from the world at large that often coincides with foster care. Their lives, and Jamal Willson's, also illustrate the frustration that often accompanies attempts to reintegrate into society. The experiences of Norah, Marcus Bellows, Reggie Greene, and Cassandra Martin with authority both inside and outside of prison—its complacency, its frequent hypocrisy, its role in shielding the mainstream from those who are not part of it—represent the experiences of many, not only those with a history of incarceration, but also others who find themselves living on society's margins.

In this, the last chapter of my last book on children in prison, I want to set down observations I have not had the opportunity to record earlier, either in this book or in my others, and to emphasize some of what I have already written that I consider especially worth consideration.

Trauma

Poverty and the conditions that characterize it—unemployment and underemployment, the concentration of single-parent households, limited education, addiction to drugs or alcohol, mental disability, physical and sexual abuse—are noted or implied in the ACLU passage that opened this chapter. Not mentioned in it, except by the generic phrases "physical and sexual violence" and "violent crime," is the enduring impact on a child of having witnessed the murder of a parent or other close relative, or the commission of murder by a parent or aunt or uncle. In my time at Ash Meadow, I knew a number of kids exposed to these or other trauma-inducing events, including being forced to watch as one's sister was raped, or one's mother was beaten.

In Ash Meadow at any given time, 80 to 100 percent of the girls had been raped or otherwise sexually assaulted prior to incarceration, and an estimated 40 to 60 percent of the boys had.[2] When I worked in Whale Cottage, a girls' unit, I facilitated an Alternatives to Violence group with six girls—no boys— in it. Five of the six had been raped at least once before coming to Ash Meadow. Almost every girl on my caseload during the years I worked in Ash Meadow had been sexually violated before she was imprisoned. The sexual victimization of children, and the physical violence that often accompanies it, is so widespread among juveniles who become offenders (though not necessarily sex offenders) that I cannot avoid thinking that it is a major factor in producing criminals.

When I worked in Swan Cottage, I took up reading to boys who wanted to be read to during the staff break after dinner. I had recently read Rebecca Brown's *The Gifts of the Body* and felt it would be an excellent vehicle for getting the boys to experience the emotion of compassion. It was. Even boys I had believed were hardened beyond hope were moved by Brown's recalling her time as a home-care aide for people too debilitated by AIDS to care for themselves.

At Whale Cottage, a girls' unit I worked in after I left Swan, I read *The Gifts of the Body* to six or seven girls during my break, as I had the boys at Swan. The book was a success at Whale too. I followed it up with a young adult novel, *Why Me?* by Patricia Dizenzo, about a girl who has been raped and how she comes to terms with the ways in which the rape has changed her view of the world as well as her relationships with her family members. Toward the end of the story, Jenny, the protagonist, finally finds the courage to tell her mother what happened, but asks her mother not tell her father.

I did not understand why Jenny did not want her father to know—after all, she had told her mother—and I asked the girls why Jenny would be afraid of her father's finding out. Every one of the girls said Jenny was afraid her father would blame her. That was also why she had delayed telling her mother: she believed her mother also would blame her.

I had known that girls often blamed themselves for their victimization, and that this self-blame was often reinforced by society's institutions. I had known a girl whose church, at least its elders, told her she was herself responsible for her uncle's taking sexual liberties with her; they refused to call it rape. After all, she had admitted that she had not screamed. They did not believe that she had been too frightened to scream. And I had gone to high school with a girl who had been made pregnant by the man who raped her, a man she knew as a friend of her family. Her doctor accused her of lying, of trying to sully the reputation of the man she said was responsible and who was highly regarded in the town. This girl's life, too, was irremediably changed, driven in part by self-loathing.

I do not know why I had not generalized from my knowledge of what had happened to these two girls (and to women I later came to know), but I had not. Perhaps it was because I learned of these events one at a time. Perhaps I thought of them as anomalous. Even though I had been fond of the two girls I had known when I was younger, and of the women who had suffered similar trauma, I was not prepared for seven girls together telling me that being victimized again by people they trusted, people who had power over their lives, was their experience too. Perhaps it was their acceptance of how their lives had been damaged and the sadness I perceived as accompanying that acceptance that got to me.

Boys' experience of rape and its aftermath was in some ways similar and in some ways different from that of girls.' In the case of rape by an older relative, several boys said their grandmother or mother told them not to tell anyone because it would make their family look bad if outsiders knew. One boy told me his mother brushed off his telling her that his uncle, her brother, had raped him, saying it was no big deal, he had done the same thing to her when she was small.

I did not know boys to blame themselves. They felt, rather, that they had been "unmanned," as one boy put it, by the experience. They felt that a kind of power had been taken from them that they could not recover. The boy who used the expression, "unmanned," believed his rape by his grandfather was what drove him to try to charm and seduce girls.

I knew a boy whose trauma arose from experiences with older girls. When he was five, he was raped by his babysitter who also used him sexually in other ways, then passed him on to some of her girlfriends. He was in a treatment group I co-facilitated, and after telling this much, he began crying and withdrew from the session.

Another boy was eleven when he was seduced by a woman in her thirties. He was sixteen when he confided in me about it. He showed no signs of trauma, but often wondered, he said, what she saw in him that attracted her.

Drugs

I used to ask kids on my caseload, soon after they arrived at Ash Meadow, what events had preceded their committing their offenses. Eventually I came to realize that the use of drugs or alcohol was integral to the commission of most juvenile crimes. In many cases, smoking marijuana enabled the kid to do his crime.

In Swan Cottage, we had a boy who had beaten a woman at a bus stop badly enough to hospitalize her, even though she had relinquished her handbag as soon as he started hitting her. When I asked him why he had been so brutal—in the cottage he was such a gentle kid—he said it was the weed. He had been with two older girls who dared him to take the woman's bag, and when she refused at first to let go of it, he just started hitting her. Emotionally, he hadn't felt a thing.

I learned to wait at least four months after getting a kid from the outside before trying to characterize his personality. The effects of marijuana linger, and it took four to six months for them to wear off enough for me to determine whom I was dealing with. Reggie Greene acknowledged himself as heavily dependent on marijuana. He saw himself as using it primarily to dampen his emotions, particularly the ongoing grief he felt over the deaths of his sister, members of his gang set, and others.

Several kids, particularly gang kids I talked with, saw marijuana and alcohol as integral to their criminal actions because of their use as a connection with friends who would insist that they do something—a drive-by, a robbery—after everybody was high. Some of the gang kids I knew described the use of weed before doing a drive-by and alcohol afterward in almost ritualistic terms.

Violence

Gang violence is sometimes perpetrated to defend territory, particularly territory the gang has claimed as important to its drug-selling operations. Often an act of violence by one gang set is retaliation against another set for injury it has done them. The desire for revenge "is what keeps us going," one young man told me.[3]

But violence among kids is sometimes perpetrated for no reason other than to relieve stress. Recall Reggie Greene's telling me that if he were on the outside he would beat somebody up to relieve the stress he was feeling—that is, his grief from losing his auntie in a house fire, and the grief coupled with anger he felt over the murder of his sister and the killing of six of his homies by other gangs.

Another boy told me he did drive-bys sometimes when he was angry, though he had to be very angry, as after an argument with his mother. He didn't have to be angry with the person he was shooting at, he only had to be angry enough to want to relieve the stress of his anger by shooting at somebody. It wasn't important to him if he hit someone or not; just the act of firing at him was sufficient.

Another boy told me the same thing. What relieved his anger was not actually shooting someone, but shooting at someone, and sometimes not even shooting at a person, but just shooting, at a bottle, for example.

Modeling

Four of the six young people I've written about in this book—Norah Joines, Reggie Greene, Marcus Bellows, Kyle Payment—had a parent or stepparent in prison. This is an unusually high proportion, four out of six, but there is truth in the idea that crime often travels through families.[4] As Kyle Payment noted, his father was a model for his behavior; he even chose to commit the same type of offense his father had committed.

In Whale Cottage, we had a fourteen-year-old girl who, after her mother disappeared, had dropped out of school to raise her three younger siblings. She was in prison for selling drugs. Her siblings were in foster care and it was her hope that she would be able to get them out of foster care and bring them to live with her when she was released from prison.

She was devastated when she was notified that her sister and brothers had accused her of physically abusing them. The thought that they felt she had mistreated them after she had sacrificed her future for them, leaving school when she was doing so well there in order to work so that they would have food and a place to live. She admitted that she had hit them, sometimes using a shoe or a belt, but how else were they to learn if they did something wrong and were not punished in this way? After all, it was how her mother had punished her.

A boy I knew in Swan Cottage followed his father's model to the extent of threatening his sisters with a knife, just as he had seen his father threaten his mother. (Yet, when I pointed out that he was modeling himself after his father, the boy denied it.)

Marcus Bellows, however, did not know his father was in prison until after he was released. Some people say that children inherit a propensity for unlawfulness from their parents, as though there is a gene passed from one generation to the next that propels its carrier into a life of crime. The more reasonable explanation is that the social environment that produced crime in one generation also produces it in the succeeding generation, the environment including the earlier generation's modeling behavior.

Kids generally seek to attach themselves to someone older, someone with more experience than they have themselves in navigating a world that at times threatens to overwhelm them. If parents are not available, kids will look for others to guide and advise them.[5] We see this in Cassandra Martin's relationship with Shari; Reggie Greene's with his older cousins; Jamal Willson's with at least two young men, though older than Jamal, who steered him into trouble and tragedy; and Marcus Bellows' with the OGs of his gang set.

Events Out of One's Control

Norah Joines' story presents an example of how an economic or medical issue may result in criminality. Norah was born into an economically comfortable middle-class family. After her parents divorced, Norah's mother's alcoholism, neglect, and abuse led to Norah's going to live with her father. Her father's stroke shortly after he retired sent Norah into foster care where her foster mother was also neglectful and emotionally abusive. Recall that Norah was raped by her mother's boyfriend who also threatened her life, and then raped a second time by a friend of Norah's foster mother. Norah became involved with a gang and participated in fights against other gangs. Ultimately, an act of violence against her foster mother resulted in a long prison sentence.

The sequence of events that brought her to prison shows how the social environment determined, in large part, the direction Norah's early life would take. Note, too, that the help and encouragement she received as she entered her twenties helped her to adopt a more conventional, legitimate lifestyle.

Kyle Payment's mental illness—however it has been diagnosed, it is clear, as Kyle indicates, that he has suffered from a mental disorder—has resulted in his assaultiveness which in turn has resulted in his being locked away for most of his life. This is not unusual in the United States where, because we no longer have sufficient facilities to house and treat the indigent mentally ill, we rely on prisons to house them and, in a very few cases, treat them.

Education

After *Why Me?* I looked for another book to read to the girls in Whale Cottage and decided on one of Primo Levi's memoirs. He used short, declarative sentences and he would be easy to understand, despite the weight of his subject matter. I thought he might provide the girls with a model for retaining hope when life seems especially cruel.

I was stunned to discover that the girls didn't know the Nazis were Germans. The only Nazis the girls had heard of were Americans. They thought Naziism was a variety of American racism. They didn't know when World War II was fought, even that their grandfathers may have fought in it, and they didn't know which countries fought on which side. They had never heard of the mass murder of Jews.

When I asked them what eras they had studied in their history classes, they said they had never had a history class, or if they had, it had been where they talked about what was in the newspaper and learned how government worked.

These girls were not unintelligent and they were not mentally disabled. They were uneducated, although they were passed from one grade to the next and graduated by their schools.[6]

Boys fared no better. I had a boy on my caseload in Wolf Cottage who was unable to read anything but his name and a few one-syllable words. Finally I was able to find a teacher who agreed to tutor him on her own (unpaid) time when school hours had ended for the day. After four months the boy was able to read at a fourth-grade level, well enough to enjoy thrillers and crime fiction.

I had another boy who was failing math. His teacher did not require students to learn the multiplication tables, but taught them to depend on a calculator. The boy could not afford to buy a calculator and our cottage did not have any. The teacher was unwilling to change his teaching method, if it could be called that, but the school psychologist arranged for a tutor from the outside to come to the prison to teach the boy multiplication and division, relying on memorization of the multiplication tables.[7]

Haves and Have-Nots

In Wolf Cottage, I knew a boy who, watching a sitcom on television in which the family lived in a stately two-story house with multiple bedrooms, a large garage, and a spacious lawn, asked me, "Jerry, do people really live like that?"

People did, in fact, and they do, less than two miles from where he lived in Seattle, and less than a mile from where he sold crack.

Kids generally knew when they were deprived of things other kids had, and of the means to get them legally. One boy, doing time for robbery, told me, "I'm not stupid. I knew I was doing wrong." But he wanted what other kids had and he could not get them any way other than to take them from somebody else.[8]

Marcus Bellows explained his resentment of Oren in terms of haves and have-nots. Oren's family had money enough to spend some of it on him and to travel. Marcus felt Oren was humiliating him and the other boys in the cottage by bringing up the fact of his family's comparative wealth when he knew the others didn't have what he had. Marcus' response was to punch Oren when he thought he could get away with it.

The occurrence of a burglar defecating in an obvious place—the middle of the living room floor, or on a bed—in the house he is robbing is well known, at least among those who commit burglaries and those who arrest them and prosecute them. The explanation most staff I worked with at Ash Meadow assumed to be valid is that the burglar's anxiety in conducting the robbery causes him to relieve himself before he can get to a toilet. Perhaps this is true in some cases, but kids told me they defecated where they did in order to soil what they couldn't have, so that the owners couldn't enjoy it either. Some kids said they hated people who had more than they had, even if they didn't know them personally.

A boy once told me that his mother, though she had a respectable job that her relatives and neighbors envied, still couldn't always provide for her children. Sometimes there wasn't food enough and they had to fill their bellies with warm water. When the boy began selling drugs, he would leave a roll of cash on the kitchen table for his mother once a week. She didn't ask him where he got the money.

Cassandra had to provide for herself and then, after her daughter was born, she had to provide for her daughter too. She saw her choice as between selling her body and selling drugs, and she opted to sell drugs.

Reggie wanted money because he wanted what the older boys he knew had, and once he began earning money from selling marijuana, he wanted independence. Later in his life, after he left the juvenile prison system, he held a legitimate job, but lost it when the business he worked for closed. He couldn't find another job and returned to selling drugs.

Influencing Factors in Staff Decisions

One of the things I've tried to show in my books on Ash Meadow is the porousness of the boundaries separating prison from the outside. A way of demonstrating this idea is to show how a staff member's personal life can influence the decisions she makes regarding someone who has limited ability to defend herself.

This is illustrated in Cassandra Martin's story where a staff member at

Peacock Cottage admits to her that she, the staff, agreed to send Cassandra to maximum security because she was hurt when Cassandra appeared to reject her overture of friendship.

Another staff member at Peacock, the one who apparently instigated Cassandra's transfer, was afraid of her because she was large, black, and willing to voice negative opinions, not because her behavior called for her removal from the cottage. Thus, in the same cottage Cassandra was victimized twice by staff carrying emotional baggage into the prison with them.

Early in my career in Wolf Cottage, my supervisor wanted to transfer a boy on my caseload, Lawrence, to another institution because she considered him a danger to the women on staff. He had been badly abused by his mother, and my supervisor believed he might transfer the anger he felt toward her to other women, especially those who held power over him.

I argued that we should retain the kid because, while it was true that he harbored conflicting emotions concerning his mother, he had done nothing to indicate that he might assault a staff, male or female. I lost the argument and Lawrence was transferred.

Weeks later, my supervisor told me that a man she had known when she was younger had tried to kill her. Afterward she learned that, as a child, he had been beaten by his mother and had been taken away from her and placed in foster care. This was also Lawrence's background, and it was her earlier experience of being attacked that she acknowledged made her fear Lawrence.[9]

While most staff were at least competent, some were not. A few should not have been working with children in any setting, much less a prison where the kids have few means by which to protect themselves. Some staff targeted individual kids. Recall the associate superintendent who stripped Cassandra of her status when she was in Whale Cottage, and the staff of Peacock doing the same earlier in Cassandra's time in Ash Meadow. Recall, too, the administration's preventing Norah Joines from transferring out of maximum security in spite of her exemplary behavior and the institution's regulations permitting her transfer.

I have often wondered what these staff told themselves in order to justify the abuse of their authority. But of course they wouldn't see themselves as abusive or their actions as unjustified. There were exceptions. Danielle Priest blamed herself for Cassandra's transfer to maximum security, and I haven't forgotten my taking Kyle Payment to the floor when I didn't have to.

Some staff seemed to assume that once a kid was in the system, he might as well consider prison his calling. Some worked to confirm the rightness of their beliefs. An example of this was Celia Barney, the associate superintendent who attempted to undermine Cassandra's efforts to find work after her release from prison.

Celia had never worked in a cottage but, like some other staff, both administrative and cottage, appeared to believe some kids were simply "bad." I once heard her allude to a boy on my caseload as "a bad apple"; she had never met him, his original offense was not particularly egregious, and, as it turned out, the additional offense he had just confessed to had been perpetrated by his brother, whom he was trying to protect. Celia sometimes took it upon herself to punish some kids beyond what was required by regulation: it was she who blocked Norah Joines' transfer out of maximum security.

I suspect that Celia's underlying intent was to establish herself as the equal to those associate superintendents who had cottage experience. This, I believe, was the case with another associate, newly transferred from one of Ash Meadow's sister institutions.

At a sentencing hearing on a fourteen-year-old girl, he represented Ash Meadow. At issue was whether the girl should be sentenced as a juvenile or as an adult. She had committed a serious offense, but she had never committed any other offense and it was clear that she had perpetrated her offense under pressure from her mother. She was a good student and a gifted athlete. The prosecutor wanted the judge to sentence her as an adult, but the judge was reluctant. Then the associate from Ash Meadow told the judge that if the girl was sentenced as a juvenile, she would be eligible to be transferred to a group home in two years. He said, too, that rehabilitative treatment was offered to residents, but they were not required to participate in it.

Both of these points were untrue—the girl wouldn't have been eligible to transfer to a group home for at least four years, if at all, and she would be required to participate in all treatment groups her cottage staff thought necessary or beneficial. The judge decided that the girl needed to serve more than two years in prison, especially if she could refuse rehabilitation, and sentenced her as an adult.[10]

Why had the associate lied? He was, as I noted, new to Ash Meadow, and the other associate superintendents considered him a lightweight. I knew this because I had heard two of them talking about him during a break in a meeting I attended. Like Celia Barney, I believe, he wanted to establish his credentials as their equal.

The Innocent

A few kids were in prison for crimes they probably did not commit.

Several kids said they took the fall for an older kid who had more to lose—that is, he would serve more time, if convicted—than a younger kid who did not already have a criminal record. One boy, for example, said he took the place of someone older who had told him he would have to serve only a few weeks whereas he, the older boy, would go to prison for years. The younger boy confessed to having committed the offense, a robbery, and was sentenced to two years.

A girl I knew took the fall for her boyfriend on a charge of armed robbery and got five years. She was pregnant when she was arrested and gave birth to her daughter a few months after she entered prison.

What convinced me that these kids were truthful was that they did not blame anyone but themselves for the choice they made to go to prison to protect someone else. They did not aver that anyone else was responsible for their decisions, that the police had tricked them into confessing, or that their attorneys had not represented them adequately.

The boy above seemed amused at the irony of his situation, that he had confessed to a crime he hadn't committed in order to keep another boy from serving the sentence he himself was now serving. The girl was angry with her now ex-boyfriend who, after their daughter was born, began seeing some-one else. His rationale was that, after all, she, now his ex-girlfriend, was in prison and he was not.

Another case is that of a young man who got twenty years for a murder his girlfriend committed. She was tried as a juvenile and received a six-year sentence on other charges, while he was tried as an adult. I knew about the intricacies of this case because the girl eventually confessed to cottage staff to having committed the murder herself, but had allowed her boyfriend to take responsibility for it out of loyalty to her. (She was not charged with murder; either the prosecutor did not believe her or he was not interested in exonerating the young man.)

Suicides

There were three suicides in Ash Meadow during my years there: a boy and two girls. The boy's suicide was likely accidental. He tied his shoelaces to his window latch and then around his neck, probably seeking partial stran-gulation in order to experience the high of oxygen deprivation. But he vomited and, apparently in a panic, tried to run to his door at the far end of his room but ran out the length of his laces and was jerked back, falling and breaking his neck. He was thirteen and had one week of his sentence left to serve.

The girls were older, sixteen and eighteen. Both had been depressed for some time.

In addition to the three completed suicides, there were hundreds of attempts or "gestures"—self-mutilation such as a girl cutting on her arm, or a boy putting broken glass in his mouth[11]—mostly in the mental health unit, but also in other cottages, including two of the cottages where I was working. The attempts I was involved in preventing were genuine; they were not gestures done to make a point or to elicit sympathy. These kids wanted to end their lives.

Once, in a staff discussion in which Ash Meadow's superintendent was present, I said that a kid's suicide was the worst thing that could happen at Ash Meadow—we had just had our second—because it affected everybody. Everybody, kids and staff, even kids and staff who hadn't known the victim, felt somehow responsible. The superintendent looked at me as though he had no idea what I was talking about. I wondered if the administrators did not share the sense of guilt cottage staff and so many of the kids felt.[12]

Reentry

Because they are too young to live away from the authority of their parents, or parent substitutes, most kids leaving prison return to their family. Unlike many adults getting out of prison, most do not have the problem of finding a place to live.[13] Their problem results from being returned to the same neighborhood and family that likely contributed to their incarceration in the first place. A number of boys told me that the men in their families, and also the men and older boys in their neighborhoods, expected the younger boys to serve time just as they themselves had. Enduring incarceration had become a kind of passage into manhood.

So much in life depends on whom you associate with, whom you meet and what is going on in your life when you meet him or her. What would have become of Cassandra Martin after her mother expelled her from her home if she hadn't met Shari? What would Reggie Greene's life have been like if his older cousins had not sold crack cocaine, or had not been in a gang? But Jamal Willson's story shows that a gang affiliation is not necessary to become involved in criminal activity. What is common to Reggie and Jamal and Cassandra is the association with someone older, which, in part, led to criminality and then to prison.

But kids may have little choice in deciding whom they associate with. Recall Norah Joines telling me that she and Guilllermo, her then boyfriend, also recently released from prison, were able to live together because her parole officer was not enforcing the rule in her parole contract that prohibited her from associating with other felons. The reason was that there were so many living in and around the housing Norah and Guillermo could afford that the rule could not be enforced.

There are exceptions to kids returning to their family and neighborhood. I knew one boy, diagnosed with schizophrenia, whose mother was dead and whose father wanted nothing to do with him, who was released to parole and became homeless.

A few parole officers in the juvenile system permitted parolees to sit in the lobby of their office during the day because they had nowhere to go when they weren't in school and they were in peril of reoffending if they hung around with their old friends. At night, if the parole officer could not find placement for them, they were on their own. I asked one parole officer where a particular kid, one who was clearly mentally ill, spent his nights.

"I don't ask," he said. The boy had given a sister's address as his home of record, but the parole officer was certain he didn't live there.

Other kids, like Reggie Greene, lived in a motel if they could afford to, or with friends, moving from one to another when they started getting on each other's nerves or when the friend could no longer afford to house them.

Sex offenders have more difficulty finding housing than others recently released from prison.[14] If they have victimized smaller children and there are young children in the household, the offender will likely be prohibited from residing with his family. There may also be pressure, even violence or threats of violence, from neighbors to keep the offender from living in their neighborhood.

Marcus Bellows, who was convicted of a sex offense, was an only child (also, his victim was not a smaller child), so he was able to return home. (I have no information about neighbors' reactions, if any, to his moving back with his parents.) But others were placed in group homes or foster-care homes that would accept sex offenders, at least until they reached adulthood. I knew one young man, a Level III offender—one likely to reoffend—who had refused to participate in treatment at Ash Meadow and so was denied admission by group homes when he was released, and became homeless. Another, a Level I offender—at low risk to reoffend—was released from his group home on his eighteenth birthday. He had no family and spent the ensuing six years alternating between homelessness and staying with friends or in a shelter for short periods of time.

*　*　*

I sometimes eat or have coffee at a restaurant that hires parolees. I once witnessed an incident where a cook verbally humiliated the day manager because he had asked him to perform a task the cook felt was beneath him. Not long out of prison, he apparently believed the manager was trying to disrespect him, and retaliated in kind. The cook was a large man who, simply by his presence, dominated the physical area around him, and he obviously intimidated the manager, which, of course, was his intent. After the confrontation, the manager called the cook's parole officer who then spoke to the cook. The cook did not finish his shift. I never saw him again.

Obviously he had made a mistake. What he had done to try to preserve his dignity in prison worked against him when he did the same thing on the outside.

While the incident I just described involved an adult recently released from prison, he could as well have been a juvenile. When I worked in Swan Cottage, we released a young man who had little going for him. He had not finished high school or completed his GED. He had prepared for it, but after failing a test, he lost confidence in himself and gave up studying. He was not able to live at home because he and his mother's boyfriend could not tolerate each other. He was able to find work at a fast-food restaurant. He regarded this kind of work as a comedown in that he had been able to earn a lot more money before incarceration by robbery and by stealing cars for their parts.

One day the manager belittled him in front of the other employees. The boy went back to where he was living with a friend, obtained a car and a handgun and returned to the restaurant in time to observe the manager leave at the end of his shift. He forced the manager into the car and shot and killed him.

*　*　*

The young people I've written about live in a world they have little power to affect, whether in or out of prison. There is Reggie Greene, losing his job and returning to selling drugs; Norah Joines entering poverty as a consequence of her father's stroke; Cassandra Martin losing everything again and again and again, including, ultimately, custody of the daughter she was devoted to; Kyle Payment whose untreated mental illness works repeatedly to extend his prison tenure. Of course, almost all had the ill luck to be born into the lower strata of the American class system with its concentrations of drug and alcohol abuse and addiction, domestic and neighborhood violence, lack of effective supervision of children, joblessness and underemployment, housing instability, untreated or inadequately treated mental illness, and poor education.

In Wolf Cottage, I knew an African American boy, one of the most intelligent kids, in terms of IQ, ever to have come to Ash Meadow, whom I encouraged to go to college. The only college he had heard of in Seattle was the University of Washington, which he believed to be racist, and didn't want to go there. He had never heard of the other universities or the community colleges that serve thousands of Seattle students.

But the community colleges could also offer a challenge to would-be students unaccustomed to administrative manners. I released a young woman to parole in time for her to register at a community college for the fall term. After spending two hours in line, she got up to the window where the clerk had just placed a sign saying the office was closed and giving the number of the room where students should go next to register. The young woman, already frustrated and feeling a loss of confidence among students with whom she felt she had nothing in common, who she felt were all smarter than she was, left campus and didn't return. I learned about her experience when she was arrested again for selling crack and returned to Ash Meadow.

Herman Boats, the director of Swan Cottage when I worked there, told me once that where the common view among psychologists and social workers was that kids who went to prison had a negative self-image, his own view, based on his experience as an adolescent gang member, was that kids who were into crime, especially gang kids, usually had a positive self-image because their criminal behavior was reinforced by their peers, and rewarded in terms of money and the things money buys.

In a social situation where you, the reader, and I would feel at ease, they would feel that everyone was staring at them because they were where they didn't belong. But in their own neighborhood or other areas where they knew what to expect from people, doing what they had learned to do well, or studying how the older kids became successful at what they did, they would be able to feel successful too, as well as a sense of belonging.

*   *   *

As I was writing this chapter, I read Bruce Western's book *Homeward: Life in the Year After Prison*. I was pleased to find that our thoughts regarding offenders are similar, though we have used different techniques to reach our respective destinations, his sociological, mine a mix of literary and anthropological. Both of us have tried to "humanize" those we have written about—he writing about adults, I about children—to try to persuade our readers to acknowledge them as part of the larger community, as no less human and deserving of dignity and respect than we and our readers are, by showing how crime and punishment are embedded in the context of their lives, but showing also that, with help, they are capable of change.

"It is not police, courts, and the threat of punishment that create public

safety, but rather the bonds of community produced by a raft of social institutions—families, schools, employers, churches, and neighborhood groups,"
Western writes,[15] and I agree.

But Western appears to believe it is possible to restore the bonds of community to American life.[16] I do not. I wish I did, but I do not.

Twenty-plus years ago, I was talking with a colleague from Ash Meadow
about what could be done to help those we released from prison, meaning
to the neighborhoods they had come from and the people whose examples
had contributed to their going to prison.

We were frustrated, my friend and I. A couple of years earlier he had
taught a young man—I'll call him Clelland—some mediation techniques and
encouraged him to try them instead of preparing himself for the worst case.
The day after Clelland was released, he learned that an old enemy from a
rival gang was looking for him. Clelland went, unarmed, to talk to him, to
try to convince him that it was in both their interests to put their enmity
aside. As he approached the other young man, who was waiting for him at
the entrance to a small grocery, Clelland put his hands up, palms open, to
show he was not carrying a weapon, and the other boy drew his gun from
his pocket and shot him, killing him.

My friend and I made a list of things we thought needed to be done to
ameliorate violence and the crimes it attends in the United States. Parents,
many of them, needed training in parenting; kids needed to be kept in school,
though they might be difficult or even threatening; jobs that allowed families
to thrive needed to be created; free, or at least affordable, drug rehab programs
needed to be created and made available to whoever required drug rehabilitation; health care, including mental health care, needed to be made affordable.

The list was not comprehensive, but it was a start. Could we implement
job creation and parent training and the other items on the list, we would
discover other things that needed rectifying. We would, if successful, be
remaking American society into one that was more just, more equitable, less
harsh to those less fortunate.

But there was a rub: we were talking about the restructuring of American
society. Who would pay for it? Certainly not those who, at least financially,
would have little, if anything, to gain. Certainly those wealthy enough to buy
the favors of senators and congressmen and even presidents would not will-
ingly give up some of their wealth and the political influence that goes with
it. Neither of us could imagine the United States, known throughout the
world for its ethos of personal greed, taxing itself to make life more bearable
for a minority without political power.

While Western appears able to imagine this happening, I am not. I wish I were able to envision a more just, more egalitarian society, but I am not able to see it as something possible. I wish the United States had the political will to re-open society so that the least among us could themselves envision a life of possibility rather than further degradation, but I see little evidence of such resoluteness in our political arenas.

A decade ago, I wrote: "In a just world, every child would have the opportunity to reach maturity without fear of being killed or brutalized, but that would be another world."[17] The children in the part of the world the United States comprises need another world, not our own.

Glossary

AA: Alcoholics Anonymous.

ADD: Attention Deficit Disorder.

Aggression Replacement Training: A ten-week class, based on cognitive behavior theory and moral reasoning and designed to reduce recidivism among juvenile offenders and those at risk of offending.

ART: Aggression Replacement Training.

Ash Meadow: A prison for juveniles in Washington State.

Case manager: A rehabilitation counselor.

Central Isolation: Isolation cells monitored by closed-circuit television and specially constructed to withstand physical abuse. They were located in the same building as the Security Office and the Health Center when I worked at Ash Meadow.

CPS: Child Protective Services.

Craft room: A room in each cottage designated for the teaching and practicing of crafts such as beadwork and leatherwork. The craft room was also used for facilitating small treatment groups.

Crane Cottage: One of two cottages where sex offenders went through a course of treatment designed to keep them from reoffending. This type of treatment was highly effective. Tracking sex offenders for five years following their release from prison, the Washington State Institute for Public Policy found that only 3 percent reoffended. See "Sex Offender Sentencing in Washington State: Recidivism Rates," August 26, 2005, www.wsipp. wa.gov.

DOC: Department of Corrections.

DSHS: Department of Social and Health Services

Elk Grove: A sister institution of Ash Meadow.

GED: General Educational Development. A set of exams, which, if the student passes them, allow him to be awarded a high school diploma equivalency certificate.

Group home: a residence housing juvenile offenders under the supervision of adult counselors. Living in a group home, residents may hold jobs and attend public or technical school.

Head: Bathroom.

High profile: A resident who meets all of these criteria: 1. His offense is one of the following: murder in the first or second degree; first-degree manslaughter; first-degree assault; first-degree rape; first-degree robbery; first-degree arson; first-degree kidnap. 2. The minimum length of his sentence is eighty weeks or more. 3. His offense has a "high impact" on the community. 4. Community response to his offense is high.

In-and-Out Program: A program whereby a resident is allowed out of his room only when other residents are in their rooms. A resident on such a program may or may not be permitted to attend school. It is used to protect other residents from the resident on the program, or to protect the resident on the program from other residents.

JRA: Juvenile Rehabilitation Administration.

Jumped in (also called "beaten in"): Initiated into a gang. A prospective member is beaten by those already in the gang. Less common since the beginning of the twenty-first century.

Jumped out (also called "beaten out"): Beaten by other gang members when a member decides to leave his gang. A ritual rather than punishment.

Lower court: The part of the Ash Meadow campus that included a playing field, an asphalt basketball court, and a volleyball set-up, located about four hundred yards from upper campus. See "upper campus."

Maximum release date: In Washington State, a sentence range is awarded by the court to a juvenile convicted of a felony. The maximum release date is the latest the resident may be released from prison. The minimum date is the earliest the resident may be released. The length of his sentence is linked to his behavior while incarcerated.

MAYSI: Massachusetts Youth Screening Instrument: Questionnaire given to residents within thirty days after being assigned to a cottage. When completed, it provides an idea of the emotional state of the resident.

Max: Maximum security

Minimum release date: See "maximum release date."

NA: Narcotics Anonymous.

Off program: A resident's confinement to his room for having committed a behavioral misdeed.

OG: Initially, the initials stood for "original gangster," but have since come to indicate "old-time gangster" or "old gangster."

OP: See "off program."

The outs: Outside of prison.

PC: The weekly cottage staff meeting. Most cottages hold them on Tuesday afternoons, beginning while their residents are still in school. When residents return, they are locked in their rooms until the meeting is over. Meetings last two to three hours.

Purdy: A town in Washington State. The approximate location of the Washington Corrections Center for Women.

Quiet time: From approximately 6:00 to 6:30 pm. Beginning after supper when cottage details are completed and residents are locked in their rooms, and ending thirty minutes later. This period is considered staff's break time, but is usually used to try to catch up on paperwork, to conduct individual counseling with residents, or to do housekeeping chores. It is also the time residents most commonly attempt suicide.

Resident: Inmate or prisoner. Used interchangeably with "student."

The Rivers: A sister institution of Ash Meadow.

Set: A subset of a gang. In this sense, a gang may be regarded as an aggregation of sets.

Tables: One of the most restrictive of cottage punishments. On Tables status, a resident is required to spend all of his free time sitting silently and alone at a table in the dining room, while other residents may watch television in the living room, play cards or board games, talk with one another, or go outside.

UA: urinalysis. An examination of a person's urine to determine whether or not he or she has recently used drugs.

Upper campus: The part of the Ash Meadow campus containing the administrative and support services, including the administration building, Social Services, the Health Center, the Security Office and Central Isolation, the cafeteria, the school, and the gymnasium.

Woodbyrne: A sister institution of Ash Meadow

Youth Group: Campus-wide treatment group for gang members.

Zone: Each cottage has four zones, or corridors, radiating out from the living room, dining room, and kitchen, which are located centrally. Zones are numbered 1 through 4. From the front door, facing into the cottage, Zone 1 is to the immediate left. Then, counting clockwise, there are Zones 2, 3, and 4. As the cottages are rectangular in shape, Zones 1 and 2 are located to the left of the common areas, Zones 3 and 4 to the right. Each zone had four bedrooms during the years I worked at Ash Meadow; due to renovation, there are more bedrooms now. Each room has a unique number in the cottage. Zone 1 was composed of Rooms 1 through 4; Zone 2, Rooms 5 through 8, and so on. Each zone had one bathroom, or "head," shared by the residents of that zone.

Chapter Notes

Introduction

1. See Jerome Gold, *Paranoia & Heartbreak: Fifteen Years in a Juvenile Facility* (New York: Seven Stories Press, 209), 141–142. There were two other incidents, six years apart, in which a staff member assaulted a resident, not in attempting to restrain him, but apparently intending to harm him. See *Paranoia & Heartbreak*, 170, for the first incident. The second is described in *In the Spider's Web* (Mill Creek, Washington: Black Heron Press, 2015), 109–117.

2. I did look up the statistics on imprisonment in the United States for the purpose of writing this introduction. Shannon et al. estimate that 3.11 percent of the adult population of the United States, 7,304,910 people, have been or are in prison or on parole as of 2010, and 8.11 percent of the adult population, 19,022,636, are convicted felons. See Shannon et al., "The Growth, Scope, and Spatial Distribution of People with Felony Records in the United States, 1948–2010," *Demography* 54 (October 1, 2017): 1795–1818. See Tables 1 and 2, 1805 and 1808, respectively, for statistics cited above. Adults are defined as persons eighteen years old or older (Shannon et al., 1809).

The authors point out, "Not everyone with a felony conviction goes to [state or federal] prison ... and many more will serve time in [a county or metropolitan] jail or on probation. Indeed, changes in sentencing constitute one reason for the recent decline in the size of the prison population" (1797).

According to the Office of Juvenile Justice and Delinquency Prevention (OJJDP) Statistical Briefing Book (SBB), on October 26, 2016, a national one-day count of juveniles in residential placement facilities was 45,567. Residential placement facilities include prisons, jails, and detention facilities as well as private facilities such as group homes. These statistics include juveniles held in adult jails and prisons. In 2014, 4,200 juveniles age seventeen or younger were held in adult jails. One thousand were in custody in adult prisons operated by the states in 2016. In 2016, 282,200 delinquency cases resulted in probation rather than incarceration.

3. Others I have written about in my books have asked that I use their real names. I have always resisted doing this, aware that a moment's celebrity may became a curse in the longer term, when one would prefer anonymity. But celebrity is only one motive for wanting one's real name used. Another, related, motive is the desire to have one's life, at least in some of its aspects, documented as proof that one actually existed.

4. See Jerome Gold, *In the Spider's Web* (Seattle: Black Heron Press, 2015), 191–192, footnote.

Chapter II

1. Clare eventually transferred out of Wolf Cottage. I was sorry to see her go. Although she was sometimes afraid, she tried to get past her fear, and I admired her for that. But in a situation where things were moving very fast, her thinking became muddled and she found it hard to focus. She knew this about herself and, in fact, it was she who told me. She transferred to a girls' cottage, but was bored there and finally left the system altogether.

2. I had known a boy in Swan cottage when I worked there who told me he had been raped by a member of his own gang set while others in the set held him down. The emotional release that accompanied his relating the incident to me convinced me that it had happened. The rape was not part of an initiation; the boy had been in the set for a year when it occurred. After my experience with Marcus, I came to believe that rape of a set's younger members was more common than what outsiders heard about.

Chapter III

1. Many of the kids I knew at Ash Meadow had not attended high school before being locked up. Some had not even gone to middle school. High school or middle school is usually where one learns about such things as government and voting, assuming the school offers a civics class.

Chapter IV

1. See Jerome Gold, *In the Spider's Web* (Seattle: Black Heron Press, 2015), 56. This book focuses mostly on Caitlin and, to a lesser degree, Sonia during the years they spent at Ash Meadow.
2. At that time, Whale was a boys' cottage. It had been a girls' unit two years earlier, when Cassandra Martin was there. Cassandra's story is recounted in another chapter in this book.
3. See the chapter on Marcus Bellows in this book.

Chapter V

1. See Jerome Gold, *Paranoia & Heartbreak: Fifteen Years in a Juvenile Facility* (New York: Seven Stories Press, 2009), 287–290.
2. See *Paranoia & Heartbreak*, 306.

Chapter VI

1. Jerome Gold, *Paranoia & Heartbreak* (New York: Seven Stories Press, 2009), 238–239.
2. While I and staff who assisted me were the only people to teach ART in Ash Meadow, it was taught more widely in two of our sister institutions, The Rivers and Elk Grove, and in the juvenile probation and parole systems.
3. *Paranoia & Heartbreak*, 242.
4. *Paranoia & Heartbreak*, 303.
5. *Paranoia & Heartbreak*, 279.
6. *Paranoia & Heartbreak*, 293.
7. Norah had done well in Wolf Cottage; Kyle had not. She had achieved Honors Level; Kyle had not. She was a favorite of most of the cottage staff; Kyle was not. And she was set to transfer out of Wolf Cottage.
8. Kyle said in a television interview in 2016 that all of the charges brought against him while in prison concerned assaults against corrections officers. See Rachel Belle, "Washington Inmate Shares the Dangers of Being in Solitary Confinement Since He Was 13 Years Old," mynorth-

west.com/washington-inmate-shares-the-dangers-of-being-in-solitary-confinement-since-he-was-13-years-old. The title is misleading. Kyle may have been kept in isolation for most of his time in the adult system, as he says in the interview, but this was not the case when he was in the juvenile system.
9. Kyle Payment's letter to me of August 1, 2013.
10. My letter to Kyle Payment of August 10, 2013.
11. It was not unusual at Ash Meadow for kids to engineer a situation so that staff had to take them to the floor. The accepted explanation by staff generally, and by at least one of the psychiatrists, was that the kids were so starved for physical contact with adults that some of them would rather be taken down than have no contact at all.
12. Kyle was initially charged with car theft, but incurred additional charges for offenses committed while in prison.
13. Kyle's letter of August 15, 2013.
14. My letter of August 25, 2013.
15. Kyle's letter of August 30, 2013. In a letter five years later, I asked Kyle to explicate several of the terms he used in this letter. He wrote back, in his letter of August 15, 2018, explaining that the inspiration for the essay was his having been betrayed by someone he had trusted, another inmate and formerly a friend. The point of the essay, he wrote, is that prison promotes self-centeredness among inmates.

> Prison fosters a certain way of living, thinking, and believing. What is perceived to be right, moral, and upstanding in society is often not right, moral, or upstanding within the prison context. Take, for example, you are walking down the street and see several people severely beating one man. What do you do? In society we are taught to do one of several things, that is, immediately intervene, attempt to help, or call the police. Often times this is defined as heroic, honorable, and the right thing to do. (Obviously, what else comes with this act of valor is helping identify suspects, testifying in court, etc.)
>
> In the prison context, if this happens, the honorable thing to do is, don't make a scene, act as if nothing is going on so as not to cause further commotion, alerting the guards to the problem, and if confronted by the guards, deny knowing or seeing anything, thus remaining honorable....
>
> Now, isn't this ultimately "immoral"?? I sure hope so!...

In short, the prisoner's ego [sense of himself?] derives from, and [is] a direct result of the prison political landscape, the racial divide, so-called honorable and righteous acts, and [wanting to remain] popular by conforming to the likes of others.

16. It is not clear if Kyle is talking about one staff member or more than one. Below he uses the pronoun "they" to indicate only one. At Ash Meadow, the word "staff" was used as either singular or plural.

17. Kyle's letter of September 9, 2013.

18. My letter of September 15, 2013.

19. See Jerome Gold, *In the Spider's Web* (Mill Creek, Washington: Black Heron Press, 2015) for more about Caitlin Weber and Sonia May.

20. Kyle's letter of September 14, 2013.

21. My letter of September 22, 2013.

22. Kyle's letter of September 18, 2013. I don't know what Kyle means by "ego" here.

23. Kyle's letter of September 26, 2013.

24. Kyle's letter of September 29, 2013. In his 2016 interview (see Rachel Belle, mynorthwest.com/Washington-inmate-shares-the-danger-of-being-in-solitary-confinement-since-he-was-13-years-old), Kyle said he had two psychological evaluations since he'd been in solitary. "Both of them say I'm a product of what is called the SHU [Special Housing Unit] Syndrome…. They wonder why I'm acting the way I'm acting. It's because I'm in solitary. I'm unable to exhibit forms of self-control when my anxiety starts up or I start getting too stressed out or feeling like I'm being pushed into the corner." According to this article, Dr. Stuart Grassian performed one of the evaluations.

Grassian described the symptoms of SHU Syndrome as including "hypersensitivity to external stimuli; perceptual disturbances, hallucinations, and derealisation experiences; affective disturbances, such as anxiety and panic attacks; difficulties with thinking, memory and concentration; the emergence of fantasies such as revenge and torture of the guards; paranoia; problems with impulse control; and a rapid decrease in symptoms immediately following release from isolation. Taken together, Dr. Grasssian proposed that these symptoms amount to a pathopsychological syndrome" (Gali Katznelson and J.Wesley Boyd, blog.petrieflom.law.harvard.edu/2018/0117/solitary-confinement-tortuee-pure-and-simple).

Grassian notes also that solitary confinement "often results in severe exacerbation of a previously existing mental condition, or in the appearance of a mental illness where none had been observed before. Even among inmates who do not develop overt psychiatric illness as a result of confinement in solitary, such confinement almost inevitably imposes significant psychological pain during the period of isolated confinement and often significantly impairs the inmate's capacity to adapt successfully to the broader prison environment" (Stuart Grassian, studiesonsolitary.file.wordpress.com/2012/06/grassian-declaration).

25. My letter of October 28, 2013.

26. Kyle had watched a tape of Sonia's clemency hearing on TVW, the state channel. Her hearing had been attended by members of her family and also by several staff from Ash Meadow, including school staff, who spoke on Sonia's behalf.

27. Kyle had mentioned this book in an earlier letter. Its actual title is *The Lucifer Effect: Understanding How Good People Turn Evil.*

28. Kyle's letter of November 4, 2013.

29. My letter of November 18, 2013.

30. Kyle's letter of November 21, 2013.

31. My letter of December 10, 2013.

32. Kyle's letter of December 13, 2013. I never learned why the paralegal, after encouraging Kyle to call him, did not respond to him.

33. Kyle's letter of June 2, 2014.

34. My letter of July 10, 2014.

35. My letter of August 23, 2014.

36. My letter of September 4, 2014.

37. The actual date was August 5, 1949.

38. My letter of September 28, 2014.

39. Kyle's letter of October 2, 2014.

40. Until this letter, Kyle had consistently misspelled "Sonia," using a "y" in place of the "i." This was the only time he spelled it correctly. He must have searched through my letters for something to write about, as I had searched his, and realized he had been misspelling her name.

41. My letter of November 11, 2014.

Chapter VII

1. The events leading to my departure from Whale Cottage are recounted in detail in Jerome Gold, *Paranoia & Heartbreak: Fifteen Years in a Juvenile Facility* (New York: Seven Stories Press, 2009), 223–229.

2. Some staff in other cottages were trained as ART instructors and began to teach it, but their cottage directors did not support them and they all discontinued their ART programs within a few months of starting them.

3. This episode is described in Jerome Gold, *In the Spider's Web* (Seattle: Black Heron Press 2015), 109–117.

4. I was interviewed by officials from the Juvenile Rehabilitation Administration about what I may have witnessed in Swan Cottage when I worked there years before, and about my opinions on some of Herman's decisions. One question concerned an allegation that Herman had physically abused a boy in Swan. I had been present when Security moved the boy to Central Isolation from the cottage, the occasion when the abuse was supposed to have occurred. There had been no abuse, and Herman was not in the cottage. I was also asked my opinion on Herman's disciplining a subordinate staff member for having lied to him—about what, I do not recall. My view was that, if the staff had lied to him, Herman had behaved properly.

I remember thinking that the questions, in sum, seemed unrelated to one another, and that the interviewers seemed embarrassed about asking them.

5. For an example of Clara's targeting cottage staff, see *In the Spider's Web*, 168–174.

6. Readers interested in Caitlin's story and in my relationship with her should read *In the Spider's Web*.

Chapter VIII

1. ACLU Foundation, *False Hope: How Parole Systems Fail Youth Serving Extreme Sentences* (www.aclu.org, 2016), 26.

2. While I am aware of no formal study that cites these figures, administrators at Ash Meadow commonly used them in meetings and conversations. I think they are probably accurate. At least they match my own estimates based on what kids revealed to me.

3. Jerome Gold, "What Keeps Us Going," *Prisoners* (Seattle: Black Heron Press 1999), 72–73.

4. See Fox Butterfield, *All God's Children: The Bosket Family and the American Tradition of Violence* (New York: Avon Books 1996).

5. In a session of Alternatives to Violence, a treatment group I facilitated for kids who had committed a violent crime or a crime that carried a high potential for violence, such as robbery or residential burglary, the kids in the

group came up with six conditions that make for "violence in people." This list arose from their own experience and observations. (See Jerome Gold, *Paranoia & Heartbreak*, 320–321.)

1. Single-parent families where the parent does not have time [often owing to the demands of her job] to supervise her children.

2. The parent is addicted to drugs or alcohol and neglects her children.

3. Violence is present in the household or neighborhood.

4. Drugs are used in the household or neighborhood.

5. Violent behavior is accepted as normal.

6. Adults and teenagers lack jobs, which leads to theft and robbery and the violence often employed in committing these crimes.

6. Jerome Gold, *Paranoia & Heartbreak: Fifteen Years in a Juvenile Facility* (New York: Seven Stories Press 2009), 217–218.

7. *Ibid.*, 167.

8. *Ibid.*, 96.

9. *Ibid.*, 257–258, 261–262.

10. Jerome Gold, *In the Spider's Web* (Seattle: Black Heron Press 2015), 201–202.

11. This may have been a genuine suicide attempt. The boy appeared to be about to swallow when his mouth was forced open by a staff member.

12. See *Paranoia & Heartbreak*, 66–67 for an account of a suicide that was prevented.

13. Those coming out of prison as adults, eighteen years old or older, may encounter difficulty in finding housing. Norah Joines' story provides an example of this. Those leaving prison as children, but children who have no family, may be placed in foster care or left to shift for themselves.

14. See Angela Hattery and Earl Smith, *Prisoner Reentry and Social Capital* (Lanham, Maryland: Lexington Books 2010), 59–61, 134–135.

15. Bruce Western, *Homeward: Life in the Year After Prison* (New York: Russell Sage Foundation 2018), 181.

16. *Ibid.* See, for example, 186–188.

17. *Paranoia & Heartbreak*, 16.

Bibliography

ACLU Foundation. *False Hope: How Parole Systems Fail Youth Serving Extreme Sentences.* www.aclu.org. 2016.

Alexander, Michelle. *The New Jim Crow: Mass Incarceration in the Age of Colorblindness.* New York: The New Press, 2010.

Anderson, Elijah. *Street Wise: Race, Class, and Change in an Urban Community.* Chicago: University of Chicago Press, 1990.

Bartley, Nancy. *The Boy Who Shot the Sheriff: The Redemption of Herbert Niccolls, Jr.* Seattle: University of Washington Press, 2013.

Belle, Rachel. "Washington Inmate Shares the Dangers of Solitary Confinement-Since He Was 13 Years Old." mynorthwest.com/washington-inmate-shares-the-dangers-of-solitary-confinement-since-he-was-13-years-old. April 26, 2016.

Bing, Leon. *Do or Die.* New York: HarperCollins, 1991.

Bourgois, Philippe. *In Search of Respect: Selling Crack in El Barrio.* New York: Cambridge University Press, 1995.

Bourke, Joanna. *Rape: Sex, Violence, History.* Berkeley: Counterpoint, 2007.

Buford, Bill. *Among the Thugs.* New York: Vintage Books, 1990.

Burchard, Rachael J. *The Missing Friend: Teens with a Parent in Prison.* New York: Energylife, 2002.

Butterfield, Fox. *All God's Children: The Bosket Family and the American Tradition of Violence.* New York: Avon Books, 1996.

Canada, Geoffrey. *Fist Stick Knife Gun.* Boston: Beacon Press, 1995.

Coates, Ta-Nehisi. "The Black Family in the Age of Mass Incarceration." *The Atlantic,* October 2015, 60–84.

Conover, Ted. *Newjack: Guarding Sing Sing.* New York: Random House, 2000.

Finnegan, William. *Cold New World: Growing Up in a Harder Country.* New York: The Modern Library, 1999.

Frankl, Victor E. *Man's Search for Meaning.* New York: Pocket Books, 1963.

Freud, Anna, and Dorothy T. Burlingham. *War and Children.* New York: Medical War Books, 1943.

Gaines, Donna. *Teenage Wasteland: Suburbia's Dead End Kids.* Chicago: University of Chicago Press, 1998.

Godsey, Mark. *Blind Injustice: A Former Prosecutor Exposes the Psychology and Politics of Wrongful Convictions.* Oakland: University of California Press, 2017.

Gold, Jerome. *In the Spider's Web.* Seattle: Black Heron Press, 2015.

Gold, Jerome. *Paranoia & Heartbreak: Fifteen Years in a Juvenile Facility.* New York: Seven Stories Press, 2009.

Gold, Jerome. *Prisoners.* Seattle: Black Heron Press, 1999.

Grassian, Stuart. "Psychiatric Effects of Solitary Confinement." https://studiesonsolitary.file.wordpress.com/2012/06/grassian-declaration. 2006.

Hattery, Angela, and Earl Smith. *Prisoner Reentry and Social Capital: The Long Road to Reintegration.* New York: Lexington Books, 2010.

Herman, Judith Lewis. *Trauma and Recovery.* New York: Basic Books, 1992.

Hill, Eleanore. *The Family Secret: A Personal Account of Incest.* New York: Dell, 1985.

Hill, Karl G., Christina Lui, and J. David Hawkins. *Early Precursors of Gang Membership: A Study of Seattle Youth.* Washington, D.C.: Office of Juvenile Justice and Delinquency Prevention, December 2001.

Humes, Edward. *No Matter How Loud I Shout: A Year in the Life of Juvenile Court.* New York: Touchstone, 1997.

Jankowski, Martín Sánchez. *Islands in the Street:*

Gangs and American Urban Society. Berkeley: University of California Press, 1991.

Katz, Jack. *Seductions of Crime.* New York: Basic Books, 1988.

Katznelson, Gali, and J. Wesley Boyd. "Solitary Confinement: Torture, Pure and Simple." blog.petrieflom.law.harvard.edu/2018/01/17/so litary-confinement-torture-pure- and-simple. January 17, 2018.

Kerman, Piper. *Orange Is the New Black: My Year in a Women's Prison.* New York: Spiegel & Grau, 2011.

Kotlowitz, Alex. *There Are No Children Here: The Story of Two Boys Growing Up in the Other America.* New York: Doubleday, 1991.

Le Blanc, Adrian Nicole. *Random Family: Love, Drugs, Trouble, and Coming of Age in the Bronx.* New York: Scribner's, 2004.

Lerner, Jimmy A. *You Got Nothing Coming.* New York: Broadway Books, 2002.

MacDonald, Michael Patrick. *All Souls: A Family Story from Southie.* New York: Ballantine Books, 1999.

McCall, Nathan. *Makes Me Wanna Holler: A Young Black Man in America.* New York: Random House, 1994.

Mendel, Matthew Parynik. *The Male Survivor: The Impact of Sexual Abuse.* Thousand Oaks: Sage, 1995.

Page, Kathy. *Alphabet.* Toronto: Biblioasis, 2014.

Parent, Marc. *Turning Stones: My Days and Nights with Children at Risk.* New York: Harcourt, Brace, 1996.

Rhodes, Richard. *Why They Kill: The Discoveries of a Maverick Criminologist.* New York: Vintage Books, 1999.

Rodriguez, Luis. *Always Running: La Vida Loca: Gang Days in L.A.* New York: Touchstone, 1993.

Rodriguez, Luis. *Hearts and Minds: Creating Community in Violent Times.* New York: Seven Stories Press, 2001.

Sapphire. *Precious.* New York: Vintage Books, 1997.

Shakur, Sanyika. *Monster: The Autobiography of an L.A. Gang Leader.* New York: Penguin Books, 1993.

Shannon, Sarah K.S., Christopher Uggen, Jason Schnittker, Melissa Thompson, Sara Wakefield, and Michael Massoglia. "The Growth, Scope, and Spatial Distribution of People with Felony Records in the United States, 1948–2010." *Demography* 54 (October 1, 2017): 1795–1818.

Shaw, Clifford R. *The Jack Roller: A Delinquent Boy's Own Story.* Chicago: University of Chicago Press, 1966.

Sikes, Gini. *8 Ball Chicks: A Year in the Violent World of Girl Gangs.* New York: Anchor Books, 1997.

Simmons, Rachel. *Odd Girl Out: The Hidden Culture of Aggression in Girls.* New York: Harcourt, 2002.

Stephenson, Bryan. *Just Mercy.* New York: Spiegel & Grau, 2014.

Venkatesh, Sudhir. *Gang Leader for a Day.* New York: Penguin, 2008.

Walker, Jan. *Dancing to the Concertina's Tune: A Prison Teacher's Memoir.* Boston: Northeastern University Press, 2004.

Western, Bruce. *Homeward: Life in the Year After Prison.* New York: Russell Sage Foundation, 2018.

Zimbardo, Philip. *The Lucifer Effect: Understanding How Good People Turn Evil.* New York: Random House, 2008.

Index